Warrior for Justice

The George Eames Story

Kathy Andre-Eames

Foreword by Dale Brown

To Terry, My beloved sister & friend —

Kathy André-Eames

PELICAN PUBLISHING COMPANY

GRETNA 2015

Library of Congress Cataloging-in-Publication Data

Andre-Eames, Kathy, 1946-
  Warrior for justice : the George Eames story / by Kathy Andre-Eames ; foreword by Dale Brown.
      pages cm
  Includes bibliographical references and index.
  ISBN 978-1-4556-2064-7 (hardcover : alkaline paper) – ISBN 978-1-4556-2065-4 (e-book) 1. Eames, George, 1933-2012. 2. Andre-Eames, Kathy, 1946- 3. African American civil rights workers–Louisiana–Baton Rouge–Biography. 4. Civil rights workers–Louisiana–Baton Rouge–Biography. 5. Interracial marriage–Louisiana–Baton Rouge. 6. National Association for the Advancement of Colored People. Baton Rouge Branch–Biography. 7. Civic leaders–Louisiana–Baton Rouge–Biography. 8. African Americans with disabilities–Louisiana–Baton Rouge–Biography. 9. African Americans–Civil rights–Louisiana–Baton Rouge–History–20th century. 10. Baton Rouge (La.)–Race relations–History–20th century. I. Title.
  F379.B33A64 2015
  323.092–dc23
  [B]

                              2015011760

All photographs by the author unless otherwise indicated

Printed in the United States of America
Published by Pelican Publishing Company, Inc.
1000 Burmaster Street, Gretna, Louisiana 70053

Warrior for Justice

George Eames

"When you're up to your eyeballs
in muck and bullets, do muck; then do bullets."

—Stuart Wilde

"The Revolution never sleeps."   —G. Washington Eames

"And before I'll be a slave
I'll be buried in my grave
And go home to my God
And be free."

—Old Negro spiritual, anonymous

"Now cracks a noble heart—Good night, sweet prince,
And flights of angels sing thee to thy rest."

—*Hamlet*, William Shakespeare

CONTENTS

Foreword

How does one begin to describe George Eames? Probably the best way was my first contact with him. I was walking off our home court after a loss in 1973 and I heard a voice shouting at me, "Hey Coach Brown, better get yourself some brothers on your team." I immediately went over to him, face to face, and told him, "Listen buddy, I am doing my best to recruit the best players I can and color has nothing to do with it, so wise up."

The next day my secretary called and told me the president of the Baton Rouge NAACP was on the phone asking to talk to me. I thought that loud mouth last night called the NAACP to report my conversation with him. I aggressively answered the phone and heard, "Hey, man, this is George Eames and I like your style."

I said, "Do I know you?"

And he said, "I'm the guy you got so mad at last night at the game and I would like to help you if I can."

Our first meeting went well and I could tell he was sincere. From then it was clear to me that he was very outspoken, committed, abrasive in some ways, and fearless. From that day on, he did his very best to let black players know they would be treated with fairness and dignity if they came to LSU.

It was interesting that an equal number of blacks, like whites, did not like George, probably because he was far from smooth. He was brutally blunt, highly opinionated, and demanding. However, he was also a true warrior for justice and never tried to impress anyone—but only spoke what he really believed in his heart.

If you met him only one time, you probably would not like him, but if you knew him like I did, you would then see that he gave his entire life to fighting any form of injustice for anyone.

George Eames was ornery, stubborn, controversial, opinionated, and bossy; but also honest, fearless, tenacious, loyal, truthful, and fully committed that all humans should be treated fairly.

There might be some who wonder why I would write the forward to this book, on this controversial man's life. My answer would come through a quote by Dr. Martin Luther King, Jr. when he said, "Many voices and forces urge us to choose the path of least resistance and bid us never to fight for an unpopular cause."

—Dale Brown
LSU Basketball 1972-97

Chapter 1

Growing Up with Racism

Approaching seventy years of age, I have one dream, one cause, one delight: to serve the will of God. I have lived by this teaching my whole life and tried to hold nothing back. As I prayed about the movie that George's great-nephew, Cleveland Bailey, Sr. wanted to create about my life with George, I determined that I would not hold back anything of my story, except some minor details that might be embarrassing to family or close friends. I entered more deeply into prayer, only then opening my scriptures and found one of my favorites, Psalm 40:

> Here I am;
> Your commands for me are written in the scroll.
> To do your will is my delight;
> My God, your law is in my heart!
> I announced your deed to a great assembly;
> I did not restrain my lips;
> You, Lord, are my witness.
> Your deed I did not hide within my heart;
> Your loyal deliverance I have proclaimed.
> I made no secret of your enduring kindness
> To a great assembly.[1]

I believe with all my heart—nothing that happens to us in our lives is an accident. Nothing is a coincidence. God's hand is in every tiny detail. He does not create our suffering, but He permits it. Out of evil, He works only goodness. Only He can see the final result. He delivers us. With enduring kindness, He helps us to work out the complex, beautiful patterns of our lives. One day, for all of us, what was done in darkness will come into the light. If not now, then in eternity.

Born in 1946, I was a child of racist times in the South. I was named Theresa Kathleen Andre in a hospital in New Roads, Pointe Coupee Parish, Louisiana.

My parents, Roy and Emily, were living with my father's parents at that time. My father's relatives were proud that they were Cajuns and that my great-great-grandfather was the first citizen of the parish to volunteer for the Confederate Army. My godmother and Daddy's youngest sister, Doris, showed me a ring that he or another relative carved from a button while in a Yankee prison!

My mother's father, Achille Altazan, was a barrel maker or a cooper like his father. Leaving school in the second grade, he taught himself to read and write. He loved playing the violin and writing stories.

My maternal grandmother was a teacher; my grandfather's mother was a midwife who nursed local folk during the yellow fever epidemic that scourged Baton Rouge and Louisiana for decades before 1905. My grandfather remembered his mother, "Mon," stripping down in the yard, bathing, and boiling her clothes there to avoid bringing the dread fever into her home.

I grew up in a little town in West Baton Rouge Parish, Brusly, LA. Unlike my old Confederate ancestors, I would be just as proud to break the color barrier as they were proud to enforce it!

My consciousness of the color barrier emerged during my childhood and early teen years; several incidents then partially shaped who I am today. Some early memories were of my grandparents.

In Erwinville at the home of my paternal grandfather, Harry (whom we called "Papa") folks used to sit on the front porch, the "gallery," which ran across the front of the house. Here I heard many stories. Papa told everyone sitting on the front porch, "All niggers steal."

Papa had hired a domestic to help Po Mom, my grandmother Olea, with household tasks. My grandfather was a farmer, so cooking had to be done for all the children and field hands. The family alone consisted of ten children, eight children born to Papa and Po Mom plus Po Mom's two young siblings who were orphaned when Po Mom's father killed himself. I think the servant's name was Millie. Papa described how he caught Millie stealing rice, "She had a little hole in her apron pocket, and she left a trail of rice as she moved around the kitchen."

After driving or walking down the lane, visitors usually climbed the

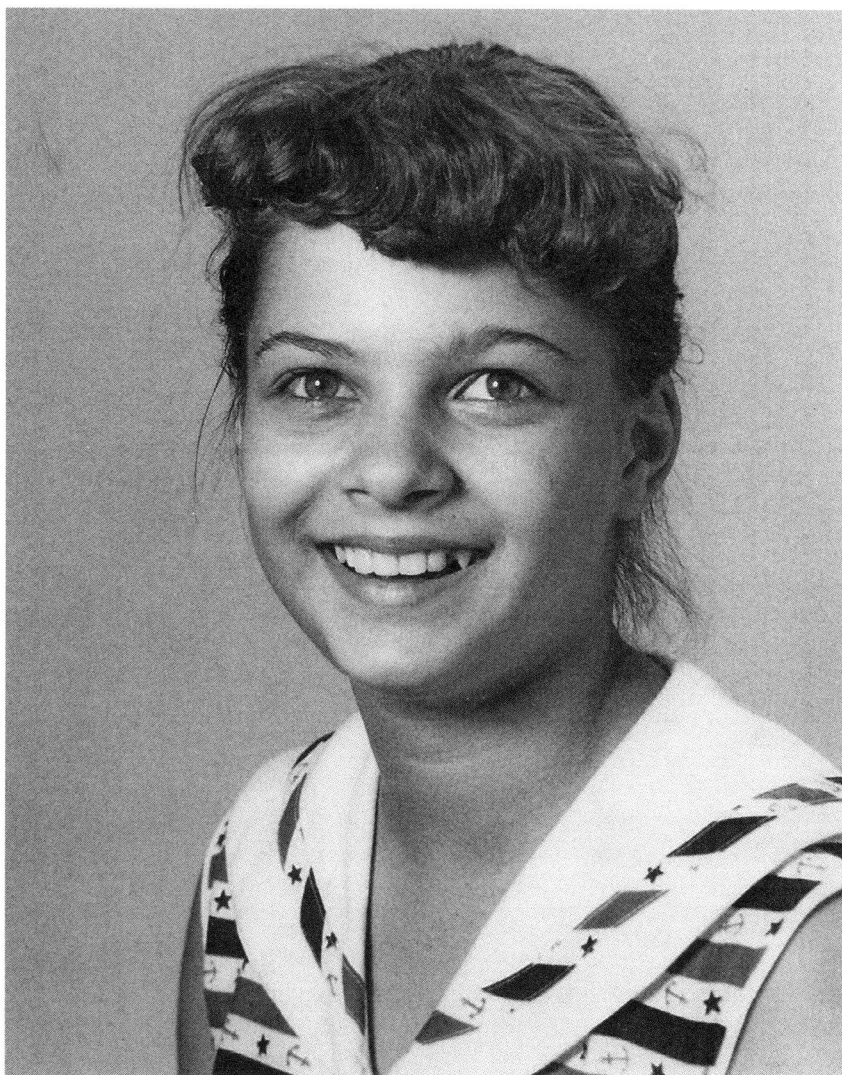

The author at ten years old, fifth grade

steps to sit in one of the rocking chairs on the front porch. Uncle Bill, who still lived on the place, was a frequent visitor. As a young child I knew him—he was already advancing in years. He loved all the grandchildren because, as one of Papa's black hired hands, he had seen all the children of the family grow up and had worked with them as youngsters. Whenever Uncle Bill walked down the lane to visit, I noticed that he never walked onto the gallery; he always sat on the steps, even though rocking chairs stood empty on the porch. I also noticed how he called everyone "Mister." Mr. Harry, Mr. Roy, Mr. Earl. He even called me Miss Kathy. I thought that was funny—after all, I was just a little girl! His wife was Aunt Hess. Nobody ever called him Mr. Bill. My brother and I knew him as Uncle Bill, but I knew if I had called him Mr. Bill, my father would have corrected me.

When I was nine or ten years old, in 1955 or '56, my father walked into the kitchen in our little house in Brusly. Slapping some leaflets down on the table, he told my mother that he would be going to his Southern Gentlemen meeting that night.

J. B. Easterly in Baton Rouge started this segregationist organization in April 1955, and another branch sprang up in Lakeland, Louisiana (Pointe Coupee Parish, where my father was born and grew up), in Oct. 1955. Over the years I remembered that name, Southern Gentlemen, and wondered if it might be a euphemism for the Ku Klux Klan. But no, this was the Klan minus the hoods and violence. No less dedicated to the preservation of the status quo of segregation in Louisiana, the Southern Gentlemen, a semi-secret group, vowed to use legal means. Closely affiliated with the White Citizens' Councils of Mississippi, they were just as vocal.[2]

In the *Times News* of Hendersonville, North Carolina, on Oct. 25, 1955, one newsman explained that the Southern Gentlemen declared Baton Rouge "off limits" to returning black veterans. The organization predicted that Baton Rouge would be "overrun" by 140,000 returning Negro veterans who were scheduled to participate in Operation Sagebrush, a series of post-World War II maneuvers at Fort Polk, LA. They feared that these soldiers would "pour into our beautiful capital city."[3]

Then on June 26, 1956, J. B. Easterly told a cheering crowd from the state capital steps where they were holding a rally, "We want to go on living our own sinful way. We don't want to go to heaven because our mamas and papas are down below. We want to do this in a peaceful way, but we are going to stay segregated in Louisiana— come hell or high water."[4]

*****

George Eames would tell me later that he was mustered into the US Army in April 1953. Upon his honorable discharge in June 1955 and his return to Baton Rouge, he was trying to decide what to do with his life.

Tragedy would strike. One fateful night in March 1956 George was on his way home from either work or night school at Spaulding Business College. Suddenly, a white businessman—fearing that George was a "Peeping Tom"—shot him. The climate in Baton Rouge at that time created many potentials for violence.

The shooter was Alvin B. Cole of 187 W. Garfield. He and his wife had had a bad experience with a young black man about a week or two before that fateful night of the shooting. A black stranger had exposed himself to her, the Coles said; the police were called, but no one had been apprehended. Due to this incident, they were on edge and defensive.

George was passing by their home on adjoining property that had long been used by the public as a shortcut through the block. Cole told the police that they believed the same man had come back; Cole insisted that the police refer to their own records, citing this as the reason for his use of his weapon.

Cole was never arrested.

Neither was George.

Assistant DA, Scallan Walsh wrote a letter to the Veterans Administration, explaining that "...this office has never been convinced that the injuries sustained by George W. Eames, Jr. resulted from his own willful misconduct. This accused was found shot and in a paralyzed position some eight or ten feet from the premises of Mr. Cole on a portion of the property used by the general public as a means of ingress and egress....for the above reasons no charges have ever been filed against George W. Eames, Jr., and none will be filed by this office."[5]

Though this letter exonerating George clearly reached the Veterans Administration, they still denied him veterans benefits. Their refusal consigned him to live in dire poverty for some years following his release from the hospital.

Despite constant requests from his mother, Alsie Eames, on

George's behalf, neither one of them received anything other than denials from the Veterans Administration.

We did not even know about the DA's letter for many years. It was not until Milton Altazan, my mother's brother, who worked for the VA at the old state capitol building, opened George's file. I believe it was in the 1980s that he sent us a copy.

This information was precious to both of us. The shooting and subsequent news articles had effectively destroyed George's good name and reputation. The so-called "news" even followed him to the hospital as he fought for his life; other patients sometimes referred to him as the "Peeping Tom." His reputation in Baton Rouge when he was released from the hospital was no better. George had to live and work under these circumstances for the rest of his life. He would fight to prove that his character was not reprehensible. It was an uphill battle taking years.

During his three-year stay in the VA hospital with no income, he always had money in his pocket. George told me that he "hustled" to make pocket money, mostly by betting on sports events. He baited racist white patients to make extravagant bets on games or even particular plays in a game, such as the outcome of a turn at bat, while he made conservative bets.

Only twenty-three years old and ever fun-loving, he amused himself with mischievous pranks. For example, rolling about the hospital on a gurney that he propelled along by pushing sticks, he would cover himself with a sheet and wheel into a corridor like a corpse rolling along by itself. Or he would take a rolling leap to the back of an elevator, running into the back wall. His head was a mere two inches from the edge of the gurney, but other passengers didn't know this and they squealed in fright that he might be injured.

His compassion often overtook his foolishness, however, as he usually spent mealtimes feeding other veterans who could not feed themselves. Prejudiced nurses occasionally neglected the black veterans. Sometimes when he saw a patient in distress, he called attention to the nurses who were lollygagging, "These people need help!" he said. Doctors would sometimes ask him to talk to other veterans, who, depressed at being in the hospital a couple of months, would be encouraged by George's cheerfulness after his own stay of two years, or more.

When he left the VA Hospital in New Orleans, his favorite nurse, a white lady, told him "Junior, I know you would like to go back to Baton Rouge and avenge yourself on that white man who shot you. But what you ought to do is to make sure that an incident like this never happens again to any other young black man." This path George deliberately chose. He wanted justice for his people, so he put the shooting behind him and moved forward.

Despite all he went through, I never saw any evidence of bitterness or hatred against white people. He hated prejudice, not individual people. His attitude and values were more than acceptable to me.

✳✳✳✳✳

George had begun work to desegregate the school system before he was shot. The original lawsuit against East Baton Rouge Parish to desegregate the school system had been filed Feb. 29, 1956. On June 13, 1956 (after George was shot), depositions of the plaintiffs were filed, including George's deposition, taken before he had been shot.

The Louisiana Legislature passed additional Jim Crow laws in 1956, among them the Recreation Statute prohibiting any mixing of the races in athletic "training, games, sports or contests," dancing or social events (a law which would adversely affect LSU and the Sugar Bowl).

The Public Carrier Statute segregated buses.

The Employment Statute demanded separate restroom facilities, separate eating places and even separate eating and drinking utensils!

The Public Accommodations Statute separated all public parks, recreation centers, and playgrounds.

In 1957: "All public schools to be racially segregated."[6]

What a sweet irony that George would see these prohibitions overturned later, as we worked in the seventies and eighties to desegregate the school system and the athletic program at LSU.

Discovering Race in My Childhood

I was about ten in 1955 or 1956, when the locals were hotly contesting these rousing racial issues. My family lived in Brusly. One day a black man walked about three miles to our home to ask my father for help. He lived in a rundown shack on Cinclare Sugar Plantation. It was Christmas time, his wife was sick, and he had no money. My father gave him a few dollars to buy medicine; when the man left, my father told me, my brother, and my mother, "I want you to gather some things together for this man's Christmas. Kathy and R. J., you find some toys for his children; Emily, see if you have a couple of dresses and a purse for his wife, and I'll give him a couple of shirts and some khakis as well as some meat from the freezer and some fig preserves." What we gathered filled a number three tub. I gave a doll.

My seven-year-old brother and I were excited because Daddy was letting us go with him to deliver the gifts. When we entered the man's home, I was stunned. The house was heated by a wood-burning fireplace of dilapidated brick; newspapers plastered every inch of the walls in an attempt to keep cold from coming through the cracks. The man's wife was covered up to her neck in the bed that was in the small living room, and two young children cowered behind their father's legs. I handed my doll to the little girl, and her father picked it up to look at it more closely. "Ain't a thing wrong with it! Ain't broken or messed up or nothing!" the man marveled. I realized, even at my young age, that he was shocked that white people would give him or his child anything that was not broken or unspoiled. His attitude humbled me, affecting me profoundly.

At about the same age, I missed the bus at school one day and decided to walk home, a long distance of about four miles for a little girl. You have to understand the unique way our community is laid out, even today, as far as I know. The homes in unincorporated Back Brusly, where my family lived, were not segregated. Leaving "Front Brusly," the incorporated township where the school is located, I crossed the highway into Back Brusly.

Walking along the road skirting sugar cane fields, I found several white homes, then a black one or two, then a couple of white ones, and so on. Not that these people ever socialized together. No, but they were neighbors and let one another be. Children didn't play together as far as I know. Yet as I walked down that blacktop road, tiring more by the minute, I came upon a large Cajun-style house, unpainted, and set far from the road where I knew black people lived. My father had instructed my brother and me that these were unsavory characters, that the women there had lots of babies with different men.

I saw a little girl in the driveway about my age, and I made up my mind I was going to talk to her, so I said hello. "What's your name?" I asked.

I have no idea what she said. I had the hardest time understanding what seemed to be a name I had never heard in my life, "Louvinnie" or some such.

"What school do you go to?" I asked next.

"Lukeville," was plain enough. I knew it was the local colored elementary school.

"What did y'all do for May Day?" Now I hoped for real information; my own school had done some decorating and planned activities with the children.

"...the maypole," she responded.

Astounded, I could understand only "the maypole." Here I was, being brave to talk to this child from a dangerous family, and despite my best efforts, I understood not one word. She spoke a totally different language. Her dialect was so thick that it created a barrier between us. I walked on, thinking that this communication would be much more challenging than I had ever dreamed.

Another incident in my childhood gave me early insight into race relations. About nine or ten years old, I was in the family car on the ferry, which carried people and vehicles back and forth between Port Allen and Baton Rouge across the Mississippi.

On the Baton Rouge side, we suddenly heard a scream. We could see from the car a black man stabbing a black woman in the chest with a long-bladed knife. They were a few yards from us where passengers were boarding.

A few seconds later my father was stepping out of the car, muttering to himself, "I need a pipe or something...I can't believe all these men are just going to stand around and see this woman be killed!"

My mother was pleading, "No, honey, no..."

Daddy was going to rescue the colored woman! Because I didn't want Daddy to be stabbed, I began to plead with him, too. I was excited, frightened, and proud of my father. Daddy never totally exited the car because someone had called the police who had quickly responded.

I never believed that Daddy hated black people. I remember that
one of his brothers, Elmo, a deputy in Port Allen, had been shot
in the stomach by a black man. Another uncle on Mama's side of
the family—George Bourg, also a Port Allen deputy—had been
stabbed while trying to make an arrest. Many of my family worked in
law enforcement and had seen some of the worst sides of the black
community. That kind of experience, distrust of blacks, was difficult
for them to overcome.

Understand this: my family and my parents, especially, were God-
fearing people, good Catholics. I was raised to be obedient to God and
man. I participated in Mass every Sunday, learned my catechism, read
spiritual books like the life of St. Theresa of Lisieux, and prayed daily.

Both my mother's and father's families were hard-working,
honest, plain folk who treasured their families, their homes, and
their honor. Our entire social life revolved around family and family
occasions. Believing in honesty and fair dealing, my father often said
that a man's word was his bond. Utterly committed, faithful, and
charitable, Mama was a prayerful person. It seemed to me they were
the salt of the earth. Both of them were affectionate disciplinarians
to my brother and to me.

As a little girl, I adored my father. I saw no wrong in him or in
Mama. They both encouraged me in school and taught me to work
in the yard and in the home. Living in the country, we raised much
of our own food, milked cows, slaughtered our own chickens and
beef, canned vegetables and fruit. We dressed simply, and enjoyed few
luxuries. While doing all this work at home, Daddy worked at a plant
in Baton Rouge, first as a pipe-fitter and later entering management as
a supervisor. He loved pipe-fitting but knew management would give
him a more secure income for his family. I don't know how he did it.

We lived frugally. I remember going to about one or two movies
a year in Baton Rouge. They were available, but we just did not go.
Having lived through the Depression, my parents saved. I received
a twenty-five cent allowance each week, all of which I placed in the
collection basket in church each Sunday.

When Daddy put in a garden, he set aside a little section for me
and my brother. We planted what we wanted. I remember pulling
little carrots from the ground in my part of the garden, washing them
off in the yard, and eating them outside. We hoed and pulled weeds,

raking leaves in the fall. During pecan season, we picked pecans, stowed them in sacks, and earned our own money by selling them to the pecan man when he drove by in his ragged old truck. Once, my brother and I helped Uncle Harry in Erwinville pick cotton for an entire day. I dragged my sack along for hours. We were paid by the pound, and I could later appreciate what it meant to pick cotton, my back aching, being hot, sweaty, and itchy and pricking my tender fingers on the dried cotton husks. I helped Mama to pluck chickens, to can fruits and vegetables, and to clean the house. I raised my own calf on a bottle; my brother and I acquired numerous pets, including a miniature Shetland pony, horse, lamb, goat, rabbits, and the like. Dogs were ever present, and a couple of cats.

Daddy was hurt badly in the fall of 1956, I believe. A drunk driver collided with my father in a terrible automobile accident; Daddy remained in the hospital for a week or maybe a month. Our Uncle Gerald (Mama's younger brother) and Aunt Rosalie moved to our home for the duration to care for R. J. and me as well as for all the animals. Having helped my uncle feed the chickens, as little as I was, I still climbed into the barn to drag bales of hay to the door to feed Daddy's cows. I broke the bales apart, and scattered them about for the cattle to eat.

In the fifth grade I entered a contest sponsored by the local newspaper and won a bicycle. My brother also had a bicycle; we always played with toys of all kinds and sporting equipment. After Daddy set up a basketball goal in the yard, we played basketball as well as softball, football and badminton. I broke my wrist when I was twelve while scrambling for a ball.

Active and strong, a good student making As and Bs, I was a confident child, mature for my age, and considerate of others, as my parents taught me to be. They were proud of me, and I was proud of myself. Through all the years of my childhood, I never experienced any kind of conflict except the normal arguments with my brother. I saw little conflict between my parents.

I was a sweet, obedient little girl for the most part. I earnestly strove to be the best I could be in everything.

Naturally, I wanted to be holy too, like St. Theresa. I felt close to God. When my grandfather asked me what I wanted to be when I grew up, I told him, "Either a teacher or a nurse or maybe a nun."

In recent years, I remembered an incident which occurred when I was twelve, in 1958. It remained a vivid image in my mind—it reveals my tenacious grasp of justice as a child. I wrote about it in essay form:

With Truth and Justice for All

Could I really have been the good, sweet child that I think I was? Even Mama would confirm it. She remembers me the same way that I do. Except for minor infractions once in a while for which she usually swatted me with a wet dishrag, few incidents called for major steps from her or my father. Probably for this reason, these ancient occasions for which I was chastised stand out clearly in my memory, fully detailed pictures complete with gestures, faces, and words. Their tiny details rear up certain and sharp, although I normally have a terrible memory for events that happened as recently as two or three days ago.

When I was twelve, for example, my mother's sister and her five boys were visiting from Texas. On these annual visits, my brother inevitably stuck with Jamie, one year my junior, and the other boy cousins, whoever were old enough to play with them. I clung closely to my Aunt Faye and Mama, the women folks who huddled over coffee in the kitchen. As they clucked along, I clucked with them, or at least listened, hanging over the sugar bowl absorbing their woman talk. A bonus was Aunt Faye's baby boy—one of them had been born just months ago—each time she visited, it seemed to me. Since Mama had no babies, I loved to cuddle and carry Craig, then Kevin, Christopher, and finally Mark. Christopher probably was the one toddling about when I suffered my first injustice.

My brother and my cousins had been pestering the heck out of me on this visit. All of them were obnoxious, dumb boys of eleven, nine, eight, and such; and all of them were equally dedicated to the exquisite torture of sensitive girls of twelve.

I had taken all I would take from these fools. I hauled off and socked my brother. Naturally, Mama had not seen a single picky thing the boys had done to me, so when she saw me strike R. J., she yelled at me.

We were in the living room. I stood in front of that old green vinyl chair to the left of the black and white television. The plastic curtains blew gently at the window from the attic fan. I stood like a rock. Mama repeated her command: "Get on your knees, Kathy. Come on; get on your knees right there. Now."

The punishment itself gave me no trouble. I had been forced to my knees when I was four, five, or six. But not in front of my aunt. Aunt Faye was the one I drank coffee with and whose babies I lugged around.

I was embarrassed and felt righteous, refusing to obey. I held my head high. I didn't yell or cry or fuss, but I made it plain that I would not do what Mama commanded.

"No," I insisted. "I didn't do anything wrong." I felt like a martyr. One in front of a firing squad. One being stoned by an angry mob. Or a poor innocent girl thrown to the lions. This was injustice. I was properly indignant. No, I would not kneel. I held my ground.

Mama couldn't believe it. I could take that. It was harder to take my Aunt Faye sadly wagging her head at me—but I wouldn't give in. How could I? Justice and Right were on the line. I would never betray Justice! Not me!

"Wait till Daddy gets home! I bet you'll get on your knees then," Mama said.

I knew I'd get on my knees then, Justice or no Justice. I'd have to, or Daddy would whip me, and I've always been terrified of my father with a size 40 belt in his hand, but I intended to hold on as long as possible.

This was my contribution to the welfare of Truth and Justice. To this day, I feel the same way about it, as stubborn about it today as I was then.

Chapter 2

A New Environment

When I entered high school in 1960, I wanted to become a nun, or rather, a Catholic sister. First, let me clarify the difference between a nun and a Catholic sister. A nun lives a much more cloistered life, usually in a contemplative order, for example, the order of the Poor Clares or the Carmelite nuns. Sisters, on the other hand, mingle more with the public and are not strictly cloistered, though they also lead prayerful lives dedicated to God. Both nuns and sisters take vows of poverty, chastity, and obedience.

My school of choice was a prep school for aspiring religious, St. Mary of the Pines in Chatawa, Mississippi. The School Sisters of Notre Dame who ran this school were teachers, and I wanted to be a teacher.

Uniquely designed, this Catholic boarding school was divided into two sections. One was for the ordinary boarders, students from across the country but mainly the South, South America and Central America, one student even from South Africa, and a few day students.

The other section, where I lived and studied for the four years I was there, was called the Aspiranture. Here young women from thirteen to eighteen years old lived in community, learning about the order of the School Sisters of Notre Dame.

Aspiring to be Catholic sisters ourselves, we received education different from that of the other girls. We dressed differently too; regular boarders wore navy skirts with white blouses whereas aspirants wore navy jumpers with white blouses—we all wore black and white saddle oxfords. The total number of girls in the Aspiranture in any given year was no more than twenty-five to forty, with forty being an extremely high number. With such a small group—ten freshmen, for example—we became quite close to one another and formed deep friendships.

Some students may have registered to enter St. Mary of the Pines in the sixties to escape the integration that stirred the nation into an uproar. At the time I entered this school, fall 1960, civil rights was not the issue that it would later become. We entered for the education we could receive, some of us wanting to become Catholic sisters. Later in the decade, on the grounds of this school, the Klan burned crosses protesting the nuns' hiring of black kitchen workers. How asinine was that! I couldn't understand why we had no black students but figured they couldn't afford the tuition.

I was serious about my religious vocation. I loved and lived life intensely in the Aspiranture. We lived a modified version of the way the sisters themselves lived, without any vows, of course. We rose at about 6:15 a.m. and had twenty minutes to dress and meet in our study hall for community morning prayer. Freshmen, sophomores, juniors, and seniors sat in ranks, with seniors in the rear of the room. The seniors were our role models—we admired and imitated them. We had a short private meditation of 15 minutes—after which we all put on our veils, which we wore with our uniforms—and went to Mass in our chapel for 7:00. The regular boarders wore "beanies" to Mass. Some of the girls who had kitchen duty hurried out immediately after Mass to help serve breakfast.

Even as young as we were, aspirants observed "the Great Silence" with no talking except for what was absolutely necessary from night prayer the evening before till after breakfast. During breakfast, one of the juniors or seniors read to us from the lives of the saints or other inspiring books. Our dining hall was in a building separate from that of the boarders. They, of course, talked at all meals and kept no Great Silence. We talked during the other meals of the day.

I was fascinated by the way the sisters handled dining and cleaning up the tables afterward. All large convents followed this procedure. Our director, one of the sisters, established table settings at all of the tables with assigned seats for all the girls. This was to eliminate confusion, to save time, and to teach us tolerance for one another. She also assigned each aspirant to serving duty for at least one meal a day each week; at the end of the meal, the servers brought small pans of hot, soapy water; a dishcloth; and a drying cloth on a plastic tray to each table. The girls at each table washed, dried, and reset the table for the next meal, returning the pans to the sink and putting everything away.

Our spiritual director, one of the sisters, encouraged us to practice mortification in individual ways. Mortification is the act of subduing bodily desires, enabling self-discipline and self-control. For example, I often ate my toast dry with neither butter nor jelly or ate cereal with no sugar. I made small sacrifices which honed my self-discipline and self-control.

Our school day began at 8:00 a.m., and the sisters expected excellence from all of us. Our teachers were sisters with the exception of our much-loved physical education teacher, a single woman. At our all-girls school, we enjoyed a lively athletics program: basketball, softball, volleyball, square dancing, archery, swimming and tennis. St. Mary's offered us a large swimming pool, where one of our boarders worked out constantly for the Olympics. A small lake on our campus provided us with several canoes and flat bottom aluminum boats which we could use after school for our own pleasure, and on field days we often had boat races along with other tournaments. We won honorable mentions, ribbons, and trophies. Classes competed with great gusto—freshmen against seniors, sophomore against juniors— with most of our tournaments featuring final four events!

After school, we enjoyed a relaxing break: a snack, a walk around the grounds praying our rosary, usually in a group, and about an hour for recreation on our large and beautiful campus.

After a 5:30 supper, we generally walked on the wonderful country road that weaved among the pine forests there. Then we returned to study hall for a couple of hours. We took turns showering during the study period. Then we recited the night prayer together, beginning the Great Silence, and we were ready for lights out at 10:00 p.m.

Our dormitories shifted through the years depending on the number of aspirants in the different grade levels. During my first year there, because our juniors and seniors numbered only four in each grade, a relatively small dorm room housed each group. My freshman group had our dorm on the screened porch of the outer part of our two-story building. We could close the windows in inclement weather, but we still suffered with the lack of air and no heat in the winter months. These porch dorms had neither heat nor air. A furnace provided heat to most of the rooms in the winter, and none of the buildings had air conditioning. This taught us personal discipline and mortification. In the winter, I can remember having to defrost my washcloth in order to wash my face!

The way we lived may seem excessive today, yet we learned about ourselves and others. We gained discipline, maturity, and a sense of responsibility. I wished that my peers outside of our school would have been able to have such an experience.

Our director, Sister Optata, or Sister Richard Marie, provided weekly spiritual teaching. They stayed with us aspirants throughout the day and slept in a small private room or cell near us at night. We were supervised 24/7.

On both Saturday and Sunday evenings the sisters rented G or PG movies for us, and those of us who could afford to lose the study time delighted in this diversion.

The sisters permitted special visiting times for the aspirants with the regular boarders, but for the most part, we remained secluded to ourselves because we were, indeed, like little sisters.

On Sundays we enjoyed long walks. Saturdays were big cleaning days, but we often relished weenie roasts with the marvel of endless S'mores! Warm afternoons and Saturdays gave us plenty of time for swimming. We could have visits from parents or other friends and relatives once a month on a Sunday, usually picnic visits on the grounds.

One of the worst offenses at this school was smoking! With all the old wooden structures, smoking, even owning matches, was virtually criminal behavior. In my senior year, one of the senior aspirants was caught smoking. This scandalized the entire school, and she was sent home for such a grievous infraction. One boarder in my senior class was found to be pregnant during the year and was also sent home. These were rare occurrences.

We loved our life in Chatawa. Our eyes filled with tears at graduation. Some graduates returned to career or business opportunities in their native countries. Many went to college or business schools, and a few entered the religious life, as I did.

"No Such Thing as a Black Lady"

Because St. Mary of the Pines was in southwest Mississippi, I often rode the Greyhound bus home and back to school on holidays. This freed my parents from having to drive there and back. One fall when I climbed onto the bus from school, since it was quite full, I walked to the back and sat next to a black lady. I was not afraid but I was fascinated to be sitting with the coloreds. As we stopped along the way at different bus stops, I noticed the black people pointing to the back window where they saw me, and pointing at me. I realized why—whites didn't normally sit among blacks; so I just smiled and waved at them.

When I reached home, my parents asked me about the trip. I told them that it was fine and that because the bus was unusually full, I had taken a seat in the back with a black lady. Daddy corrected me, "a black *woman*."

I acknowledged, "Yes, that's what I said, a black lady."

Daddy corrected me again, "a black woman. No such thing as a black *lady*."

Suddenly it dawned on me what he was saying. For years now, I had been developing my own moral character, my own little spirituality, and prejudice had no place in it. In my innocence, at ages thirteen and fourteen, I would go in to my spiritual advisor, Sister Optata, and explain how my father was. I would describe my father's faulty, but stubborn, reasoning; she would then tell me which arguments I could use to enlighten him. The next time I went home, when a situation or conversation came up, I would practice on him. He usually shot me down brutally and quickly. I never gave up; though I might not have been able to change his thinking, I certainly grew in my own private convictions.

At St. Mary of the Pines I was somewhat isolated from events happening in the "real" world. For example, we students saw virtually no television during the school year. This changed in my senior year when President Kennedy was shot. Imagine all these teen Catholic girls enthralled with a young Catholic president and his young family. We all adored John, Jackie, Caroline and little John-John.

I was a senior in Latin class when the president was assassinated. Instantly, the word flew from class to class.

Everyone was upset; our students from Latin American were hysterical. In Central and South America, our school ranked as one of the highly-recommended schools in the United States for teaching English and business skills. Girls from Honduras, Venezuela, Guatemala, El Salvador, Nicaragua, and others were sent here by their wealthy fathers or uncles, presidents and leading officials of these varied countries. These students began weeping, talking quickly and loudly in their native languages.

The sisters endured several troubled minutes with hysterical Latino girls before they discovered what it was that disturbed their students so. Being from countries often subjected to violent political turmoil, the girls were terrified that the huge United States would experience a military coup or equally horrendous violent takeover—and that they might be trapped here, never again to see their families. Imagine their amazement when Lyndon Johnson was smoothly sworn in and events proceeded calmly through the funeral.

Classes were suspended. For days we leaned forward, all glued to the few televisions in the school. We watched each mesmerizing minute, following Black Jack—the president's riderless horse—then the horse-drawn caisson bearing his casket through the streets of Washington, DC. We shed tears at little John-John's salute to his fallen father, and the stalwart courage of our first lady, Jackie, standing patiently with young Caroline and him.

Because I was sequestered in this quiet environment with few televisions, which we seldom watched anyway, I really did not have the opportunity to follow the civil rights struggle in the sixties as many of my peers on the outside did. I was not affected in any way. I caught a few glimpses of news during the summer but didn't really follow the full import. Then when I entered the convent in the fall of 1964, my teachers immersed me in religious instruction; we seldom watched television. The older nuns followed the news religiously [pardon the pun!], but we students did not.

The year Dr. Martin Luther King, Jr. was assassinated, I was an upper graduate student. One of the nuns entered our study hall, asking, "Would any of you like to attend an interdenominational memorial service for Dr. King in Dallas?" I volunteered, along with a handful of other young sisters. On the dais sat Jews, Protestants, blacks, and the Catholic bishop. I remember thinking that the service was beautiful, and for the first time I linked my arms with others to sing, "We Shall Overcome." Though touching, it was not life-changing for me; I really did not grasp the full significance of what had happened. I knew that blacks were fighting for their rights, and I agreed with that. I wanted them to have the same rights that I had. But other matters had priority in my life.

While teaching in Morrilton, Arkansas, 1968-69 and even the year before that, I had been giving serious thought to my life in the convent.

I loved God no less, but had begun to find the life too restrictive.

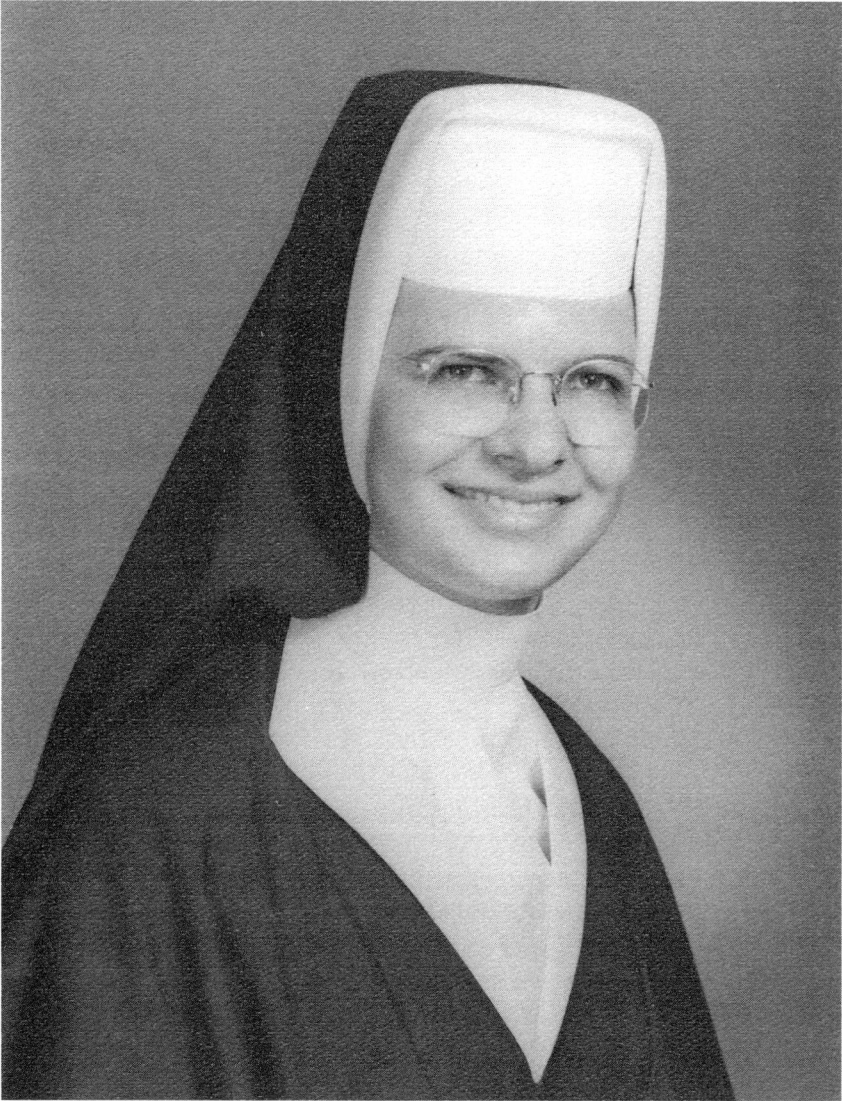

1969—Author, Sister Bernadette, before I met George Eames, Jr.

At the same time, I had begun to regret my degree in music. Uncomfortable with performing for church services, I had realized even before I graduated that memorizing the body of music which I would need as a musician was difficult. I'd forget pieces as I learned new ones. This caused me untold misery. But greater still were the restrictions of the lifestyle itself. While I had loved Chatawa and my first three or so years in the Motherhouse while learning about the religious life, my natural inclinations were to learn more about people in general and other cultures. I felt the convent would prevent this kind of growth.

Throughout my whole life so far, I had focused on becoming a religious. Now I agonized over the decision to leave, yet I still felt it was the right decision for me.

Throughout my high school and college years I had been writing poetry, a hobby about which I deeply cared. Though not masterful, my poems showed my love of language and imagery. During the spring of my year in Morrilton, months before I would leave the convent, I sent a poem to Dr. Louise Cowan, head of the English Department at the University of Dallas. She wrote me back, acknowledging the potential she had observed in the poem. Furthermore, she told me, "You are a poet, and you deserve the opportunity to develop this talent. I am offering you a full tuition scholarship to earn your master's degree in English." Now I knew where I would be going, and I had an option which would replace the burdensome degree in music.

I was under vows from July 29, 1966 through July 29, 1969, at which time I had fulfilled my religious obligations and was free to leave. I was asked by my superiors to take one last assignment, to teach in the Upward Bound program at Southern University that last summer; I explained that I would have to leave on July 29 because I had received a scholarship to begin my graduate work at the University of Dallas in the fall. They agreed that they could find someone to fill in at the end, for about two weeks.

I returned to Baton Rouge from Morrilton, Arkansas, where I had taught fifth grade in the Catholic school there.

I lived at St. Gerard Convent in Baton Rouge while I taught at Southern University. I spent weekends at home. My mother and I scrambled to assemble some kind of wardrobe for my year in Dallas. Still under vows, I wore absolutely nothing but my habits at the time. I taught on Southern campus in religious garb.

Chapter 3

Breaking Free

Although I had not yet studied English as a graduate student, I was assigned to teach English in the Upward Bound Program. This was my first prolonged exposure to many black people—the experience excited and scared me a little. I immediately sacked the Southern Lab library for works by black authors.

I remember being most impressed with Gwendolyn Brooks and loved the earthy humor of Langston Hughes. Giving my little classes compositions on simple topics. I soon discovered the truth about much of black education in the South. I was supposed to encourage these young high school people to aspire to college. Many of them didn't understand what a sentence was, or a paragraph; spelling was atrocious. Grammar was a hallucination.

I was lost, without a clue as to how to begin to remedy their skills. I tried to write encouraging notes on content. Poverty was apparent in their writing, in the way the students described their homes, families, and expectations. They taught me more than I taught them.

One student, Joe—a tall, dark boy with a magnetic smile—warmed up to me quickly whereas most of the other students eyed me distrustfully from a distance. During breaks, Joe began talking to me every day. As time came for me to leave, I couldn't do so without telling him something. I didn't want him to think I was just abandoning him. I told him that I had to leave the program early because I was leaving the convent and returning to study in Dallas. He pleaded with me, "I don't understand. Why do you have to leave the convent? Couldn't you just study as a nun?" He was hurt, and I knew why.

Joe may have thought that I was abandoning my values—my concern for black people. I might have been the first white person that he had been close to, so I explained as best I could that what I stood for would never change, that I would be the same person with the same values, and that I would never forget him.

Obedience to my superiors would end on July 29, but obedience to my God would never end.

Daddy did not accept my teaching at Southern. What I did not know till years later is that when Mama told Daddy that I would be teaching black teenagers on Southern University campus, he flew into a rage. He was so agitated that he threatened to come to the convent and forcibly remove me. Mama pleaded with him, "Honey, don't you understand that Kathy is still under her vow of obedience? She's doing this because she took a vow of obedience!"

Daddy gradually calmed down; and after I left the convent and Southern, he left me alone. I thought Daddy was unusually quiet, but because I was busy trying to prepare myself for school, I pretty much ignored his reserve. I had no way of knowing about his smoldering rage and Mama's complicit silence not telling me how he felt. Daddy's anger would erupt in the future, blasting my family apart. Permanently.

How I Met George

Daddy and Mama drove me to Dallas. I loved graduate school from fall 1969 through May 1970. Earning my master's degree with straight As, I was delighted to land a job of instructor at LSU for the fall 1970; and that spring, the *Mediterranean Review* even accepted one of my poems for publication!

I moved back in with my parents, bought a used car from them and began my first semester at LSU.

I grew unhappy after a couple of months. I needed to be with young people in a different environment, so I began looking for apartments. At the Studio Arms near LSU, the apartment manager told me that one of their renters, Marsha, was searching for a roommate. We met, liked one another, and I moved in with Marsha. After a couple of months, Marsha was packing to go home to Oklahoma for Thanksgiving. She told me, "By the way, you may receive a phone call from a friend of mine, George. He works at the NAACP office, and I met him when I called for some advice about how to handle some of my black students— especially the boys. Just tell him I went home for Thanksgiving."

Thinking little of it, I continued my own plans to have a close friend stay with me at the apartment during Thanksgiving week. She was Sister Sharon, a classmate and friend of several years and a fellow School Sister of Notre Dame; and I planned to visit with her some of the local historical places such as the Audubon home and plantations in and near St. Francisville, Louisiana.

On a Saturday night after 10:00 p.m. the phone rang. George wanted to know if Marsha was there.

"No, she went home to Oklahoma for the holiday," I said patiently, "but what are you doing calling somebody so late at night? It's after 10:00!"

George was nonplussed, "What are you doing going to bed at 10:00 on a Saturday night?"

"That is absolutely none of your business!" Incensed, I hung up on him.

Sunday morning, George called to apologize. I accepted—at least he had the decency to apologize for his rudeness.

To my chagrin, he called me again on Sunday night. Monday night—again.

"How long are you going to keep this up?" I asked him.

"As long as I need to," he answered simply. I had to laugh; we began talking.

Marsha had told him she was living with an ex-nun. He was curious. He proceeded to recite his Catholic prayers for me: the Act of Contrition, the Hail Mary, and others. When I asked him how he had come to know these, he told me that a couple of cute little nuns used to visit him in the Veterans Hospital in New Orleans when he had first been shot, and they taught him. He learned the prayers and pretended to be interested in the Catholic faith because he wanted them to keep visiting him!

He was excited when I told him I had a nun visiting me. "What are you two going to do for fun?" he asked.

"We're going to visit some of the places in St. Francisville." I had never been there and wanted Sister Sharon to see them.

"You mean the plantation homes that the slaves built?" he asked incredulously.

"Of course, I know that the slaves built them, and I give them every credit for doing a beautiful job!"

"You must be a Klucker!"

"I have no idea what you're talking about," I said. This set him off. We continued to talk and argue. I finally made up my mind that I had to meet this hothead, who was, nevertheless, a fascinating man. I wrote down his address and the directions to his apartment. It was a part of his family home that he shared with his sister, Gloria.

When he answered the door, he was in a wheelchair. I did not know he was handicapped. He would never mention it on the phone.

I kissed George on the cheek and had a seat. He told me later, that when I kissed him on the cheek, he thought to himself, "This is one sweet girl." All his defenses crumbled.

We talked for a long time. When George insisted on sitting on the sofa with me, he moved from his chair to the sofa by simply lifting himself. Then I insisted that I had to sit in the wheelchair. I needed to accept it and to be comfortable with it. I sat in it and rolled myself around while he laughed at me.

I had never dated in high school and dated little in graduate school; I had had maybe three or four formal dates. Though the young men were intelligent and likeable, I felt nothing but general friendly feelings for them.

I felt much more when I met George. The attraction was deep, mutual, and physical. I began telling him, practically from the day we met, "Slow down! Slow down!" The relationship moved quickly.

To me it seemed from the first, permanent, inevitable, and destined.

George Shares the Story of His Early Years

George shared the story of his early years with me. I compiled this story for his bio page of his Web site, Mr. Civil Rights. Here is George's story, in his own words:

I was born on March 12, 1933 to my mother, Mrs. Alsie Buckner Eames, and my father, G. W. Eames, Sr. My mother was from Wilson, Louisiana; and she attended Alcorn University in Alcorn, Mississippi. My father was born in St. Francisville, Louisiana. I'm sure that my father went to some grade in high school because he was able to master the Bible. He became a Baptist preacher. My mother was a school teacher, teaching primarily in Pointe Coupee Parish, East and West Feliciana Parish, and retiring from St. Helena Parish.

I was the baby boy. I had two older sisters, Gloria Honore Buckner Eames, three and a half years older than me, and Joy Mae Eames, about two and a half years older than me. My mother had eight miscarriages.

My childhood was exciting because I had a chance to travel to all those different places with my mother and my two sisters, so I created my own lifestyle, imaginatively and otherwise. I had to do that because my oldest sister, Gloria, felt that she had to rule the roost. I had to figure out how to outsmart both of them because Joy Mae went along with whatever Gloria decided to do to me.

I recall back home in Baton Rouge Mother had gone to tend to some business. I think I was around four years old, and both of them were beating up on me. I knew Mother had hidden her famous .38 pistol in the closet, out of my reach, of course. I think I climbed up on a chair or something to reach the pistol. I didn't have any idea how to pull the trigger or anything like that, but I knew that the pistol was something that I could use to stop them from messing with me. When I pointed it in their direction—our property was sixty feet by one hundred fifty, with the house sitting close to Van Buren St—so I don't know what distance Gloria had to run to get to the back fence. But whatever distance it was, that was where she ran screaming. I don't remember which way Joy went, but I know that they got the message.

When Alsie Buckner Eames came home, they told her everything that Junior had done, but didn't mention anything they had done to Junior. Mother caught hold to me and turned me every way but loose. I couldn't talk plain, but I was trying to explain to her what had happened to me while she was gone. And I stuttered so bad I couldn't get nothing out! I never did think about doing that again.

Before I reached school age, Mother was teaching in Pointe Coupee Parish, Gloria and Joy went to school in the little one-room school house, and I went with them.

Every year we would come home to Baton Rouge in the summer, not for the whole summer, because in the country the Negro kids had to go to school according to the sharecroppers' schedules on the white plantations. Mother's schedule was always based on the white plantation owner's schedule.

When I was five, I would watch how this white plantation owner ruled and owned everything. That was near Lettsworth, Louisiana. I used to watch how he treated the old black men. He called my mother "Elsie." He owned the General Store, he was the head of the school board in

Point Coupee Parish; he was in charge of everything as far as I could tell as a five year old. He would come around to see what everybody was doing. I don't know what his name was, but I know one thing, my Mother wasn't afraid of him. And I guess I took my cue from her.

Mother had a 1937 or 1939 Pontiac. Mother would leave the three of us in Pointe Coupee Parish on a Friday and tell the Negro neighbors who lived about a half mile away to check on us—that she would be back on Sunday because she had to go home to check on my daddy who, at that time, was working at the Standard Oil (before the big layoff).

Believe it or not, the way we would entertain ourselves, was me trying to cook cornbread—because I liked cornbread with clabbered milk with the cream on top. The mistake I made in trying to make the cornbread, instead of putting baking powder, I put four to five spoons of soda. That was the prettiest cornbread I had ever seen in my life! Crust pretty brown. Cornbread yellow. Put it in the buttermilk with sugar on top. Commenced to bite down on the cornbread—taste nothing but soda! Of course Gloria and Joy had a field day laughing 'cause Mother had left the cooking to Gloria. That was the end of my cooking days in Pointe Coupee.

But here comes the scary part. Our little whitewashed house with two rooms, outdoor toilet, slop jar inside for the night, was near a railroad track. When we heard the train coming, we would peek through the crack in the wall and see the hobos hiding from the conductor on the train so they could hop on the freight cars. That was our amusement, and the scary part was seeing the hobos close by, though they didn't know we were there.

I think that we moved from that particular house in Pointe Coupee Parish and moved to another area. That's where we were close to the Atchafalaya River levee where the plantation owner had fenced in a portion of the levee for his cattle and livestock. He had many animals with chickens, guineas, ducks, geese, pigs, goats, sheep, horses, mules, and jackasses. As a five year old, my brain told me, "How can this be that this white man has all this and the Negroes have nothing?"

I used to see this white man opening and closing this great big ol' gate across the road from where we lived, about a half mile away. So, for some reason, unknown to me to this day, at five years old I rose early one morning and opened that big gate—and I let everything out that wanted to leave! That white man told my mother what I did, and my mother whipped me, of course, and she whipped me bad. When that season ended with the sharecroppers, that white man told my mother, "Elsie, you are the best Negro teacher that's ever been in this parish, but I don't want that boy of yours to ever come back here again!" So mother was fired or dismissed from that parish after working there for at least three or four years or more.

When school started in Baton Rouge, we came home to stay with Daddy at 161 Van Buren St. Mother registered me and Gloria and Joy at Reddy St. School on the corner of Napoleon and Reddy St. My first grade teacher was Ms. Eva Scott.

If you recall, I mentioned that I stuttered. When my teacher would give us an assignment to read at home, I would memorize the first line in my first grade book; the next day, I would hold my hand up. If she didn't call on me, I couldn't say a word. I would just stutter, and the kids would laugh at me.

In my little mind, I hated school. I used to get into all kinds of trouble. They would punish me, whip me so much that my mother asked them just to send me home. That's when she decided to put me in Blunden Home for Orphans 'cause she figured that would be better for me to learn. My mother spoke the best English of anyone I've ever known, and she loved to read. She would read to us, teach us how to spell. Joy was the best speller. Gloria could read so good. Joy could read. But I couldn't. I could read to myself, but I couldn't explain myself to people. When I tried to talk, they would laugh. But this one thing I could do—I could draw and I could write, and when I could speak, it made sense—getting it out was the problem.

"I Quit School in Seventh Grade"

I quit school in seventh grade. I became a hustler. I worked at all kinds of odd jobs, grocery stores, shoeshine parlors, motor inn hotels, dish washing at restaurants. I learned how to gamble, shoot dice, play cards—I was a real good pool hustler.

Then it dawned on me, but by that time I was about two years behind, and all my friends around me were going to school and doing good. My mother sat down and talked to me.

"You got to go back to school," she said. My father told me, "If you ever want to get any money from me, you have to go back to school."

Joy was going to Southern Lab School, Gloria was married and had gone to school to become a beautician, and I was a nobody. When I went back to school, I made the honor roll in a Ms. Wilson's class. Seventh grade then was Junior High School, and it was housed on

McKinley High School campus in the annex building on the corner of East Blvd. and Louisa St. A lot of my friends that I grew up with were in high school.

I said to myself, "Self, you have to make something out of yourself. You got to do better than this." I did. I began to study; I still stuttered, but I took my time to explain myself. I really loved history and social studies. I wanted to know everything I could about how we survived slavery and stuff, so I would challenge the teachers and debate them on subjects that I knew something about. Like I told you, I was a hustler. I knew how to trap them because they figured they were smart, but I was cunning—and still am.

My experience in high school gave me some of the best years of my life. There was a coach named George E. Mencer who took me under his wing and treated me as an equal. He wanted me to get involved in all the sports. The reason I couldn't play football was that when I was ten years old playing sandlot football, a larger boy broke my leg, and that hindered my speed, I thought. But he talked me into playing basketball because I was six feet, one inch and I could jump. But I came into basketball later because I liked football better as a little boy. One of my teammates named John (Molly) Daniels and Raymond Brown, D.J. McCrae, and Earl, "Ig," Thomas taught me the techniques of the game. I played two seasons at McKinley High School through tenth grade.

Then I quit and went to work. Mother had retired, my parents had separated, Joy was in college, and I was kind of on my own. I liked to dress. I was good-looking, couldn't nobody outdance me, couldn't nobody outfight me, and couldn't nobody outdress me. It gave me my pride.

George Is Drafted into the US Army

And when I went to register for the draft at eighteen years old, they didn't believe that I was eighteen. So I had to get a new birth certificate, and the birth certificate came back and it read Race: W. That's how it remains to this day. When I made twenty, I was drafted by the US Army.

I went to New Orleans for the physical examination, passed the physical, came home to wait to be called up to be inducted. Went back to New Orleans to the induction center, and that's when you have to stand in a line and take the oath, and make one step forward. You are in the military. That night we were on the train to San Antonio, Texas to the reception center at Fort Sam Houston, Texas. That morning at 5:00 a.m., pouring down rain, I had slept "ready roll"—had on my blue suit, burgundy shirt, blue socks, blue suede shoes. I felt a kick at the bunk. It was a Negro sergeant at the end of the bunk. I was on the top; and a white boy named Jack Edwards, who I grew up with (we had been inducted at the same time), was on the bottom bunk. But the other inductees had already fallen out for the head count. I heard them, but it was raining! So I didn't move.

This Negro sergeant had come back to see that everyone was out but me. So he asked me, "What in the hell do you think you are doing?"

"Uh, it's raining out there," I said, knowing I have on my suit and blue suede shoes.

He told me, "Recruit, it don't rain, g– d– it in the Army; it rains on the Army." And he commenced to turn the whole bunk over on me. That caught my attention. He asked my name; I had no rank or serial number. And after the head count, I was called out to report to the mess hall at 0500 hours the next morning. I was on what you call "KP"—kitchen police—on pots and pans. For three days and three nights running, I was on KP. They broke me into not doing it my way, but doing it the Army's way; and I think we were in the reception center at Fort Sam Houston for ten days. We were taught how to stand, how to salute, how to march— always with the left foot first—we were issued our GI uniforms, given Army haircuts, and issued a flying twenty. That flying twenty enabled us to buy toilet articles, cigarettes, a couple of beers. The beers were Colt 45 brand.

We tried to talk to the Mexican girls who worked around the commissary, but they totally ignored us. We didn't speak their language, and that was the first time a Negro from the South had even looked hard at a Spanish girl or a white girl. But "you're in the Army now"—you figure you got some privileges.

Early one morning, we heard all these military orders, "Fall out! Dress right! Cover down! Young soldiers, you are getting ready to go to Fort Bliss in El Paso, Texas for your basic training."[2]

✳✳✳✳✳

This was as far as we wrote. I typed *To be continued...*, but the events of the next three years stopped me from typing further. I regret this omission deeply. I would love to have more of his story in his own words.

George was too busy living to write it down. Our writings were notes, press conferences, letters, lawsuits, complaints, commendations, civil rights matters, speeches.

Everything personal simply had to wait.

***** *

Through my teen and early adult years I had suffered from depression, I found later that I had a chemical imbalance which caused it—easily resolved with a daily dose of natural vitamin B complex. When I met George, however, I was still struggling with it. As I came to know him, I found him so full of *joie de vivre*, gratitude, and joy for life despite his handicap and personal problems. I felt I wanted to be with this man for the rest of my life. His eyes, lively, full of devilment and fun, enchanted me completely.

I could not tell my family about my growing feelings about George because of my father's prejudice and family history.

As much as I hated it, I lied to them. Mama, as mothers are more apt to do, asked if I had met anyone interesting. I gave her partial truths—a man called Frank. I used "Frank" because George used to call me "blind Frank" sometimes, and I retaliated by calling him Frank in return. Frank "worked out of town" a lot and somehow was never available to meet my parents. Once I slipped and referred to him as George. Confused, Mama asked, "I thought you said his name was Frank?" I hastily explained, "His last name is George." Mama was not entirely comfortable with this explanation, and said nothing more. When she called me early one morning, and received no answer, she asked, "Where were you?" I had a dog and taking him out to potty was always available as an excuse. I spent evenings with George and returned to my apartment early in the morning.

Gloria was George's sister who lived upstairs. Her reaction to this white woman coming and going constantly was totally negative. She was frightened, and warned him, "Junior, you've already been shot once. Now you're carrying on with this white woman! If the Klan finds out, they'll blow up Mother's house with all of us in it!" George didn't back down, telling her to mind her own business. She was skeptical of me for years. She even told him, "She's probably just trying to get our money!"

"What money?" George said.

I found George's living conditions appalling. His apartment in the family home consisted of a single bed in one room with tiny

2000—Here is the G. Washington Eames, Jr. homestead where he lived until 1979.

kitchen and bathroom with a large footed tub. What disturbed me most was the kitchen. Dirty dishes were always piled in the kitchen till Gloria would have time to wash them. She usually brought him a meal each evening.

Dirty dishes—I could fix easily enough. But the counters and cupboards! Peeling, flaking wood, roach droppings, and all the rest. Gloria was never much of a housekeeper, but George was immaculate, both in the house and in his personal habits. Yet George couldn't reach the areas that needed attention, so I bought oilcloth, thumbtacks, roach tablets, cleaning agents, and rags, I began to work on the kitchen. After cleaning all the horrible counters, I covered them with oilcloth. As I worked, George kept telling me, "Get out of that kitchen, woman!" When I finished, the whole apartment was much more presentable.

The two couches, black and orange, looked decent, but I couldn't understand the heavy black corduroy drapes that darkened the whole apartment. George told me proudly, "One of my friends made them for me. Don't you think they're sexy?" Sexy? I found them dusty and dreary, but they stayed up a while longer, pulled back so that light could enter.

The bed was irredeemably small and lumpy, with springs that stabbed. To my surprise, one night I saw a new full-size bed with a new headboard and a chest of drawers. He had bought the set on time at a local furniture store and would pay it off with his tiny disability income.

George struggled with very little income. It horrified me. He had been denied a veterans pension because he had been "engaged in wrongdoing" at the time he was shot. That was in 1956. He didn't even begin to receive a small disability income from Social Security till sometime in the sixties. I can't imagine how he lived. He had no medical insurance at that time. Because he was in his thirties, Medicare would not kick in for years. When he was ill, he called on Dr. D'Orsay Bryant. Doc was a gynecologist, a close friend and NAACP associate, who did what he could.

When I met him, George was suffering from a severe bladder infection; he also drank Mylanta constantly. Though he had been drinking cold drinks or sodas with his food, I began making fresh lemonade for him every day; the bladder infections lessened. The longer we were together, the less Mylanta he drank, until he stopped completely. Perhaps his sensitive stomach was caused by stress. I didn't know.

Our relationship was sometimes bumpy. While I fixed supper at his apartment or just watched television, he talked on the telephone with friends and relatives; at least he would explain that they were "cousins." After forty-five minutes of such a conversation one night, I left without saying good-bye and returned to my apartment. I didn't appreciate being ignored for long. Of course, he called me immediately and patched things up.

✶✶✶✶✶

We talked frankly about his past, how he used to stutter badly in school and how his peers laughed at him. Even when he later went into the US Army, he stuttered. When he made corporal, his commanding officer told George's men: "I know Eames stutters; you may not understand everything that he says, but that which you understand, you must do. He knows what he's talking about."

George always had a huge ego when it came to clothes. His father didn't want to buy the kind of clothing that George wanted when he was a boy. He felt compelled to look good—George would later be known by everyone as a sharp dresser—so at thirteen or so, he told his father, "You don't want to buy me the kind of clothes I want? Fine, I'll buy them myself." George worked a shoeshine stand and other odd jobs as a teen and bought everything he needed to look good.

Later, from his wheelchair, he would tell me, "I got to look good. When people look at me, I don't want them to say, 'Look at that poor man in the wheelchair.' I want them to look at me and say, 'That man sho' know how to dress!'"

One of George's practices bothered me intensely. He stole. First, he often bought "hot" items. Then, when he went shopping, I knew him to switch tags, putting a cheap tag on a more expensive item. I argued with him about it and came to understand that for George, these were guerrilla tactics. Blacks constantly bucked up against a white economy that seemed designed for everyone else's needs but theirs. The Veterans Administration had denied his pension which he deserved. The white man gave nothing away unless it was inferior, broken, or spoiled. (I remembered the doll which I had given the poor black man from Cinclare Plantation.) As time passed, I worked with him to stop stealing. As he gained prominence in the NAACP, I convinced him that he should do nothing to dishonor his position and the organization. He loved civil rights passionately and would do nothing to jeopardize the organization. He stopped stealing.

The Topic of Marriage Comes Up

The topic of marriage came up. One day I asked, "George, how is it that a good-looking man like you has never been married?"

"I was," he replied.

I learned that he had been married in a Baptist wedding.

"Does it bother you?"

It bothered the heck out of me. I was a Catholic; good Catholics don't marry divorced people. Here I had thought I was standing on the highest moral ground; now I find out the church that I loved would not accept this relationship.

If I found out earlier, more than likely I would have broken off our relationship.

Now I couldn't. I was in too deep.

We talked briefly about his previous married life. On May 8, 1961, he had married Lucinda Turner. They separated around January 29, 1964 and lived separately with no reconciliation in those intervening years.

The divorce was finalized February 3, 1966.

He described how his wife used to cry all the time as she realized she would not have children. And how when she became mad at him, she moved his wheelchair where he could not reach it.

I determined in my own mind that this was no marriage at all. George explained that his divorce decree stated that no children had been born of their marriage—but she had become pregnant either during their breakup or right after. She never told her children that George was not their father, and they continued to think that they were George Eames' children.

I was attending the Catholic Chapel on LSU campus at that time. One Sunday evening as I sat in the pews near the front by the altar, I suddenly realized that all the white people were moving in, some into the pew where I was. They would undoubtedly move away if they knew I was in love with a black man. Suppose George had been sitting beside me? What about the church in Brusly where I had gone for years as a child? That one would be even worse.

I was uncomfortable with the prejudice I perceived in the church. I left before the Mass could start and didn't go back. For years.

Chapter 4

Rape And Outrage

George and I had fallen deeply in love, but I had not yet moved in with him. For appearances sake, I maintained an apartment. We generally concealed some aspects of our relationship, at least from my family. Then an incident occurred in September 1973 when I was 26 years old—something completely unexpected, shocking, and terrifying.

I had just dressed and was ready to go to George's apartment, when suddenly I heard a man trying to break into my apartment. I immediately called the police. While I was still on the phone, he tore through the door, grabbed a butcher knife from my kitchen, pulled the phone from me, and slammed it down. I stalled him as long as possible, but he made me retrieve my car keys, forcing me drive to a deserted house where he assaulted me.

My father's worst fears were coming true: a black man was raping his only daughter.

I tried to talk my way out of this. Acting friendly, I asked the attacker if he knew George.

Nothing stopped the attacker. After several assaults, the man left me hogtied in a closet and slammed the door. He left me nude, bleeding, tied up, and terrified. How would I get out of this? That closet door seemed solid as it closed. I was afraid and exhausted. I think I dozed on the dirty carpet in the closet; I soon awakened.

I was determined to get out of the closet and find help. I finally managed to free my hands from my feet and began kicking the closet door. It gave. I hobbled to a window. Was the man still there? In a quandary, I feared that the attacker would return, assault me again, and possibly bring others with him.

I had to leave. But how? Who would be on the road this early in the morning? Then I found that the thick glass on the windows of this old house would not break easily. My hands were tied behind my back. Finally, I opened one window.

I called "Help!"—every time I saw headlights. I was careful to keep any hysteria from my voice.

A car stopped. "Where are you?" he asked.

"I'm tied up in this house. I've been raped," I said calmly.

"I'm sorry, lady, but you're going to have to show yourself—this could be a trap. I'm a security guard hired to patrol Plank Road."

"I'm going to try to reach the back door." I hopped as best I could to the tiny screened back porch where I showed myself in the back door. He was waiting with his flashlight.

It was the most humiliating moment of my life.

"Oh, my God!" he swore. He cut the ropes from my hands and feet; he gave me his raincoat.

The rapist took my car.

I gave the investigating officers this information and a description of the man, "He wore a bandanna covering his hair, a camouflage shirt or jacket. He was about my height with a slight build, and his voice was soft."

They recognized him, Donald Ray O'Connor, and went to his house.

Luckily I had memorized my license plate number. Police found my car parked nearby, with my car keys in the suspect's pocket. Police had been observing him for some time. They had suspected that he was a serial rapist, but did not have enough evidence to arrest him until then.

That spring, 1974, we went to trial. Nervous and unsettled, yet confident, I testified. When I saw Donald Ray O'Connor's young, tiny wife testify that he had been with her the whole evening, I felt sorry for her—but not for him.

As I recall, none of my family were with me in court. George did not come. I would not have been comfortable with any of them there. I don't think anyone was there with me except for members of the prosecutor's office.

I did not return to court for the sentencing. I read that the judge sentenced him to 40 years in prison, if I remember correctly. In 2014, I was notified that he was being released, but I did not fear him. I figured he would be as glad to stay away from me as I was to stay away from him.

What I found more shocking and upsetting, however, was a knock on my door in January 2015.

Another man is in prison in New Orleans, serving time for a similar rape in a neighborhood close to where my own rape had occurred. The attorney claims that this rape, too, was probably committed by

Donald Ray O'Connor, who had not yet been imprisoned at the time this other rape took place. Then he told me that in my case, O'Connor had been found guilty of *armed robbery*, not rape.

I was aghast. All these years I felt I had helped to put away a serial rapist. Why would they sentence him for armed robbery? All the evidence was there for rape, had been laid out for the jury and the judge—why?

How did this happen? The only reason I could think he was convicted of armed robbery—which it certainly was, also—was perhaps because armed robbery carried a stiffer penalty at the time. The attorney took my deposition; I insisted that as far as I was concerned, the rape in 1973 was the primary crime, and the theft of my car was secondary.

After the Rape

But to return to September 1973, my father's reaction to my rape frightened my family. In a rage, he threatened to kill the rapist. He would hollow out a Bible, to put a gun in it, and pose as a minister to enter the jail where the man was being held. My father wanted to kill him. Family members restrained him and calmed him down.

I moved in with my godparents for a few days; they helped me to find a new apartment and move.

When I was able to return to George, we talked it through. He was kind but unusually quiet. He wondered: How many black men had been tortured and hung, castrated and killed for such perceived offenses? Mainly, he wanted to feel sure that I had not been mistaken about the man's identity, his description, clothing, and voice. I was sure. The police found my keys in the man's pocket mere hours after the assault.

This violence did not interrupt my relationship with George. After all, he had nothing to do with it. Still, my experience had been traumatic. For over a year I felt insecure. Any door was vulnerable to someone who wanted to attack you. I felt so vulnerable that I lost all interest in sex. George was affectionate, but cautious with me.

*****

Before the rape, around 1972, when I finally told Mama that I was dating a black man, she was horrified and warned me. "Kathy! Don't you realize that no white man will ever want to touch you if you date a black man?"

"Mama, if any white man doesn't want to touch me, that will be great since it will help me eliminate any men I wouldn't want to associate myself with anyway. Let me tell you something. Nothing and no one can interfere with this relationship. Not because he is black. Not because he is in a wheelchair. He has the moral right and I have the moral right to pursue this relationship wherever it takes us as a man and a woman. This is the moral truth of this situation. I don't know what will happen. The relationship may come to nothing. It may lead somewhere. But I will not break it off just because he is black. You can take it or leave it."

What disturbed me most was not that Mama disapproved of the relationship—but that she disapproved of it for all the wrong reasons.

Daddy Said: "My Daughter Is Dead."

An amazing transformation happened to my father around 1973 or 1974. He attended a *cursillo*, a religious retreat where he had some kind of conversion experience.

Mama called me, excited, "Daddy is back from his *cursillo*, and Kathy, guess what! He's changed. He told me how he went up in the front of church and talked to one of the black men who were there. He said he apologized to the man about everything he ever did to hurt black people. And he cried! Maybe we can tell Daddy that you're dating a black man. Let me try to talk to him. I'll call you later."

She did call me a couple days later, crying, "Kathy, don't come home! Daddy has gone crazy. He's driving around with a gallon of whiskey and his pistol looking for you. I don't think he's even going to work."

I was terrified. I switched cars and moved to the outskirts of Baton Rouge to stay with a former LSU student and his wife, both of whom had become close friends. I stayed away from George's apartment for weeks. I was afraid I might lead my father to George.

When Daddy calmed down, he and my natural brother, R. J., would have nothing to do with George and me. My adopted brother—Brett, then a young teenager—was simply confused.

Daddy said, "My daughter is dead. I never had a daughter."

My brother, three years younger than me, said virtually the same, "My sister is dead. I never had a sister."

R. J. was close to Daddy and felt essentially that I had ruined the family, especially my father's life. He was protective of Daddy, thus had to deny me forever. He has never relented.

Chapter 5

LSU

In 1972, George went to an LSU basketball game one night. I don't remember going with him that time. Head basketball coach Dale Brown had just been hired.

Everyone was curious about Brown and he was in the news. Years later, Kevin Cook interviewed Dale for an article in *Playboy* magazine published in April 1990. The article explained why Dale was not a racist and how he had met a black activist, George Eames, who helped him recruit black players for the LSU basketball program.

Here is the story about Dale Brown and how he and George began a lifelong friendship.

Dale Brown had a rough childhood. He was abandoned by his father before he was born. As a young child Dale watched his mother struggle to find meaningful work and decent housing for herself and her child. His empathy, ever with his beloved mother, motivated Dale to become a fighter, to identify with all those victimized by society and cultural bias. Growing up in the Dakotas, Dale eschewed racism. As a matter of fact, Dale told Kevin Cook, his interviewer, about an AAU tournament in Montana, when the Native Americans came out in colorful headdresses. He said, "Man, I want to go warm up with them!"[1]

As the new head coach at LSU, Brown wanted black players but had no idea how to recruit them. LSU was shaped by the Jim Crow laws of 1956. LSU was another victim of racial bias, and for decades the school could neither recruit nor even entertain black athletes at its campus. Dale explained to writer Cook that he had wanted to recruits blacks, but they were leery because of Louisiana's historical racism. It wasn't till he met George that he had any results.[2]

How natural it was that these two would team up. So how did they meet?

George, a devoted fan of all sports, had been attending basketball games at LSU. He was a lone black face in the crowd. One night in 1972 he was sitting courtside. The Tigers were losing badly to Alabama. At halftime as Dale passed him on the way to the locker room, George yelled, "When are you going to get some blacks on this team and win some games?"

Seething with frustration, Dale suddenly turned around, knocking down the rope and poking George in the chest with an angry finger.

The two differ a bit on what was said next.

George told me that Dale had said to him, "If you can find me some blacks with the balls I got, I'll play 'em."

Dale told me in 2013, "That's not what I said. I told George, 'When the brothers got as much pioneer spirit as I got, I'll play 'em.'"

The next day, George called Dale and told him, "Remember me, Coach? I'm the brother in the wheelchair that you grabbed last night. When can we get together and turn around this athletic program of yours?"

Both Dale and George were committed to changing the playing field for African-American students, not only in basketball, but in other athletic and academic areas of student life. They didn't have a smooth working relationship at first. However, because Dale had LSU's blessing to desegregate the basketball program and to secure the black talent needed to improve the team's performance on the court, with George's encouragement, they met to discuss a strategy that would work to desegregate the basketball program.

Thus began the long road trips to other parts of the state, attending games and visiting homes of prospective black recruits. George also insisted that Dale go to the local high school games, especially to his alma mater, McKinley High School, where he himself had once played basketball for Coach George Mencer, his hero.

On those long road trips, they enjoyed meals at historic Louisiana restaurants such as Pat's Fisherman's Wharf in Henderson, Louisiana. They shared stories of their childhood experiences, families, and solidified their relationship as they began to understand one another better.

Their initial working relationship grew into a solid friendship. George watched many practice sessions, discussing with Dale individual players, their strengths and weaknesses. George had long been going to the games; I began going with him and loving every minute of it.

I remember visiting Dale and Vonnie and young Robin (their daughter) in their home, celebrating several Christmases with them at their home or ours.

Still, those two hardheads were constantly debating, planning, strategizing basketball ploys and policies.

Active in the local branch of the NAACP, George was neither president nor vice president when he met Dale. He was only the office manager, but as his dedication grew along with his prestige and success in the organization, he became one of Dale Brown's staunchest allies. George solicited life memberships in this flagship civil rights organization from Dale himself, and from LSU Athletic Director Joe Dean. Dale attended banquets of the organization, helped with fundraising, and served as keynote speaker on several occasions.

Dale Brown's Role in Desegregating LSU

George gave an interview with Eyeline Films regarding Dale's role in desegregating Louisiana, particularly LSU athletics.

George declared, "In 1974 Dale Brown was the first white in East Baton Rouge Parish to join the local branch of the NAACP, and in 1976 he became the first white life member of the NAACP." George explained, "At that time the NAACP was the most hated organization in the state of Louisiana. Consequently, it was the worst organization a white man could be involved in. When Dale Brown became involved with me, and they found out how aggressive I was, that made him become the same target I was. A Ku Klux Klan member called me about four hundred times one night, repeating over and over, 'Nigger, nigger, nigger, nigger, etc.' I called the FBI and they investigated, found out who had called, and stopped it. Dale Brown had similar calls, so much so that he had to change his phone number. He couldn't even give out his phone number; that was just how bad it was."

I remember the night Dale recruited Ron Abernathy, the first black assistant basketball coach at LSU. In 1975 Dale desperately wanted to recruit young Durand "Rudy" Macklin from Louisville, Kentucky for LSU. Going up to Louisville, he noticed a talented young black coach—Rudy's coach, as a matter of fact. He thought to himself, "That young man certainly knows how to handle himself

1983—Dale Brown with his wife, Vonnie, is receiving his life membership certificate from life membership director Dr. Edward Muse of the national office of the NAACP with George.

and his team. I need to recruit him, too! Rudy and Coach Abernathy—what a conquest!" Dale was no fool. Rudy would more willingly come to Louisiana if his coach came with him.

In 1976 at 2:00 a.m. one morning, a long distance phone call came from a frustrated Dale Brown, "George, I'm trying to convince Ron Abernathy to come to LSU, but he's heard some awful things about the Klan, right there in Denham Springs. Please tell him that what he's heard is not true. That there is no curfew for blacks in Baton Rouge, that the Klan does not run Baton Rouge—but that you do!"

Dale later explained to me, that before he would involve himself too deeply with George, he went to Ossie Brown (District Attorney from 1972-1984) to find out how George Eames had been shot in 1956. Dale said, "Ossie closed the door, and told me that it had all been a cover-up. The man who shot him was upset about another man. George had never done anything wrong, but was a victim, in the wrong place at the wrong time."

Even sixteen years after they met, George was still disgruntled with the LSU athletic department. Though he and Dale had desegregated the basketball players, George wanted better representation in all departments. George held a press conference, starting a commotion on campus and in the press that would not soon be resolved. The next day, February 25, 1988, Karen Didier reported that although local NAACP head George Eames had held lengthy discussions with then Chancellor James Wharton on LSU hiring practices, he felt that nothing had yet been achieved. Wharton disagreed, of course, insisting that the black faculty members had more than doubled to forty-three black faculty members out of the more than 1000 total faculty.[3]

I had helped George to prepare his notes for the press conference. George's complaint was that LSU had "no black athletic counselors, no black athletic advisers, no black athletic coordinators, no recruiters on staff for football, baseball or track for men or women." His notes continued: "No blacks serve in the position of associate athletic director, as coach or assistant coach in baseball, track and field or women's basketball. No blacks serve as the head of an academic department on the campus."

He continued: "We're not trying to destroy Louisiana State University. We're trying to build it into a multi-racial university that all citizens can respect. We're not asking to take over the institution. We're asking for parity." Although George did not specify specific employment goals or a time period, he wanted written assurances that these needs would be addressed. In his typical style, he smiled when asked by the reporter, "I'll answer you in the words of an old black spiritual: 'How long?' Not long." In keeping with NAACP tactics nationwide, George mentioned that the organization had more than one way to bring pressure for compliance, including a boycott. He had already forwarded a copy of his findings to the national office and to the US Department of Justice.[4]

Other Louisiana press followed this story eagerly: "LSU officials answer racism charges," appeared in the *Alexandria Daily Town Talk*. In addition to the discussion reported by the *Advocate*, Alexandria's press alluded to George's remark about LSU being a "plantation" with a "plantation" mentality, in that the all-white triangle at LSU would not allow blacks to play the positions of quarterback, center, or guard.[5]

After Chancellor Bud Davis left the press conference, in response to questions about whether LSU manifested any racist attitudes, Coach Brown said that the university was "not without racism."

Damning the university with faint praise, the Chancellor had

informed the press that Carolyn Collins had recently been appointed
the first black dean of a major division at LSU. Dale commented that
one black appointment in a state with a 40 percent black population
should be called what it is...racism. Mike Archer [head football
coach at LSU 1987-1990] complained that Eames' comments were
complicating recruitment.

Next year in 1989, the New Orleans press reported the continuing
action against LSU, Tim Ellerbee, "NAACP pushing for changes," the
New Orleans Times-Picayune. The New Orleans media described the same
press conference, noting that Eames explained that the black football
athletes did not feel entirely comfortable in approaching the all-white
staff about their problems; that the fans did not accept them; that anyone
observing LSU rivals located in Michigan, Alabama, Ohio State, Notre
Dame etc., could see that they treated their players differently; and that
at one point in the 1989 season, black players and fans had discussed
a possible boycott which had never materialized. (Clearly, the message
George implied was that such a boycott would indeed materialize in the
future if conditions for black athletes did not change.)

LSU Athletic Director Dean insisted that although LSU was not,
at that time, winning football games, the university certainly did not
have racial problems, but that "George Eames has pushed for us to
hire more black people, but that's his job."[6]

The article relayed that George was specific in his demands that
the athletic department open all positions on the football team
to black athletes. I was with George when he planned the press
conference and had helped him to write his notes. These included
his favorite discussion of the "white triangle," a pet peeve of his; "You
see, a football team has what I call the triangle, and if you're a black
athlete you need not apply. LSU has no black guards, centers, or
quarterbacks." His contention was that the triangle constituted the
leadership or "brains" of the team, implying that a consistently all-
white triangle indicated that the all- white coaches had no confidence
in the intellectual ability of blacks to succeed in these positions.

George also promoted LSU's hiring of reputable black coaches
and administrators to serve as role models. Then he put in a plug
for his friend, Dale Brown, "If they have problems now, the football
players have to go to the head basketball coach, Dale Brown!"

George lamented the position of the black football players, given the current atmosphere on campus. "That's not the way it should be. The LSU family has embraced the black basketball players. The black football players don't have the same family experience. That has got to change."[7]

Despite the problems that he had described, George was pleased with the press conference. He expressed hope that, although for years among blacks it seemed clear that LSU was not the school where blacks should play football, with LSU's attention to the problem, the recruiting of the best black talent in the country could only improve.

Though LSU officials disagreed with George, they also felt that the meeting had been productive and insightful.

What the press did not hear and would not be able to report was a conversation before the press conference. As was often the case, George was late, nearly an hour, for a press conference which he had called. Dale met him outside the arena, wringing his hands. "George, do you realize you've been keeping all these people waiting? My boss, the athletic director, the press...."

George retorted, "I've been keeping you waiting? Man, don't you know our people been waiting for freedom for 400 years?"

Working together for many years, George helped Dale recruit Coach Abernathy and Rudy Macklin from Kentucky; Ethan Martin and Howard Carter from Baton Rouge, Chris Jackson from Mississippi. I remember hearing George talk of others, less famous, for whom he fought just as hard. Never forgetting how much Dale also did for the NAACP, George decided in 1991 to honor Dale by writing a letter to the university:

George Honors Dale Brown

Baton Rouge Branch NAACP
P.O. Box 2901
Baton Rouge, LA. 70821
Chancellor Bud Davis
Louisiana State University

Dear Chancellor Davis:
After a unanimous decision, the Baton Rouge Branch of the NAACP advised me to congratulate Louisiana State University head basketball coach, Dale Brown, for his humane and forthright appearance before East Baton Rouge Parish School Board in support of Dr. Bernard Weiss.

Chancellor Davis, let me personally tell you about the person whom I know as Dale Brown and the things that this man has been able to do for East Baton Rouge Parish and for the state of Louisiana since he arrived in Baton Rouge.

On many occasions in the past nineteen or twenty years, Coach Brown has touched the hearts of many black people, white people, and other people of color, both within and outside of the university community, by his untiring resources, love, and affection for his fellow man. Case in point: in 1975, when Nixon was president, this country decided that affirmative action and set asides constituted reverse discrimination against white males (cf. Allen Barkley decision, University of California Medical School & Weber decision in the trade unions of Kaiser and Geismar plants here in Louisiana); and in 1976, our bicentennial year, the national director of the NAACP, Dr. Benjamin Hooks, came to speak at this local NAACP chapter's banquet—I invited Coach Brown to attend. Dr. Hook's theme was from the old Negro spiritual: "One More River to Cross." Dale and I, along with other people of good will (i.e. Dick Gregory, Rev. Jesse Jackson, Rev. T. J. Jemison, the late Emmitt Douglas, Harry Evans, Dr. Redfield Bryan, Al Guglielmo and others of note) decided to make a difference.

And this was before Dale Brown as coach and mentor of the Louisiana State University basketball program began to win championships. He put his reputation, his job, and his family in jeopardy during that time in one of the most racist, insensitive communities in the state of Louisiana. But none of the above hindered Coach Brown from speaking out about the injustices, not only in this parish or state, but across this nation. Highly recognized by African-Americans as one of the most fearless, respected coaches in the country, with his courage and foresight, this one man has been able to change the whole philosophy of Louisiana State University.

Congratulations and warmest thanks to Coach Brown for his many achievements and to Louisiana State University for its wisdom in retaining such a courageous coach and mentor.

Sincerely,

G. Washington Eames, Jr.

President, East Baton Rouge Parish Branch NAACP

cc: Coach Dale Brown, Louisiana State University

Joe Dean, Athletic Director, Louisiana State University

Dr. Bernard Weiss, Superintendent, E.B.R. Schools

Dr. Benjamin Hooks, National Director, NAACP

Dr. William F. Gibson, Chairman of the Board, National Office, NAACP

How George Helps Poor Children

Dale was also quick to recognize anything that George accomplished on the behalf of the university, its players, or children, in general. In February 1992, Coach Brown's first black office manager, Janis Simms, (hired with George's recommendation) mailed the following message to George on LSU stationery:

Dear Mr. Eames,

The staff of the LSU men's office would like to thank you for your overwhelming support and assistance of the LSU-Texas game in the Superdome on Friday, January 3, 1992. Through your efforts of contacting the Fourth District Baptist Association, headed by Rev. Charles Smith and various community leaders in East Baton Rouge, Orleans, and other surrounding parishes, we were able to provide tickets to over 10,000 underprivileged children in Louisiana, many of whom had never seen a LSU basketball game in person or had ever been on the inside of the Superdome.

Once again, thanks for your assistance.

Sincerely,

Janis Simms

Office Manager

The twin sister of Janis Simms, Jamie Simms , would also be hired as a tutor for students playing basketball for LSU. George and I would refer to these two as our "adopted daughters." We remained extremely close to them, and visited them in Memphis and Lake Charles on numerous occasions.

As we attended many basketball games in the seventies and eighties, I gleaned the full significance of this popular sport. I wanted to share my insights, so I wrote a poem in the nineties. When I shared it with Dale, he published it in one of the programs distributed before his games:

Making It
By Kathy Andre-Eames
Lesson 1: Whatever is not entirely physical,
must be spiritual, must be vision.

Lesson 2: What begins in the mind,
may pass through the body,

but comes to rest in the soul.

Lesson 3: Play as though
your life depended on it.

Lesson 4: Play as though
your soul depended on it.
It does.

Fine coaching is the catalytic spark
that fuses intellects, the hearts of action
into a steady stream of mastery,
the blended star of a dozen small reflections.

The arena is a caldron lit from within,
steadfast with light, burning wood and string,
fire to eat the flaming hands and feet,
distended chests, the strain of shocking heat.

Boys enter. Boys from weed-jammed parks,
concrete arenas, apartment alleys, shores,
blues and bayous, crack-filled parking lots.
Far from the three point line the first scores.
Begin, boys. Cut lanes where no lanes are!
Massage the ball with your minds, massage the goal!
Hammer, boys, hammer your melting hearts
from the first sparks into blazing sheets of gold!
Play is not play in the game that is not a game;
break your backs in the vein-standing stress!

Yet, in the eyes of boys, what tenderness
survives. Boys deep in joy, arm to arm,
knee to knee—they must and do survive,
surpassing dignity, a circle of lives,
standing man to man, a circle of friends.
The roar rolls over the long court!

A lay-up by five, ten converging hands!
Thousands are lifted, generating thousands,
etching the stats in bone, surging blood,
making it. Making the women's song.
Making it. The dreams of little girls.
A flood-gathering power. Full. Strong.

George Focuses on the LSU Athletic Department

By then I was teaching English at Glen Oaks High School, home of one of the most successful high school basketball coaches in the state. I gave my poem to Coach Harvey Adger, who in turn passed it on to his team. One of my juniors, Julius, came to me. I was touched when he told me that he read my poem before all of his games to motivate himself to do well.

George later told this story, which I had heard him repeat to many other people over the years, to Patrick Sheehan and Gannon Weaver of Eyeline Films, who interviewed him for their documentary movie about Coach Dale Brown:

> LSU was the last athletic department in the United States to desegregate itself *in toto.* Case in point: I attended a football game in the early sixties when LSU, all white, was playing the University of Colorado. A black player on Colorado's team named Cliff Branch brought a kickoff back one hundred yards. All I could hear, being the only black at the game in Tiger Stadium, was "Catch that nigger!" Comments like that went on for years until the early seventies when LSU got its first black football player, Mike Williams. Then I heard, "Don't hurt Leroy!" "Watch Leroy!" "Catch Leroy!" I thought to myself, Leroy must be playing defense and offense! So I asked to see a program, and I looked for Leroy, but there was no Leroy, first name or surname. "Nigger" had turned into "Leroy!"
>
> When I met my wife to be, Kathy Andre, she was teaching English at LSU. When she came to my apartment one evening, she told me about a composition that she was grading that had been written by one of the young men on the LSU football team. He said, "I'm so glad I'm a Tiger because if you are a Tiger, you can get a job at any factory, plant, or oil rig or anywhere in Louisiana, just because you were a Tiger."
>
> With that remark, I decided that G. Washington Eames, Jr. was going to desegregate LSU's athletic department so young black men and women would have those same opportunities in the state of Louisiana. My encounters with him [Dale] were not always cordial because we did not always agree about the speed of the turnover, but his comments did not deter my mission to desegregate all of LSU: faculties, staff, students, cheerleaders, Golden Girls, players, coaches, tutors, counselors, etc.
>
> My wife, Kathy, and I went through much turmoil during these years because we were on two tracks: to desegregate the EBR Parish

School System and to desegregate LSU. Our lives were threatened daily, our house was set on fire in 1981, a bullet came through one of our windows one night, etc.

And Dale Brown also had his problems in the circles in which he traveled, especially after he became a life member of the National Association for the Advancement of Colored People and participated in all our activities:

—hiring of the first black coach at LSU, Ron Abernathy

—recruiting of Ethan Martin, the first black player from East Baton Rouge

—the first black woman hired in the Athletic Department, basketball office manager Janis Simms

—the first black tutor for LSU basketball, Jamie Simms.

The successful desegregation of Louisiana State University, which is the mecca of the state of Louisiana, opened the doors of racial harmony across this state and in our local government, especially in East Baton Rouge Parish where we now have a black mayor, a black police chief, a black school board superintendent, black people in all areas of parish and state government.

Dale and I contributed to these successful endeavors, and we have documentation to prove it.[8]

✳✳✳✳✳

In the spring of 2008, George and I attended an AAU basketball tournament at a local high school. We watched Jalen Courtney and Andre Stringer, "Mr. Basketball" of Mississippi. George and I talked to these two outstanding athletes, both high school juniors from Jackson. We learned that they were both being recruited by Mississippi State and other major colleges. This was not about to happen if George had anything to do with it! He asked them if they had been approached by LSU—no. We met their families who were there and took pictures with them. George said he would set up a meeting with them and LSU's head basketball coach, Trent Johnson. George talked to both young men in depth. He followed up during the week, talking to both of them and to Coach Johnson. The next weekend Jalen called Coach Johnson to sign on with LSU. About a week later, so did Andre Stringer.

Chapter 6

A New Love—A New Life

George and I dated carefully in the seventies until our marriage in 1977. We traveled around south Louisiana to Opelousas or to Lafayette for picnics. We often went to New Orleans, enjoying the music and culture, the zoo and City Park, Bourbon Street, the French Market, beignets, and the like. In July 1971, we had attended Louie Armstrong's funeral in New Orleans, praying that no one would see us on television. At the same time, we also attended LSU basketball games and freely visited the friends we met there.

Two little incidents reveal a lot about us during this time.

On Bourbon Street one night a white tourist was heckling a little black shoeshine boy. George noticed and yelled, "Hey, man, leave the kid alone! If you want to mess with somebody, come mess with me!" He brandished his fists from his wheelchair. The man looked up, and when he realized who had yelled at him, he walked off embarrassed.

Another time I was rolling George's chair down the middle of Bourbon Street. An older lady on the balcony above us said to a companion, "How sweet! She must be his nurse."

I told George, "We'd better enlighten her."

I kissed him, and we heard the lady gasp, "Did you see that?"

✳✳✳✳✳

We were growing more comfortable confronting the public. We had weathered a rape, violent reactions from my family, distrust and fear from his family, and shock on the part of much of our Southern society.

I figured George would never ask me to marry him, might never feel he had the right to do that.

Consequently, in the fall of 1977 I bought my own engagement and wedding ring and told him, "George, this is what we need to do next. Let's get married. On November 21, 1977, we'll be celebrating the seventh anniversary of the day we met! Let's make it official. I think you're ready, and I know I'm ready."

From the twinkle in those mischievous eyes and the grin on his face, I knew everything I needed to know.

We set the date.

Though we knew we wanted to marry, we still did not want our marriage license published in the Baton Rouge newspapers, so we went to New Orleans. I remember to this day how the official in the white shirt looked at me when I told him we wanted to get our wedding license. First, a look full of surprise as he eyed George in his wheelchair. Then reproach and contempt as he realized we were a black and white couple.

Another official in the New Orleans office dismissed us, saying, "Y'all need to go to Algiers. They'll sell a marriage license to anybody in Algiers!"

Got on the ferry. Went to Algiers. Came home, license in hand, ready for November 21, 1977, our wedding day.

*****

Our wedding itself was a small, private affair in the home of friends, Gwen and Leo Davis. It was performed by Rev. William Simon, a friend whom George had asked. My mother, and Mama's oldest sister Helen, and George's sister Gloria signed the certificate as witnesses.

My first cousin, Vee, attended on my side. George's other sister, Joy Mae, and her daughter, Debra, joined us there. Dr. D'Orsay Bryant, president of the local branch of the NAACP, good friend, Dale Brown, head basketball coach at LSU, and their wives, celebrated with us as well.

Our reception was a wedding supper at Giamanco's where I had reserved a private room. It would cost several hundred dollars, but I was prepared. On my wedding night, I ordered lobster and invited my wedding party to order anything they desired. When I went to pay the bill, Dr. Bryant had already picked up the tab.

When we celebrated our first anniversary one year later, we returned to Giamanco's, inviting Doc and Dale and their wives to

1970s—NAACP Youth Council with Chairman George Eames: Tommy Gipson, Wanda Raby, Edward Reed, Alice Nick, Carl Booker, Andrea Turnbull, A. Johnson, Ray Dunn

celebrate with us. To my amazement, Dr. Bryant picked up the tab again! I later told George we would have to celebrate somewhere else in future years because Doc would never let us pay the tab!

Our happy wedding came at a cost. I realize today what it cost my mother to be at our wedding, to remain complicit in my relationship with George, my marriage, and all that would follow. I brought her untold emotional and mental suffering because of the subterfuge, because of her fears, and because of the division in my family. Our relationship threw Mama into a war, a minefield.

When Daddy's relatives came to visit, they talked about the "niggers," casting surreptitious looks at Mama. They knew about me and jabbed mercilessly at her.

The extended family was no less painful. Sometimes relatives and neighbors as well, were polite to me for my mother's sake, but since I never knew where some of them stood, I stayed away for the most part. Rumors arose that I was pregnant. I told Mama then, "They're going to be sadly disappointed when no baby shows up!" I had neither

1983—Dr. D'Orsay Bryant with his wife, Elayne. George served as vice president of the NAACP branch with Bryant for several years. Elayne, for many years a member of the board, worked closely with George on Freedom Fund Banquets and other projects.

the time nor inclination to subject myself to their condemnation.

Even years later, Daddy tolerated me coming to the house provided I did not talk about my husband; I had to walk on eggshells.

Despite the continued aggravation of family resistance, George and I were happy with one another. We were comfortable facing the public, *any* public. We had grown stronger with the conflicts, more resilient, more determined to live our own lives, more committed to one another and to civil rights. George continued with his volunteer work with the NAACP. I began working in management at Sears in 1974, so I was able to support the family with no trouble. I never resented George's poverty or having to be the financial support of the family.

I could never have asked him to give up the passion of his life. I simply shared it in my own way.

✳✳✳✳✳

George served with Dr. Bryant as his vice president, working closely with him, arranging his press conferences, then succeeded him as president. We remained close to the Bryant family. Doc was married to the former Elaine Butler, whose sister was Jean Butler. George had grown up with them, knowing them well.

When George became one of the original plaintiffs in the lawsuit to desegregate the East Baton Rouge Parish school system in 1956, he had attended meetings with A. P. Tureaud, Alex Pitcher, Jr., and Thurgood Marshall. They met for strategy meetings in the Butler Building owned by Dr. Leo Butler, the father of Elaine and Jean. Dr. Butler's daughters would later serve on the board of directors for the local NAACP branch and work tirelessly on branch projects, notably the Freedom Fund Banquets that were held every year, usually in August.

We were co-workers; we socialized together as well, attending parties and dinners at Doc and Elaine's home, especially for the grand Easter dinner that they held for family each year. We knew and loved their children: Lud, Leighton, and their beautiful twin daughters, Sherrie and Sharon. Jean's children were also close: Lynn Whitfield, Pepper, Kimberly, and Shawne.

When George, Gloria, and Joy Mae were young children, their mother, Alsie, would bring them to the Butler home where they played with Elayne and Jean when Alsie had an appointment with Dr. Butler. Today Jean remembers George as an energetic, fun-loving little boy with an infectious smile and lively sense of humor.

George worked closely with his cousin, Robert Eames, affable, talkative, often long-winded, but a brilliant attorney and as committed to civil rights as was George himself. Robert Williams, a

1980—The author with actress Lyn Whitfield, (Jean Butler's daughter) at a social function

Vietnam veteran, could be a little unpredictable, sometimes careless about his person and dress, but an equally if not more brilliant and insightful attorney. For many years, these two men working with attorney Murphy W. Bell, were the backbone of the local NAACP legal counsel, working smoothly with federal attorneys such as Franz Marshall.

Friends Help Move to a New Home

About a year after our wedding, we bought a house. I had no money. George had no money, but since he was a veteran, we qualified for a veteran loan with no money down. What a thrill this was for us!

Terry Robiskie, football running back at LSU, and his friend, Thylon Smith, linebacker, helped us move. After the two of them had carried every single thing we owned into a truck and from the truck into our new home, Terry asked Thylon, "You want to go play a little racquetball? We'll see you later, George." I was amazed at the energy these two had!

Terry not only helped us with the furniture, but also with a huge, traditional tub similar to the claw-footed tub that George had used on Van Buren St. Wanting exactly the same type of tub, he searched till he found one and bought it for the new house. But the traditional, low, porcelain cast iron tub presently in place was securely cemented and had to be removed. It was a piece of cake for this burly football player. Donning goggles, Terry cracked the tile and cement with well-placed strokes. He lifted the cast iron tub, discarding it outside.

We had built into the front room on Van Buren St. an eight-foot bar with Formica top and cabinets below. Once moved into the new house, George wanted that bar to put into our new den. No problem. Terry and Thylon ripped the bar from the apartment floor, placed it in his truck, and installed it where George wanted it in our new house.

Over the years, George took it upon himself to keep our home in good repair. He found and hired friends and service people to repair, build, renovate or service whatever we needed. He found lawn care specialists, fence builders, concrete and aggregate workers, ironworkers, roofers, tile craftsmen, carpenters, painters, electricians, plumbers, masons and brick workers, and mechanics or painters for our vehicles. We kept our vehicles year after year, not easily able to afford new replacements. Some of these service people would accept no payment for their services or would give us deeply discounted prices. In later years Herman Brister, Jr. came whenever George called, helping us to maneuver our VCR and cable television.

George was a great cook, especially now that we were in a larger, better-equipped kitchen. Often I returned from work to find our supper on the stove, dishes washed, and the kitchen and counters clean. After we adopted Wardell, George made him watch in the kitchen so he would learn how to cook. George cleaned up after himself in other ways as well, taking great care of his clothes, polishing our shoes, dusting, and helping me in any way that he could. I did all the household tasks he could not reach, hanging all pictures, some painting, repairing doors, and the like. My talents would prove handy when I renovated our bathroom in the nineties.

2007—Police Chief Jeff LeDuff, the first African-American police chief of Baton Rouge (appointed in 2005) greets George at the National Conference of Black Mayors.

2007—George attends the National Conference of Black Mayors with the first African-American mayor of Baton Rouge, Kip Holden, elected in 2005.

*****

The NAACP office, when it was in our home, challenged both of us. George would dust and try to organize it periodically. We accumulated mounds of material: newspaper clippings for cases and possible cases; his archives included letters, documents, lawsuits, collections of evidence, membership applications, and more. Without significant help he could do little.

We found a place for a small fire-resistant safe and filing cabinets, and we used drawers in the huge built-in desk that we had put in after our first house fire.

Pictures covered the walls, collages of all our activities in the NAACP and our sports activities. Other large pictures hung there as well, pictures of George and sometimes me with our first black mayor, Kip Holden; first black police chief, Jeff LeDuff; US Senator Mary Landrieu; Lyman White; Gov. Murphy J. Foster; staff pictures of the Capital City Baseball League and Delta Baseball Association; varied basketball team pictures; enlargements of news photos, and more. Eventually we'd have colorful news clippings of President Barack Obama and his family, his election, and his inauguration. Obama was celebrated with great fervor in our household.

People were coming and going constantly during the day and even into the evening; we had several folding metal chairs for small meetings, no table but clipboards to provide hard writing surfaces, and dozens of black and red pens with highlighters as well. George's bed, our television, and my one comfortable chair took up the rest of the space.

George always knew exactly what he wanted to say, but because of his atrocious spelling, I bought him an electronic speller. He never used it—after all, he had me! I regret today that I don't have much handwritten material from him—his penmanship was atrocious! He generally dictated everything to me, and I typed it. With the computer this became much easier. I would print the first version for both of us; we would go over the type together—editing, adding material, and polishing till it was as perfect as the two of us could make it. He himself kept notebooks. He made intricate notes for all the fundraising activities for the NAACP and his baseball programs, listing dozens of possible patrons, phone numbers, and other essential information.

Our home brought many visitors—and carried some risks. We had to leave the door unlocked though we knew it could be dangerous for him. George spent hours working in bed each day, so we had to let people enter without his having to get up each time. For important meetings, George did sit in his wheelchair, dressed properly, and often used our dining room table. But for everyday business, he worked from bed. He often suffered back pain, and I believe had he not done this, he would have begun experiencing the serious problems he eventually had with wounds much earlier.

By far the most typical thing he did daily was to devour the local newspapers, the *State Times* and the *Advocate*. He clipped articles that seemed important to him—so many that he stored great stacks of them in plastic bags. We eventually put these into huge, clean, plastic trash cans which were then moved to our shed.

I threatened him that as soon as he died, the first thing I would do would be to move all these trash cans to the curb to be picked up! He warned me then that he would come back to haunt me if I threw away his "archives." I complained that because they were in no way organized, they seemed useless. George persisted; and much to my chagrin, he often located articles later that he needed for a case.

Terry Robiskie had visited us with his friends, even one of his girlfriends, when we had lived on Van Buren St. at George's apartment. Now they came to our home. George recruited Chris Jackson here, as Dale assured his mother at two o'clock in the morning at our house, that her son would be perfectly safe in Baton Rouge because George would see to it. We treated Willie Simms to Louisiana-boiled hot sausage when Dale was trying to recruit him for the basketball team. We entertained Jose Vargas and his Italian girlfriend here after he began playing professional basketball in Europe. George and I cooked a mean spaghetti, and he had the pride to tell the young lady, "I tell you what, I can cook spaghetti even better than your mama!"

"Your spaghetti was better, Mr. Eames, but you have to understand, you have better meat here in the states!" she admitted. George's great nephew Harrell, Debra's son, was here on that occasion. Through star-struck eyes, he accepted from Jose a little porcelain figurine. I had placed it on our fireplace mantel for decoration. When I asked him later if he had seen it, Harrell replied in all innocence, "Aunt

Kathy, Jose gave it to me!" I didn't have the heart to tell him that it belonged to me and that Jose had no right to give it to him! I would never ask him to part with such a treasure.

Joyce Simms invited George and me to a couple of fish fries at her home where I met her husband, James, their son, Jimmy, and her twin daughters. Joyce was actually afraid of George when she was a young girl; she thought he was bad and tough. That changed. Consequently, when her twin girls, Janis and Jamie Simms were about thirteen or fourteen years old or so, around 1975-76, she trusted George to protect her girls. He began bringing them to concerts and ball games. I was working three nights and most Saturdays. Their father, it seemed, was also busy. George filled his van with these young companions and their friends giving rides to their favorite entertainment. George had earlier befriended his young cousins and other boys. He treated the young women as daughters; they also felt that he was a second father to them. As their mother Joyce lay dying of cancer several years ago, we visited her in the hospital where he

1992—Christmas with our two "adopted daughters," Jamie and Janis Simms

assured her, "Don't worry about your girls, Joyce. I'll be taking good care of them."

George and the twins called one another daily for years, even when they moved to Tennessee and Texas; they asked him for advice and brought the men they would marry to meet us and gain George's approval! Though—like all family—they occasionally had their disagreements.

How Our Families Accepted Our Marriage

After we were married, Mama often came to visit our home, sometimes on a Sunday afternoon. On holidays, she came when she could; we exchanged gifts. This did not work with my brother. After I sent gifts to my brother's children once or twice, they were returned. I stopped.

One Christmas evening when Mama came, we saw that she had been crying. When we demanded that she tell us what Daddy had done, she told us that he had threatened to throw out all of her

1991—Christmas with my mother, Emily Andre, George, and me

clothes before she came back—and that he was kicking her out if she came to visit us.

George was upset. He insisted that I give him Daddy's phone number. Mama and I pleaded with him not to make a bad situation worse. But, being George, he called anyway.

"Roy, why are you giving your wife such a hard time just because she wants to see her daughter on Christmas day?"

I'm sure Daddy was shocked to receive this call.

"None of your g– d— business," Daddy replied.

"It sure as hell is my business!" George shouted into the phone. "If you ever lay a hand on this sweet lady again, you'll know just how much my business it is."

"You want to meet me under the bridge?—I'll make you understand."

"I'll meet you any g– d— place you want to meet. I'm not scared of you—you coward—beating up on women!"

Daddy started sobbing, apologizing. He changed suddenly and dramatically. "I'm sorry, podnuh. I know I'm wrong. I know you take good care of my daughter. I won't give Emily a hard time again."

✳✳✳✳✳

George's sister, Gloria, seldom hosted social gatherings at her home, which was just down the street from us. On one occasion, after her retirement, she invited some close relatives, including George, me, and other friends.

We sat scattered about Gloria's living room, enjoying Gloria's gumbo and friendly drinks. Laughing, telling funny anecdotes to one another, the women especially were teasing one another about men and their "man troubles." Suddenly, Jean Butler announced rather decisively, "What I want is a man who will love me the way that Kathy loves George!" The whole room laughed and agreed. My devotion to him was completely evident to all of them. I was flattered, and felt it was true. What I didn't know was that the perception of many people was identical with Jean's opinion.

Chapter 7

Civil Rights Intensifies

George became intensely engaged with East Baton Rouge Parish School desegregation from about 1978 through the eighties. On Saturday, Oct. 4, 1980 the *Advocate* published an article which would later have dire consequences for us, "Eames naturally part of desegregation suit."

Ed Cullen reported that George had long been a party to the twenty-four-year-old desegregation lawsuit. In 1956 he joined the litigants with the encouragement of his cousin, Alex Pitcher, Jr. in the suit known as *Clifford Eugene Davis Jr. et al vs. The East Baton Rouge Parish School Board et al.* George remembered talking to famous civil rights litigants, A. P. Tureaud and A. M. Trudeau, both of New Orleans; and Constance Baker Motley and Thurgood Marshall, NAACP lawyers in New York. They met in Pitcher's office in the old Butler building and he recalled how the group had moved around, knowing the dangers of what they were doing, to avoid detection or suspicion.[1] [Only eleven years later, Marshall would become Chief Justice Marshall of the Supreme Court.]

George had long been fascinated by civil rights, by the law, and by the need for civil rights activism. When Pitcher explained to him that Brown vs. the Board of Education had stated in the 1954 landmark decision of the US Supreme Court that "separate educational facilities are inherently unequal," he leaped at the chance to become involved.[2]

For years George had been telling me stories of his friends while he was growing up.

His neighborhood, believe it or not, was not segregated at all. As a matter of fact, white boys whom he knew well and played with lived there. What he had never been able to understand was why after a weekend of sandlot baseball or football, whites and blacks went different ways on Monday morning. His mother, an English teacher with a keen interest in civil rights, explained it to him. George

77

1983—The author receives a commendation from Dr. Edward Muse, from the national office of the NAACP.

respected the feistiness of his mother. He remembered that in the forties, when it was far from popular, on Election Day she drove around helping register blacks to vote. George insisted, "That's where I got my ideas from. Mama was a strong woman."

The East Baton Rouge Parish School System finally went back into court about 1975; it had been so long since he had been involved in it that George literally forgot that he was a party to the suit. George took little time to adjust to the new proceedings. He was in court to hear US District Judge John V. Parker give the school board until January 1981 to submit a desegregation plan.

By now, George was vice president of the local branch of the NAACP. George reacted when asked by the reporter how he felt. He was somewhat saddened by the thought that so many children who had passed through the unequal system since 1956 had not gained the educational advantages to which they were long entitled. The system had delayed, denied, and contained us for too long already, he said. He compared the system to President Nixon, "Stonewall it. Put off. Finagle."

The school board always wanted more time—though they knew the ruling and the outcome. It seemed to George that their intention

1981—With the revival of the East Baton Rouge Parish schools desegregation case, George made many appearances in federal court. He's shown with then-City Councilman Howard Marcellus and George's close friend, Frank Millican, a member of the EBR Parish school board.

was never to comply, but to do the same thing they had done under (US District Judge) E. Gordon West who, with school board lawyer John Ward, blocked implementation of the federal order at every turn. West called the US Supreme Court's 1954 decision, "one of the truly regrettable decisions of all time."

Of all the players, attorney John Ward most irked George. The public, including black parents, paid Ward's salary, yet he never represented their interests. Not only was this "taxation without representation," but the black community in effect had to pay double, needing also to support the litigants who did represent their valid interests.

As George warmed to his subject, he clarified for the reporter—and for me—how unfair the system had long been. Talking about the "inconvenience" of the long bus rides for the white children, he could only laugh. In his day, no yellow school buses existed. White children were given tokens to ride the city buses while black children walked. This, despite the fact that only one black high school in the parish, McKinley High School, required black students who wanted an education to cross the entire parish in most cases, as best they could—with no help from the school system. George laughed, remembering an old friend in high school. One of McKinley's football players whom they called "Zion City," had to walk from north Baton Rouge to south Baton Rouge. Living close to Baker, he had to walk or hitchhike past Istrouma and Baton Rouge high schools. Without an interstate, the only routes were Plank Road and Scenic Highway.[3]

Other inequalities made participation in school activities difficult for black students. For example, McKinley had no track. Athletes ran relays around the building "over sidewalks and bricks. Fall down and kill yourself." With no gym and with only one light on each goal, the students played in the dark, missing the layups because they simply couldn't see the basket. Students had no water fountains, no dressing room, and no football field. The team, carrying all the gear, had to walk to whatever field they could find for practice. Even the band had to practice in the street.[4]

McKinley could not accommodate the great number of black students from throughout the parish. Students had to attend in shifts, a morning shift for half of the students and an afternoon shift for the other half.

For whites to complain about the "inconvenience" of having to ride the buses was laughable. As far as George was concerned, "busing" was just an excuse for the school system to try to get around the US Constitution. Asked what he wanted, George would invariably repeat, "Justice. What do you want? That's what I want. A fair chance at the same privileges. Don't handicap or restrict me because I'm black."

George Calls for Reform at Many EBR Schools

George grew more involved with the school system, even during the tenure of Dr. Bernard Weiss. Weiss became a close friend. This led to deeper efforts at reform. The following article appeared in the *Advocate* on June 2, 1989: "NAACP president calls for federal probe of East Baton Rouge School System." Curt Eyesink reported George's charges of racist practices in nine parish high schools and in the school system's maintenance department.

In addition, one of the middle school principals, Westdale's Patsy Smack, had been arrested for shoplifting and served a probationary period. George immediately called for her job. His reason? "If this had been a black principal, she would have been long gone!" He felt a "buddy system" was in place in the school administration system, with whites in power "having each other's backs"—after all, this school system had remained under a federal court order to desegregate for more than thirty years with cases like Smack's allowed to remain secret. The problem, according to George, was the need to dismantle the buddy system and get rid of "the good old boys" who wanted no change at all.[5]

George called for a series of actions and investigations. He specified the time periods and incidents he wanted examined:

1. Zachary High and administration, last ten years. The school's principal had just permitted its first prom since blacks were integrated into the school.

2. Woodlawn High and administration, last ten years. Black students attending Woodlawn's feeder middle school somehow never make it to Woodlawn.

3. Belaire High School and administration, five or six years. George cited discrimination in choosing cheerleaders, homecoming queens, and their courts.

4. Glen Oaks High School and administration, five years. George

was asking for a federal probe into the suicide of a 15-year-old black student in the assistant principal's office. A .357 Magnum revolver was used.

5. Robert E. Lee High School and administration. George stated that he had been told by black parents that the administration intimidated blacks on campus, and he had been asked by black parents to investigate the presence on that campus of radical, right-wing "skinheads" who had been intimidating black students and spraying racist graffiti on school property.

6. Istrouma High School. There were claims by black parents that when it became predominately black, "the administration just wrote it off."

7. Baker High School, current and prior administration. George claimed he had received more than one hundred complaints of civil rights violations at the school.

8. Central High School. They claimed unfair athletic practices and coach guidelines for black students forced to work during the summer.

9. McKinley High School. The school had declining enrollment and a report that the school's notable jazz band was almost exclusively white.

10. Investigation of nepotism by whites in the maintenance department of the school system which was preventing promotions of blacks to prominent positions.[6]

George did not contact Dr. Weiss directly on these issues. Weiss acknowledged a fine working relationship with George, and his willingness to work out any problems brought to his attention.

George Seeks the Truth as He Solves Problems

Right after George was elected branch president in 1980, an elderly black man called the NAACP phone installed in our home. When he asked for Mr. Eames, I replied that George was out. He hesitated a moment, then volunteered, "You know, Ms. Eames, your husband don't have a whole lot of polish, but when he say something, everbody know exac'ly what he said!"

Early on, George's standards for the work he did in civil rights became absolutely clear to me because we discussed them. Nothing but the truth would suffice. When complaints came to the NAACP office, he did his best to investigate every allegation, interrogating those making the complaint, making absolutely sure that they were truly wronged, that they were telling the truth as far as he could ascertain. His guide was the law, pure and simple. He believed in upholding the law. He explained that the NAACP was a legal organization, that his job was to hold white people to the law, and that if the law itself was unjust, the changing of that law was a different matter and necessitated different actions—which was not his job. in that particular case.

One case I remember well because it clearly illustrated how he worked. A black woman called him one day to complain that her husband's and her rights had just been trampled by the police.

He began his patient interrogation, "What happened?"

"My husband was sleeping in his car right in front of our house, and the police arrested him!"

"Why was he sleeping in the car?"

"He'd been drinking and he just fell asleep. Then the police come along and tell him he had to leave, but he was right in front of our house!"

"Then what happened?" George asked.

"He wouldn't leave, so the police was going to arrest him and put the cuffs on him!"

"And?"

"What you mean, and...? I seen what the police was doing to my husband, and I come out to tell them to leave him alone! They told me I was interfering with a police officer and if I didn't go back in the house, they was gonna arrest me, too!"

"I'm sorry, ma'am," George began to explain to her, "but you and your husband were in the wrong."

"Wait, a minute, Mr. Eames—whose side you on? I called you for help and you telling me that I'm wrong?"

"As I was saying, ma'am, you and your husband were in the wrong because there is a law against loitering. When your husband refused to move, he broke the law. Then you came along and broke another law, interfering with an officer who was just trying to do his duty. You lucky you weren't also arrested!"

"Well, I never...!" The phone slammed down.

George Saves a Job and Helps Make Bail

George had completed only tenth grade, yet he had a gift, an instinct, and a talent for getting to the bottom of things. The only subject he had loved in school was social studies. He paid keen attention and often challenged his teachers on widely varied issues.

This loitering case was far from the last one of this sort. Numerous complaints poured in, as people left challenging messages on the NAACP phone. Many cases were more complex and took hours—if not days or weeks—to analyze. He worked methodically, trying to trace all the facts. Because of his thoroughness, he simply could not process all the complaints; he had no one to whom he could delegate this work, and the public complained when he didn't call them back. George did all he could, short of working twenty-four hour days. On the phone, leaning on his elbow in bed for the most part, he handled all of this. He could be on the phone late into the night some days. The older he became, the more his elbows would trouble him, painful and sore.

George often intervened for people's jobs.

One case which we both enjoyed involved an elderly black man named Ned. Calling first to say he had been fired, he begged to come to our home to seek George's help to recover his job.

Ned insisted, "I don' want take up all yo' time, Mr. Eames. I know you some kind o' busy." White-haired, slightly stooped, eminently respectful, Ned stood nervously holding his cap in his hands as he apologetically explained what had happened.

He worked at a meat counter in a major chain grocery store. The manager of the meat department allowed Ned, who was the assistant manager, to bring home to his dog old cuts of meat that he did not feel comfortable selling to their customers.

One evening, the general manager discovered meat in Ned's possession as he was leaving the store. He fired Ned on the spot. The next morning Ned called George, pleading that he intervene for Ned's job.

George first contacted the meat manager, determining that Ned had indeed told him the truth; he had permitted Ned to take home old cuts of meat.

Then George called and asked for the general manager. George didn't take long to sort out this case. Ned's job was restored.

The next day, Ned appeared in the NAACP office, where he thanked George profusely.

"Mr. Eames," he said before he left, "I got one more request—could you get me a raise?"

George laughed, "You better be glad for now you have your job back. I think we better leave the raise alone for right now!"

In another case, a woman pleaded with George for her son who was in jail. I don't remember the details; however, I do remember that George drove to New Orleans with her. He ultimately signed a jail bond for the young man.

Some official called George that week to say, "Mr. Eames, I see that you signed a bail bond for this young man. Do you realize that you have put your home in jeopardy—you could lose your house if this young man doesn't show up for court!"

George did not realize the implications. He asked the official if he could reverse the action, and the bail bond was overturned. George always took care not to put me or his family in jeopardy in any way; he had not realized the possible outcome of his generous actions.

My uncle Gerald Altazan, who has followed George's career and our lives for years, summed it up: "You know, when you see George on television, you almost think he's a mean man. When you meet him in person, he's about the nicest person you ever want to meet."

In the late eighties and early nineties George did a series of interviews with John Spain on his *Sunday Journal* television show. As Beth Bryant said, "John Spain hated George, but because interviews with George gave him tremendous ratings, Spain continued to invite him. Public impressions of George came from this intense adversarial relationship which they had. Every rejoinder was an attempt to overturn the other's point or position."

I knew what the viewers saw, but my own view was far different. I knew him from the inside out. George solicited no middle-of-the-road fans; either you hated or you loved him. He struggled to tell the truth as no one else would tell it and as he best knew it. Usually, blacks loved him while many whites felt unfairly castigated. George would persist, pressured and driven—his messages delivered through raw will. These brutal messages he had no patience to polish, spoon feed, sweeten, prettify, or delay.

Chapter 8

A Son at Last

Even before we were married, we had purchased a little poodle whom I named Chavis. As we lavished our affection and attention on the dog, one day I told George, "You know, it's a shame that we're giving so much to a dog when there are children who need a good home."

Newly married and in a new home, we began to consider adoption. Of course, my maternal instincts kicked in big time, and George agreed.

We wanted a child.

In the late seventies we began adoption procedures. The social worker, it was clear, had reservations about placing a child with a mixed couple. We were honest and cooperated with her as best we could, but we were also adamant that we could provide a wonderful, loving family for a young child.

She explained that she felt a child would be confused to have a white mother and a black father. We were amazed. We countered that a mixed child would find a home exactly suited to his background. Who could best help a mixed child than mixed parents? What was more logical?

We finally received that phone call we had been waiting for.

Wardell Austin Bennett was a child of a white mother and a black father, a young man in his twenties who had died of a heart attack.

Wardell was just short of six years old. Placed temporarily in New Orleans in a home for children, Wardell had been taken from his mother's home a couple of months previously. His birthday was on Dec. 20, 1979, and our visit was planned for that week, several days after his birthday.

We bought a Spiderman doll for his birthday celebrated earlier that week. After visiting Wardell in the home for about thirty minutes, we were permitted to take him to the park. We fed the ducks and marveled together at this wonderful, beautiful little boy. I believe we took him home with us just a few days later, maybe New Year's Eve. George and I were ecstatic as we brought him to Sears where I was working, introducing him as our son and buying him clothing and all the personal items he would need.

I took a couple of weeks off but had to return to work. George was a devoted father, bringing Wardell everywhere he went. Our friends and some family members were warmly welcoming. My cousins, Ingrid, Robert, and her family gave him a party.

Wardell was quiet; he had much adjusting to do.

As we lived with Wardell, we learned more about him. He spoke of his little brother, Robbie, and a baby sister, Angela, whom he loved dearly. When he cried for his family, it wasn't for his stepfather or his mother—he cried for Robbie. "I want Robbie!"

This was heartbreaking for us; we could tell him only "Baby, we don't know where Robbie is! We would find him for you if we could, but we don't know where he is."

Years later, while George was in prison, I spent a week in New Orleans, searching public records, the Charity Hospital where Wardell was born, struggling to find Robbie and Angela for him. All my attempts were fruitless. Now, after the chaos of Hurricane Katrina, the case is probably hopeless.

As we spent more time together, Wardell told some of his story. "When they came for me [the social workers who took him from his mother], I was holding on to my Mama's legs; and they had to pull and pull to get me away because I was real strong."

Wardell had emotional problems; he continued to see a psychologist for a year. Then the doctor told us he thought Wardell had progressed enough to stop treatment.

We did everything with Wardell, taking him to sports events, on hiking and camping trips, and to the movies. One year, we camped in the Garden of the Gods Campground in a tent near Colorado Springs. Wardell and I went hiking in the canyon and riding the trolley into Manitou Springs. In later years we bought a camper. George had a bed built into his long van; since he could not enter the camper, he slept in his van. Wardell and I slept in the camper. Wardell did many healthy activities with both of us or one of us or with other children and family members.

I remember a couple of humorous incidents during these early years.

George and I had a little poodle named Chavis before Wardell came to us. Just as he would do with Wardell later, George often took Chavis to the park, let him run around, and called him when he was ready to go.

Returning home from work one night, I asked George, "Where's Chavis?"

"Well, I guess he's still at the park. I called and called him, but because he wouldn't come back to the van, I left him there," George said.

I was angry and upset with George. I flew to the park, and sure enough, my troubled little dog bounded anxiously up to me.

I had no idea that George would do the same thing with our child!

This time George went to Bon Marche Mall with Wardell a couple of years later. Wardell wandered off where George could not find him. George told people going into the mall that if they saw a little boy by himself, they should tell him that his father was looking for him. It was getting late—still, no Wardell.

George left Wardell there. He drove home. When I came home a few minutes later, George told me that since Wardell had never come back to the van, he had left him there.

I flew to Bon Marche to retrieve my wayward son—much faster than I did to retrieve my wayward dog! I was mad with George.

"What could I do? He never came back," George told me calmly.

With our six-year-old son Wardell in the public school system, we were anxious for East Baton Rouge Parish school board to submit an acceptable desegregation plan after so long a time, but we certainly were not surprised. Like most other parents, we wanted progress, not disruption by abrupt changes.

Our Home Is Broken into and Set Afire

We faced another crisis in late 1980 that could have been tragic.

Wardell had come to live with us within a week of his sixth birthday, December 1979.

Our home was set on fire only ten months later in October 1980, in the week before George was to go to court. Someone or some people broke into our home. They set George's office on fire, undoubtedly hoping to destroy materials that would be used in court.

Housing was an immediate problem. The night of the fire we stayed overnight at the Bellemont, then moved back to George's family home on Van Buren St. George's former apartment there had been rented to a single, older woman. We had to make do. George could not access the only downstairs bathroom in the hall. Since the only restroom which he could feasibly use was the one in the lady's apartment, we paid her a small fee so George could use her bathroom. The only other bedrooms there were unused and dirty, having been locked up for years. I cleaned them up, made the beds, and organized the few clothes we had brought with us. All of the clothing was smoke-filled and needed washing and dry-cleaning, especially the suits that George needed for court.

The fire created many challenges for our family, our son and George's professional obligations. Our home sustained thousands of dollars of damage; we had good insurance. We faced the difficulty to keep Wardell in school, to hire workmen and supervise them, and to handle the desegregation case. All of this while living across town in the most improbable living conditions.

I placed a little dorm refrigerator in our bedroom and had to buy most of our meals at restaurants. I cannot describe my gratitude to friends and family who offered us home-cooked meals during this time.

During any extra time that I could muster, I searched for any kind of apartment that could accommodate George and his wheelchair. Fruitless. We lived on Van Buren for almost six months.

Wardell contracted the chicken pox in our temporary quarters, and we had only space heaters during the cold months with no air conditioning during the hot months. For a time, Wardell had stayed with friends and neighbors Beverly and Hayward Dixon to attend the school he had started in the fall; after all, he was in the first grade.

I knew that Wardell would probably be homesick at the Dixons. I went to a toy store and bought a huge stuffed gorilla. George loved one of Richard Pryor's stories that he shared with Wardell. He told it like this: "During slavery times, a black slave was working in the cotton field when a spaceship landed. He looked at the aliens walking out of the ship, then shaking his head, said, 'You folks better git yo'selfs back where you come from. You done landed on Mr. Gilmore's property!'" Wardell named his gorilla Mr. Gilmore because Mr. Gilmore was a bad dude.

When Wardell grew homesick, we quickly brought him back to Van Buren St. to live with us. Wardell had come to us only that previous December—what an adjustment period for him!

The Atlanta child murders exploded in the news during 1979-81. Someone had hated us enough to set our home on fire. I worried about Wardell walking home from school. Could he possibly be abducted or hurt in some way?

George spent every day that he could at our burned home, supervising the renovations and he was there when Wardell returned from school.

George and I were sitting in the bedroom one day when Wardell returned with a little friend. The day was warm and our windows were open.

We heard the little boy ask, "Wardell, what in the world happened to your house?"

Our six-year-old son replied nonchalantly, "The KKK burned it up."

We had no idea where Wardell picked up the idea—apparently he had heard someone say it—but it was neither George nor I.

At six years old, we weren't sure what our son understood of race; probably little. However, we quickly became aware of his negative attitude that he must have picked up in his earlier years. One day, Wardell referred to a child who lived down the street as "the little nigger boy."

We patiently explained that he was being impolite. We tried to impress on him that he and the other boy were both black. Wardell refused to accept it. He insisted, "No, I'm not; I'm white." This was the pot calling the kettle black.

It seemed possible that his mother had tried to pass Wardell off as a white child. After all, we thought the rest of her family were all white, and he was light-skinned. As light as I am.

We tried to orient Wardell about racial topics. One day I made some paper dolls: black, white, and tan. Then we told the story using the paper dolls. The black father fell in love with the white mother—resulting in little tan boy. Black father died (as his father died of heart disease in his twenties). White mother married a different white father and they had two white children in addition to her tan son. Tan son is moved away, all alone. Then along comes black father (George) and white mother (Kathy), and tan son comes to live with them.

I played paper dolls with Wardell several times, trying to help him to see that his natural father and adopted father were black and that his race was black as well.

It was years later, when Wardell was in treatment in New Orleans and was writing for therapy, that a single shocking fact emerged: "Robbie was black like me. Why did she [his mother] give just me away?"

Wardell had absolutely no interest in sports when he was a child, yet we tried to encourage him. He attended Coach Dale Brown's basketball camp and became a ball boy. Loving sports as much as he did, George longed to have a son to share his passion.

One night George was on the phone with Dale when Wardell, about eight years old, looked up and asked, "Is that Coach Brown on the phone?"

"Yes," George said.

"Would you ask him if I can go to Atlanta with him and the team?"

"Here. Ask him yourself," George said.

He did. Coach Brown told George to bring Wardell to the LSU bus early in the morning. I scrambled to pack a little suitcase for Wardell, and the next morning off he went with the Tigers.

During the trip Dale called George to ask him, "By the way, do you and Kathy eat a lot of lobsters?"

"Lobsters? No indeed!"

"Well," Dale said. "Wardell says you do. We went to a restaurant last night and were ordering our usual meals. When I asked Wardell what he wanted to eat, I figured he would want a hamburger or something like that. 'Lobster,' he said. Lobster! George Eames feeds you lobster? 'We eat it all the time!' he told me. We ordered one for him."

✲✲✲✲✲

Wardell played Little League, camped and rode horses with the Cub Scouts. We picnicked on Lake Pontchartrain, fished, camped in Louisiana and hiked out West. Wardell and I rode a van to the top of Pike's Peak. We continued to do our best to involve him in wholesome and fun activities.

One day George talked on the phone with someone from the national office of the NAACP. At the end of the conversation, the man told him, "Mr. Eames, you need to check. Some children been playing on your phone."

George listened for the message he had recorded; instead, he heard: "This is Wardell Eames, you m— f—! I'm bad, and you better not mess with me." What an interpretation of the original message: "I'm G. Washington Eames. You have reached the office of the

1982—George and Kathy Eames

NAACP. We'll take on anybody, any place, any time...."

*****

I was feeling increasingly distressed over the declining respect for life—especially with the number of abortions performed in our country. I wanted to protest or take a stand in some way.

The opportunity came in April 1985, over the Easter weekend. Andre and I were then attending St. Paul the Apostle Catholic Church, the little black church housed in the former Capital Theater on Capital Ave., (now Gus Young Ave.). The church was planning a Pilgrimage for Life during the weekend of March 30-31. The article published in the *Catholic Commentator* on April 24, 1985, explains: "About seventy-five persons from this state coalition of religious, civil rights, and legal activists gathered in Baton Rouge to resume their walk for life and against the death penalty."[1]

Wardell Andre Eames and I walked with the others fifty-two miles, beginning from Angola State Penitentiary to the steps of the State Capitol. Vans would pick up stragglers and drive them to the head of the line of marchers during these two days. While in the van, we had time to drink some water and bandage our blistering feet. At eleven years old, Wardell was one of the youngest marchers—if not the youngest. He walked with me and with other adults in the group, enjoying this unusual activity. After this accomplishment, I had a t-shirt decorated for him which read: "I walked 52 miles for life."

*****

Tunica Hills is a rugged outdoor hiking area near Angola, Louisiana. Nearly on the state line between Mississippi and Louisiana, the topography is unique to the state, full of deep gorges, small waterfalls, and creeks. I loved the outdoors. I had gone there on a day hike with a group in the Sierra Club. I wanted Wardell to experience this area as well; one day during my spring break in 1986 when Wardell was nearly twelve years old, I drove him and a neighborhood friend to Tunica, just the three of us. We were prepared. I carried water in my backpack, a box of aspirin, an Ace bandage and bandana, and snack foods. The boys also wore backpacks. We took our time descending the trail, which led down huge steps roughly cut into the steep hillside.

The trail ran at least three miles to a shallow pool which collected the run-off from a little waterfall. Exquisitely beautiful, the natural flora included all kinds of moss and fern.

As we reached the bottom, I stepped down a few inches to a lower area and heard a distinct snap. My ankle. I knew I had broken it. The pain grabbed me and I nearly fell. Here I was, three miles down a trail that would lead uphill all the way, steep and rough, to where I had parked the car. I called to the boys and told them what I thought had happened. They sat near me, as I suggested we eat a hearty snack and drink some water. Then, using my head, I took off my shoe, and soaked my ankle in the cool water. I swallowed three aspirins, then drew my foot out, dried it off with the bandana, wrapped it well with the Ace bandage and then the bandana. Putting my shoe back on, I would climb out as best I could.

I struggled, sometimes inching up on my butt, grabbing small trees and pulling my way up, favoring the aching ankle. At one point, other hikers came our way, and seeing my struggle, they asked me if I needed help reaching my car. I can't believe today that I told them, "Not to worry. I can handle this." I did. It took me three hours to return to the car, which I drove all the way back to Baton Rouge with a broken ankle.

Once home I dropped the boys off with the neighbor and called a friend, Gloria High, to bring me to the emergency room. I changed my jeans while I waited for her because they were muddy and filthy by my sliding along the hillside. I had done such a good job wrapping the broken ankle that there were no complications. George was completely outdone with me—he would never again hear of me going hiking! In that one day, I burned so many calories that I lost five pounds in a few hours. Yet I was proud of myself; I knew that I was tough and had the courage to do whatever I needed to do.

Our Marriage Begins to Founder

At some point in the eighties, our marriage began to founder because of the strain of parenting despite our demanding jobs. By then I was a department manager working more than 40 hours a week—away from home. George had become president of the Baton Rouge branch of the NAACP in 1980, assuming much more responsibility for school desegregation and other weighty issues.

Yet George had to be with our son much longer each day. Wardell was no longer a cooperative child in 1983 and 1984. At ten, Wardell was becoming sullen, and silent. He wouldn't talk freely to either of us. His usual answer to any question was a grunt. He never smiled. Never complained. If he left the house, we never knew when he might return, and he would do so without telling us anything.

Even events which should have been fun for father and son were a trial. Wardell couldn't have cared less about sports, and this was George's passion. He felt keenly Wardell's lack of responsiveness— no matter what we did. George longed for a son to share some interests— Wardell seemed to have no interest in anything. I sympathized with George, but didn't know what to do about it. We found nothing but sullen quiet from Wardell.

I was aware that Wardell had been traumatized in his early childhood. When we became parents, I believed that love could overcome all problems. As trouble had mounted, I had stormed heaven with tears, beating on God's door till my fists were bloodied.

Love did not prevail in these years. I was beyond shocked and disappointed. I saw deterioration rather than healing. If love, if *love* did not work, what in the world could possibly work to save us? I was without weapons on the worst battlefield of my life, and I felt lost. Absolutely helpless.

George and I had never argued about anything in our marriage before—now we had arguments about everything related to our son.

George told me at one point, "We should have stuck with dogs!"

I almost agreed with him. Feeling like a failed parent, I thought the same thing, "I guess we should have stuck with dogs."

✳✳✳✳✳

One Friday night Wardell and I sat at a little folding table eating boiled crawfish. George ate in bed leaning on his side. Suddenly he exploded in anger. George tipped over the table, throwing crawfish all over the room. I was horrified as he shouted at us.

I gathered a few items in a bag, then left the house with Wardell, driving to the home of George's niece, Debra. She was surprised to see us at night. She commiserated with me. Debra knew well how controlling George could be; he had helped to raise her.

As Wardell went to his little cousin Harrell's room, I settled on the sofa, but I would not sleep.

I agonized over this incident. I began seriously to think of leaving George—taking Wardell with me, of course.

I had long felt that George was too hard on him. I reminded George of all that Wardell had gone through. George always dismissed this, saying, "Everybody goes through something." When I told him he was too hard on him, he always responded, "A boy needs a firm hand. Are you trying to make a sissy of him?"

My heart was breaking. Wardell might indeed be a lost soul, but if I left George, I felt I would ruin his life also.

My quandary was that I was being compelled to choose between husband and son, each equally vulnerable.

I knew that without me, George would have nothing. I also knew that if I left, I would probably have no more success with Wardell than we had had together. I had no idea if I could begin to handle him by myself—more than likely not.

I had been having dreams during these years that revealed my troubled heart. In one dream, the three of us were driving to New Orleans when suddenly the van would fly over the side of the bridge crossing Lake Pontchartrain. With the van quickly sinking, I had to decide which one I would save, George in his wheelchair or Wardell. I could not possibly save both of them. In the dream, I never could make the decision.

The next morning George called to apologize, begging me to come home.

I had no choice. I returned and immediately began mopping the office. George had actually picked up all the crawfish from the floor, I know not how; however, he had missed a few, and I knew the room would smell unless I cleaned it thoroughly.

Something Is Wrong with Wardell

Despite Wardell's earlier therapy, something was dreadfully wrong. We saw it in the lying, the running away, then his stealing from us. But things would get worse.

The crisis grew. Then, at age twelve, Wardell stole a pistol from

George. He told a friend from church, "I'm gonna have to get rid of him [George]."

After this serious incident, we petitioned the court to have him put in state care again as an uncontrollable juvenile. Judge Tony Graphia, who had handled the original adoption, advised us to pursue this solution to secure thorough evaluations and assistance with him.

Wardell was eventually diagnosed with emotional and identity disorders, as well as suicidal depression. The diagnosis gave us hope. We cried with relief—to know at last what was wrong. George exclaimed, "I want my son back."

We requested custody back from the state and hospitalized him for six months in a facility in New Orleans where we visited him weekly. We participated in family therapy as well.

Wardell came home, but when our situation rapidly deteriorated, he went back to state custody.

Frankly, I was on the verge of emotional collapse from my struggles with our son. George was a firm father, so the two stayed in conflict with each other. This is not uncommon for troubled teens and parents. I quickly lost all confidence in being able to guide Wardell— or to influence his life. I was just not ready to assume custody.

After Wardell spent more time in state care, he was released into the custody of my sister-in-law Gloria.

Wardell got worse. At age 19 or so, he committed more felonies, even trying to steal Gloria's car one night.

Wardell was incarcerated at Dixon Correctional Institute.

Good things happen. Dale Brown was most kind. First, he invited us to a basketball game in Philadelphia. We flew there on our own, not with the LSU team, and stayed in the same hotel as the team. The comedian and civil rights activist Dick Gregory also joined us there.

One morning, coming downstairs for breakfast in the dining room, I saw Dale, George, and Dick sitting at the table facing the door. Dick had been elaborating on the fact that he never sat anywhere with his back to the door because you had to see who was coming at you. He leaned back and said loud enough for me and other diners to hear: "George Eames, you're the only nigger I know who travels with a double handicap—a wheelchair and a white woman!" Of course, everybody there cracked up, including me.

Chapter 9

Action on All Fronts

In 1988 George and I were both emotionally devastated by our parenting experience. In the fall 1989, I left Sears and began teaching at Glen Oaks High School. My brother, R. J., criticized my teaching in a virtually all black, inner city high school. He complained to Mama. I told Mama, "That is stupid. Doesn't he understand that every child that I reach is one less likely to knock his grandkids in the head one day?"

I was excited about teaching again. My contact with teens there did much to heal the hurt caused by our son Wardell. About the same time, probably for the same reasons, George increased his activities with youth and started Capital City Baseball for inner city kids. He said often to me, "Here I am, saving everybody else's children, and I couldn't save my own."

George worked with my school's programs, coming to talk to kids who were in the in-school suspension program, and the like. I also asked him to intervene with students of mine who were giving their parents trouble. He signed some kids up with the baseball program or youth council and also intervened with the school board in some cases.

During the early eighties, I believe, George and I were invited to the Jewish Synagogue by Rabbi Barry Weinstein to celebrate a memorial honoring those who had died during the Holocaust. We were both moved by the entire solemn celebration. George carried with him for years a little story credited to Pastor Martin Niemoller (1892-1984), who had been imprisoned in a German concentration camp:

> First they came for the communists, and I didn't speak out because I wasn't a communist.
> Then they came for the socialists, and I didn't speak out because I wasn't a socialist.
> Then they came for the trade unionists, and I didn't speak out because I wasn't a trade unionist.
> Then they came for me, and there was no one left to speak for me.[1]

As one dedicated to speaking out, George cited these lines to those with whom he came in contact. He would recite this little lesson, then point to the floor, "You see that place on the floor where you are standing? Be accountable for your space." George found it wholly unacceptable that anyone could let injustice pass him by without speaking out. He believed in being responsible, and being totally accountable. He lived by that maxim.

In August 1988, George had the opportunity to meet the new superintendent of East Baton Rouge Parish schools, Dr. Bernard J. Weiss. Thus would begin a long, enduring friendship between our families.

If the parish was to have any success improving the schools, George felt Weiss needed to understand the area he would vastly influence. George offered to drive him around the parish, and to show him the areas that were especially needy. They spent several hours together in early September 1988.

Early on, Weiss invited me and George to lunch with him and his wife, Marie, at the Camelot Club, a members-only establishment for the movers and shakers of the Baton Rouge community. Imagine the shocked response of the guests on that fateful afternoon. Weiss would hear strong criticism later for bringing "that troublemaker" to the Camelot.

These two wonderful people became "Bernie and Marie" to us as we came to know one another better. It was also during this lunch that Bernie turned to me and asked, "When are you going to come teach for me? You were born to the classroom." Of course, I gave my excuses, yet with the support and encouragement of both George and Bernie, I began the arduous task of preparing to take the National Teacher's Exam.

I did well on the test; I scored in the 99th percentile in English, the subject which I would teach. In the other subjects I scored at the 85th percentile—or higher. I re-entered the field of education at Glen Oaks High School at Bernie's request in the fall 1989.

Over the next two decades we would accept many invitations to dinner at their home, and at restaurants; many cards and letters passed between Bernie and George. During this same time, the four of us became close to Rev. James Stovall and his wife, Alice, till he died in 1997. Jimmy and Alice were a natural relationship for us. After all, Jimmy had been a lifetime advocate for civil rights, advocating for prison reform. He was appointed to the Louisiana Commission on Human Rights in 1992 and became the co-organizer and chair of the Louisiana Coalition against Racism and Nazism in 1989, working to oppose the influence of David Duke of the KKK.

Now we three couples became the knights of the "Square Table," as we called ourselves. We met once a month. Often another warrior—Fannie Godwin, our official school board watcher—joined us. We shared battle stories, victories, much laughter, and deepest affection for one another. After years of struggle, I brought this little doggerel poem, written in the meter of "The Night before Christmas" to one of our Christmas celebrations:

Revisiting the School Board
'Twas the school board's first meeting, and all through the season,
The Movers and Shakers were shaking. The reason?
Traumatic elections that took place in the fall
with many the fallen and broken and all.
The fierce competition woke many a sleeper;
the mikes sang, the phones rang from beeper to beeper.
Many mouths had flown open, wider and wider;
rougher the messages, snider and snider.
And under the skirmish, behind walls and programs,
reformers were preaching like thundering dragons.
Poor superintendent! He was caught in the middle,
the state of the parish being mostly a riddle
with asbestos-filled buildings and rain-fallen ceilings,
shortages, overages, paints that were peelings,
with Deputy Horace snuck off God Knows Where,
and the stubborn old board members hugging their chairs.
Visions of excellence haunted poor Bernie,
nay-sayed and de-layed by Hammonds, attorney.
And to add hurt to insult, the school board beside him
trampled his contract and cheerfully fired him.
The battle was lost, but the war was not over,
with faithful companions like Jimmy the Soldier
and George laying plans with Square Table discussions,
and everyone knows how these had repercussions!
From Thanksgiving to Christmas and into the New Year
with dinners and cakes! There was nothing to fear.
With backers like Kathy, Marie, and Sweet Alice,
Education must win with the King in his Palace!
So hang in there, Bernie, with six months to spare,
And 40 to Boots—why, you're up in the air
and down on the Fleet!* Hurrah for the Navy–
Congratulations in order, so please pass the gravy!

*I believe Donald Fleet was over Human Resources during this time; I remember having an interview with him before I was hired.

"That's What I Am—The Equalizer"

During the summer of 1987, we drove to Lucy, Louisiana, Terry Robiskie's hometown where Terry expected us as dinner guests. He was at his parents' home with several of the Raiders, and the next day we joined them at a professional football game in New Orleans where we sat on the field.

Dale Brown had taken George on an earlier trip with the basketball team to Las Vegas. It was now Christmas 1988. Dale knew that Wardell was still in state care and that I was pretty upset about it. Dale somehow found a sponsor to pay for us to accompany the team to Hawaii. Another family traveled with us, a little boy, Jamie Simms, who had terminal brain cancer. Everyone catered to Jamie. He was befriended by the adults as well as the whole basketball team. Chris Jackson, whom George had recruited for LSU, played on the team that year.

During our layover in Los Angeles, we connected with Terry Robiskie and his wife Cynthia and little Bryan, their baby son. We were glad to see old friends. George, Dale and I took pictures with George and then Dale holding Bryan. (Terry has been wide receivers coach for the Atlanta Falcons since 2008 and was promoted to assistant head coach in 2013; Bryan was recruited by the Falcons in October 2012.)

When we arrived at the Turtle Bay Hilton, we discovered to our dismay that our room was located in a little cabin accessible by a pebbled path. George and I could not negotiate this with his manual wheelchair. We told Dale, who arranged for us to move to the main hotel. We ate with the team, traveled to and from the arena for practice and the game, and with the others, enjoyed what Hawaii had to offer: shopping on Waikiki beach, a luau, and snorkeling in the Pacific. During our off time, George hung around the huge pool admiring all the bathing beauties in bikinis with some of the team. I ate all the fresh pineapple I could put on my plate! George, true to form, made friends with all the Hawaiians he met: officials, guests, and the domestic help. By the time we left we were experts at giving the official Hawaiian hand greeting for "Hang loose!"

Between 1985 and 1989 a television series called *The Equalizer* became popular. George liked the idea of this show. He often said of himself, "That's what I am—the Equalizer." It seemed the scales of justice would never be even. In the seventies, George's friends also called him *Ironsides* after the famous attorney portrayed by Raymond Burr.

*****

Many issues caught George's attention. He did his best to address as president of the local NAACP branch. His goals included solving problems in employment, education, local government and culture. I found a copy of his notes for one of his many meetings with his board. He came prepared with targets and goals.

NAACP Meeting of Selective Officers and Board Members
I. Call to order
II. Prayer
III. Purpose: Presented By G. Washington Eames, President
 Visit and revisit (places touched and retouched by the NAACP)
1. Casino:
   Overhead view of the infrastructure
   Points to consider,
          Hiring 50 percent black
          Ensure all that is entitled
   2. Black Churches:
   Churches need to create (if not already created) programs for job and economic development
   3. Banks:
   Target bank for low interest loans, for black homeowners and businesses
   Prospective targets
   4. Downtown development:
   Target [prospective] library "Thurgood Marshall"
   5. Mid-city development:
   Target Baton Rouge General Hospital
   Money appropriated (low interest) for community improvements
   Issues/programs for local area drug problems, etc.

Refurbishing the black areas
6. Chemical plants:
Rollins/Exxon—committing environmental racism, getting production in black areas, etc.
7. City-Parish government:
Making sure blacks are being hired 50 percent
Ensure all that is entitled
8. LSU:
All structures/organizations/departments on main campus, making sure black students receive equal education opportunity
9. Department stores:
Ensure all entitlements
10. City police/fire department:
Hiring 50 percent black
Ensure all entitlements
11. East Baton Rouge School Board:
Review all structures/organizations/departments
12. BREC:
Review all structures/organizations/departments
13. Black businessmen:
Goals – to receive at least $100-$200 to reinvest in black communities
14. Tutoring program:
Locate building & volunteers
Start up immediately
Note: allow time for questions and suggestions after the purpose has been presented.

*****

For years, the NAACP office was in our home. Hundreds of children and adults entered our home. Young adults used my washer and dryer. Some we fed. We talked for hours with troubled adults and teens. One young woman was suicidal; I sat with her for hours. During the summers George often babysat children and pre-teens for single mothers trying to secure work—or he located housing for them. Some of these families remain lifetime friends of ours. George assisted white women with job woes. A young girl, Becky Mansur, showed up sick and in conflict with her father and stepmother. We took her in for a few days till she could work out a solution with her father. It never dawned on either of us that taking time with children could be dangerous to us.

In December 1989, we began to see troubling news accounts of bombings of NAACP offices across the United States. Jewish groups joined civil rights groups to investigate and protest these bombings which were directed at public officials and NAACP offices. The incidents killed at least two people. The FBI and the Justice Department believed that white supremacists were responsible.

George's concern was grave as he realized we were at risk with the Baton Rouge branch office in our home. The office where he often reclined in his bed on the phone had a long window. It ran along the outside wall facing the street. A Molotov cocktail lobbed from the street could easily kill him. It could set our home ablaze. A close friend from George's early years, Ted Poydras, realized this. Ted got a heavy duty iron grill and installed it with heavy screws along the entire window. Projectiles thrown at the window now would bounce away from the grill. We felt considerably safer.

When George was not home, I sometimes answered the NAACP phone or the house phone. My nature was honesty, and George grew irritated when I told callers the truth about his whereabouts or when he would be returning home.

"Are you trying to get me killed? Someone could be planning to ambush me on the way home—and you're giving them the path and the time they could do it!" he said angrily. For these reasons, the local branch made the decision in 1992 to rent office space and move the office. George explained on his Web site:

"For most of the years I worked for the NAACP, I conducted all the business from my home office with only a telephone. There I also met many clients, but I felt it was not fair to my family because of the danger posed to them. Meetings necessitated strangers often coming to my house. One day a strange, extremely pregnant woman had someone drop her off at my house when I was not home. She had no way to get back home, and I did not return for some hours. Kathy had no choice but to let her in. We gathered our resources, developed, opened and dedicated a public office in 1992."

George Builds a City Baseball League

In the late eighties and the early nineties George built a tremendous inner city baseball organization, as he worked with the National League of Professional Baseball Clubs and Thomas Brasuell; WVLA Television and Cyril Vetter; Fourth District Baptist Association; EBR Parish Schools and Herman Brister, Sr.; BREC and Earl Thomas; and LSU Baseball and Skip Bertman.

By 1995 George had forty-six active teams, tutoring, providing youth jobs in concessions, refurbishing parks, and the like. George spent hours on the phone soliciting coaches from the churches, raising the funds from local businesses and organizing meeting times and schedules.

What I remember best about that time is that when I returned home from teaching, I would find George and Earl in George's office in our home working out of huge boxes: uniform pants, socks, shirts, balls, bats, and gloves. The shirts and pants first of all had to be ordered then had to be sorted into the respective teams of children and adult coaches by size. Hours of work went on till all hours, preparing for the children to play. I myself spent hours on the computer developing logos, letters, and a slogan, for the season.

Then George would be gone for hours in his van delivering the gear, meeting coaches, and developing a code of conduct. He wanted no smoking, no cursing, and only the best model behavior for all the young people. He worked tirelessly before, during, and after the season. This included traveling between the varied parks, watching the children play, and making sure all needs were being met.

Between 1989-1995, George's level of activity increased. These included banquets, not only for the local NAACP but for Capital City Baseball; organizing funds, uniforms, and coaching for forty-six teams; planning and funding a full day of activities for adults and children for Dr. Martin Luther King's birthday; and the Freedom Fund Banquet usually in August, in addition to meetings of the organization and with various public entities and parish officials like the Police Department, Fire Department, Mayor's office, and more. This left precious little personal time. George was on the phone or in the van between parks, office, Centroplex (now known as the River Center), constantly. His personal needs and family played a distant second.

1990—Jesse Jackson comes to Baton Rouge to speak on behalf of Cleo Field's campaign. He graciously signs a photo for George.

1990—George is nearing the end of one of the annual Freedom Fund Banquets. George strikes a pose so typical of him. He seems to be dreaming of additional projects!

1992—At the Freedom Fund Banquet, George is shown with Dr. Bernard Weiss in the background; civil rights attorney Johnnie Jones; and then-Mayor Tom Ed McHugh delivers greetings.

2004—Then-Gov. Murphy J. Foster brings greetings to the Freedom Fund Banquet with George.

*****

It was not easy to change the names of local streets, highways or bridges to honor Dr. Martin Luther King, Jr. This letter indicates the extent to which George and his board had struggled to honor the memory of Dr. King by naming a local street or other edifice after him:

A Proposal to Rename the I-10 Bridge for MLK
April 11, 1991
The Honorable Mayor Tom Ed McHugh
Dear Mr. Mayor:
The Baton Rouge Branch of the NAACP voted Tuesday, April 9, 1991 to rename the I-10 bridge, commonly known as the New Mississippi River Bridge, the Dr. Martin Luther King, Jr., Memorial Bridge. Primary among the several factors influencing our vote were these:

Interstate highways were developed in 1952, the mindset of the time being to connect the west coast with the east coast. Because of the constant denial of public accommodations to African Americans, mostly in Southern states and some border states, constitutional scholars researched and found a provision in the Constitution that no state could deprive minorities access to public accommodations (hotels, restaurants, restroom facilities, lodging, etc.) if these establishments procured and used in their business, products and supplies transported through interstate commerce. Dramatic demonstrations against these discriminatory practices began immediately.

East Baton Rouge Parish and the state of Louisiana were profoundly guilty of these transgressions. The NAACP (National Association for the Advancement of Colored People), CORE (Congress of Racial Equality), SNCC (Southern Nonviolent Coordinating Committee), along with SCLC (Southern Christian Leadership Conference) led by Dr. Martin Luther King, Jr, protested vigorously across this state and the nation with sit-ins, wade-ins at swimming pools, picketing, and freedom rides. After the arrests and brutalization across the South and in Louisiana of African American protesters by the police in many cases, or by white citizens who were attempting to preserve "states rights," custom, and traditions, the Congress of the United States, the Supreme Court, and the President of the United States found "states rights" to be unconstitutional with all the states guilty of discrimination; and President Johnson signed the executive order commanding all states in the United States to cease and desist any denial of African Americans' access to public accommodations.

Neither Acadian Thruway, nor I-110, or Harding Blvd, has played a significant role in the achievement of public accommodations and the rights of minorities in this city and parish.

For all the above, Mr. Mayor, our city council, and state legislators, the Baton Rouge Branch of the National Association for the Advancement of Colored People respectfully requests that this great city and parish of ours name the new Mississippi river bridge: the Dr. Martin Luther King Memorial Bridge.

Respectfully submitted,

G. Washington Eames, Jr. / President, East Baton Rouge Parish Branch, NAACP

When this tactic proved ineffectual, in 1992 he and his board supported naming Florida Blvd. in honor of Dr. King. People for a Change still fought for S. Acadian Thruway.

At this time, we believe, individuals associated with this organization began a vendetta against George in particular. This included complaining to the NAACP national office at every opportunity (often manufactured), campaigning against him, and trying to turn people in the community against George.

Chapter 10

We Play Ball

George was passionate about helping black youth gain access to college athletics. He had made major progress at LSU in basketball and football. Through the years he had also accomplished much in the school desegregation lawsuit. He now turned his attention to baseball.

The original baseball program that we revived in 1987 was the Capital City Baseball League with the sponsorship of the Fourth District Baptist Association; East Baton Rouge Parish School Board; Coach Skip Bertman and his foundation; and BREC; along with local businesses, stores, and realtors, including WAFB; Cyril Vetter, owner and president of WVLA; WIBR; the *State Times* and *Advocate*.

Willie Spooner had initiated the original program, Capital City Kids' Clinic, in 1955. This success would run for fully two decades.[1]

We hoped to rival their success in serving the inner city children and teens who were now at greater risk than ever before. To enable a superlative baseball program, George approached Eugene Young. [He retired in 2003, and had worked for BREC—Recreation and Park Commission for East Baton Rouge Parish—serving as superintendent for forty-two years.] George explained the need for many of the city parks to refurbish their baseball diamonds, restrooms and bleachers if an inner city baseball program were to be successful. Young appointed Earl Thomas to assist him. Earl would become a staunch supporter of the program and a close friend.

With beautiful baseball parks clean and ready to go, RBI (Revival of Baseball in the Inner City) representative Tom Brasuell came to Baton Rouge to inspect the fields and to review our programs. Thanks to the shrewd management of Young and the constant assistance of Thomas, Brasuell found that the facilities here in Baton Rouge were the best baseball facilities in the United States. Returning to New York, he described our program to the president of the National League; they presented a check for $10,000 to the Capital City Baseball League

111

that helped us fund our program in a first-class manner.

To help fund the 1992 baseball program, the Capital City Baseball League held a banquet in the Centroplex Exhibit hall in March 1992. The keynote speaker was LSU head baseball coach Skip Bertman. Other speakers included Southern University head baseball coach Roger Cador, and Mayor Tom Ed McHugh. George gave another speech which I helped him to write. He spoke from the heart.

Save the Children
March 13, 1992

Marvin Gaye made a plea in the seventies: "Who cares? Who really cares to save the world? ...To save our sweet world that is destined to die? Save the children...save the babies...."

Here we are, thirty years later. And our children are still dying, but ladies and gentlemen, it's obvious as I look over this audience that some of us do care. Yet where do we go from here as a people? As a race? As a nation? I'm trying to do my part. That's the reason that I felt I should contact all of you—to share in this responsibility of ours.

Baseball, softball—they're just a beginning, a quiet invitation, a summons—to bring this small community of humanity to the realization that someone must care.

You may ask, why baseball, why softball? Baseball and softball give children the opportunity to share in the discipline, companionship, and spirit of a team, a chance to work closely with an adult role model who can give quality personal attention, insist on character development, ideals of consistent reliability, and effort along with a positive attitude. In this way, care becomes physically enabling, emotionally supportive, and real to the child. That kind of care must be multiplied throughout our parish and city through the genuine concern of many minds, many hearts, many hands.

We have not yet entered the struggle in great enough numbers. Our casualties are still entirely too high. How many children should die across this country in our community or other communities before we understand that the isolation and suffering through racism, poverty, unemployment, homelessness, and insensitivity are atrocities on the face of the earth?

What our children need—what our children are literally dying for—is our presence. A boy longs to look on the face of a man who will be there for him. A girl longs to look on the face of a woman who will be there for her.

What our children are literally dying for is our touch, our understanding. If we cannot be present to them, then surely they must die. If enough of us care, however, really care, then our children must surely live. Save the children.

The Rise and Fall of Capital City Baseball

On his Web site that I created in 2009, George described his baseball program in this way:

"The program started and thrived, growing to forty-five baseball teams in the inner city that played on the 'field of dreams' at Longfellow Park, Howell Park, and North St. Park. Not only that, but the program contributed to 2,000 jobs with the assistance of the Mayor's Council on Youth Opportunity, BREC, and East Baton Rouge Parish School System. Also, at each park, six nights a week, officials calling three games a night, one scorekeeper at each park, contributed to summer income for these officials and scorekeepers, not to mention the youths running the concession stands at all three sites. Here we had forty-five baseball teams consisting of fifteen youngsters per team, totaling six hundred seventy-five young boys and girls; three officials per game totaling one hundred thirty five officials, forty-five scorekeepers, and two individuals working each concession stand, totaling 6 individuals. Can you imagine—if this program would have been able to continue, we would have had many more black kids off the street, and our communities today would be much safer. In 1991 Baton Rouge Recreation and Park Commission (BREC) won the highest award for recreation in the entire United States of America, thanks to Capital City Baseball."[2]

In the *Advocate*, Baton Rouge, Thursday, Aug. 18, 1994, journalist Joseph Schiefelbein proclaimed, "Inner city youths revived by league." "Gold trophies filling four tables in the North St. Park gymnasium brought a fitting end to a summer of baseball. Forty inner city teams of fifteen youth each had competed in three age brackets. Announcing the team winners in each bracket, executive director of the league, George Eames was proud to announce that the five-year-old league was about so much more than wins and losses. 'Our goal is to teach youth a work ethic, and baseball is a discipline game. Above all, baseball teaches cooperation, teamwork, getting along with others to accomplish a goal.'"[3]

Goals come big and small. For example, a successful first home run for Darren Clark, who flew around the bases. On such small successes great dreams are built. This eleven-year-old first baseman and pitcher could now dream of following in the footsteps of his major league idols: Barry Bonds, Cecil Fielder, Ken Griffey, Jr. and Frank Thomas.

The big leagues were equally impressed with the Capital City League. The program for reviving baseball in the inner city. (RBI), begun by the majors in 1989, gave a $10,000 grant to Capital City. George said that grant, which gave each team about $400 extra, was an excellent investment in the inner city youth of Baton Rouge, with more than uniforms at stake. The support of RBI continued throughout the school year with educational programs, mandated school attendance, and performance in order for players to participate. The RBI grant also helped to supplement the donations of business sponsors.

Starting with sixteen teams, the Capital City League planned to expand to a girls' softball league and add a fourth tier of baseball, the sixteen to eighteen year olds. The youth were probably the most impressed with the opportunity to learn new skills and leadership, to observe great role models, and to enjoy their friends throughout the long Louisiana summers.

Seated in the middle of the four tables, George recalled those who had insisted the league would never work, "The naysayers have become messengers."[4]

Unfortunately, two separate factors brought about the demise of the program. First, Leo Cyrus, Sr. relinquished the presidency of the Fourth District Baptist Association; he was one of the coalition members whose support was critical to the Capital City Baseball League. Rev. Charles T. Smith became the president.

George explains: "On or about 1994, Rev. Charles T. Smith, pastor of Shiloh Baptist Church and president of the Fourth District Baptist Association, met with me in his office at Shiloh Baptist Church, to inform me that the Fourth District had decided to sponsor summer basketball. Capital City Baseball lost our number-one sponsor of the program. As a result of that decision, we lost the influence of the black male in the black community. Baseball is the only athletic program that needs total undivided supervision of the black boy by the black man. That is the reason that I decided to bring back the field of dreams, rather than basketball or football."[5]

Then, in June 1995, the baseball program collapsed. George was incarcerated for three years, and without his leadership and constant hands-on supervision, the program ended.

When George returned to Baton Rouge in 1998, he immediately

began trying to resurrect the program under the name Delta Baseball Association.

George recalled: "In 1998, I got in touch with LSU athletic director and former baseball coach Skip Bertman. We met with a number of people and we tried to start a new league, Delta Baseball Association. They included: Rev. Leo D. Cyrus, president of the Fourth District Baptist Association; Southern University Chancellor Edward Jackson; Southern University baseball coach Roger Cador; BREC associate Earl Thomas; Herman Brister, Sr., assistant supervisor of East Baton Rouge middle schools; William 'Bill' Tucker of Tucker Realty; Effie Carter of Carter Realty; and Estelle Guillory."

George continued, "Despite great efforts on the part of many of us, including a generous check for $10,000 from the Skip Bertman Foundation, we could not get enough coaches and sponsorship to make the program a success. I returned the $10,000 check to Skip Bertman with our thanks and regrets."

I had designed the letterhead for the league.

The baseball program could not be reactivated as it was from 1987 till 1995. This had some negative impact on our community. Without activities for our inner city youth, primarily in the black, deprived areas of north Baton Rouge, Eden Park, and South Baton Rouge, Baton Rouge has experienced a sharp escalation of violence over the last few years. Crime rankings are always controversial; and there's no doubt our lack of constructive programs for black kids in the inner city has contributed to our high crime ratings.[6]

*****

Because of George's sentence, he could not work with children one-on-one. George felt the least he could do was act as organizer and director of the activities he hoped to reestablish for the youngsters. Of all the accomplishments George enjoyed in his life, nothing thrilled him more than his beloved baseball program. He grieved over losing it. The children themselves suffered the greatest loss.

George continued to express concern at what he saw happening to black inner city youth. He wrote a letter which was published in the *Advocate* on March 11, 2008, "Bring back BR youth baseball."

George learned that the Mayor's Council on Youth Opportunity was defunct, and with his own failed efforts to reestablish an inner city baseball club upon his return from prison, George searched for a way to encourage another individual or group to undertake this project.

He thought he had found his answer at the Black Assembly and Civil Rights Luncheon, hosted by attorney Ernest Johnson, NAACP, and State District Judge Janice Clark. It was chaired by his longtime friend, Joseph A. Delpit, and coordinated by Rev. Lee Wesley, his nephew. This meeting caught George's interest since one of its concerns was the black male youth.

George pleaded with 100 Black Men to reactivate an inner city baseball league. The national group has a local branch founded in 1992, and it aims to reach black youth with leadership and guidance. George suggested the type of support such a project would require. His own baseball program had included the local NAACP, the Fourth District Baptist Association, and the now-defunct Mayor's Council on Youth Opportunity (Herman Brister, Sr.) Even LSU head baseball coach Skip Bertman and Southern University baseball coach Roger Cador had worked on the league with the East Baton Rouge Parish school system. Others included WBRZ-TV (Richard Manship); WAFB-TV (Ron Winders); WVLA-TV (Cyril Vetter); and BREC director (Eugene Young).

Many churches and businesses in the community sponsored teams, and the National Baseball League gave its full support for Baton Rouge to participate in RBI [Reviving Baseball in the Inner City], with a $10,000 grant to what Thomas Brasuell called "the best baseball facilities in the entire United States." Because of our Capital City Baseball program, BREC later received an award for the best athletic program in the United States.[7]

George described details of the program, the number and ages of youth served, procurement of uniforms and such, concluding that at its height, the program contained fifty teams of inner city youth.

George sincerely challenged 100 Black Men to bring back "the field of dreams" to the Baton Rouge community. Ever mischievous and critical, George used to claim, "How can you have 100 Black Men in Baton Rouge when there aren't 100 [real] black men in the whole United States?" His ploy, the challenge, however, did not work; the baseball league would not rise under anyone's leadership.

What disappointed George more, were the actions of Rev. Charles T. Smith in leading his churches to abandon baseball in favor of basketball. That, he never could understand—abandoning an already successful and growing program in favor of something that had never even been tested.

Chapter 11

Celebrations and Speeches—New Trouble Rises

Regardless of difficulties imposed on our family, I would never have asked George to stop doing what he was doing.

Civil rights and helping black people were his passion and his life. I supported him in every way that I could. For example, when George was elected president of the NAACP branch in 1980, the position demanded more formal speeches from him. He always knew what he wanted to say. Just as we had been doing with letters, he dictated his ideas, usually in the style he preferred. Then we went over them together, editing, adding ideas, clarifying, polishing till we were both satisfied.

We did the same with press conferences and with his speeches. With the speeches, however, he wanted me to help him practice. Sometimes I would read them, giving emphasis where it seemed appropriate. I marked the speeches with a highlighter, and he practiced while I listened. When he stumbled, I corrected him and read over the difficult line or lines till he felt confident with them. Some of his friends teased him that I wrote all his speeches. This was not true. The heart of the speech was his—the topic and the chief arguments, and much of the rhetoric. My role was to polish and enrich with additional examples or better choice of words. I never wanted to alter his unique, earthy tone.

I must also tell you that I didn't always do this willingly or cheerfully! After all, I was teaching, trying to keep house, and keeping up with a recalcitrant youngster (as well as husband). Time was such a premium for me. I balked at the constant letters, notes, speeches, and more. Still, no one could say no to George. Eventually I would buckle-in, sit down with him and accomplish whatever new purpose he had for me. The worst burden that fell on us were the new legal problems. We pushed on. The speeches below represent the kinds of messages which George delivered in his speeches:

1992—NAACP branch president G. Washington Eames, Jr. delivers one of his many speeches.

"We Need More Warriors in Our Race"

[Delivered in the early eighties]

In 1954 you had a mental awakening with Brown vs. Board of Education, the foundation of the civil rights movement. The primary concern was for black Americans to be treated with human dignity: to be able to eat, to work, to use public accommodations—or simply to enjoy life.

That same year in Birmingham, Alabama, a black woman, Mrs. Rosa Parks, made a decision—not to move no more—and with that expression of human dignity and foresight, a revolution was born.

Now as I sat here looking at this audience, it occurs to me that since most of us were born then, and since most of you should therefore remember, all of you are guilty of not picking up the banner and continuing the fight for freedom. All of the doors opened in the sixties with blood, sweat, and tears are now being closed with the stroke of a pen; but baby—you thought you had it made! You put down the banner and have been celebrating since 1968. Jobs were flourishing, executive positions were opened up, legal aid was available, affirmative action was alive and well—and so was security—but it didn't last long.

Twenty years later, only two decades later, the voting rights act, fair housing laws, education, equal employment opportunities, public accommodations, enfranchisement, and representative taxation—all of these are being questioned. Just twenty years later, all of these ingredients of a happy and prosperous life are being diluted or erased from the Constitution of the sweet land of liberty.

Ladies and gentlemen—what we're lacking in our race is black men and black women warriors. All we do is pray, plea, and beg God to give us strength to overcome the white man's power over us. Now how did that come about?

When we first arrived in this country we had leaders, we had Kunta Kinte, Nat Turner, Harriet Tubman, Sojourner Truth, etc. In our generation we had Martin Luther King, Jr. and our own Emmitt Douglas. Way back yonder years we even had our own lyrics: songs like "Steal Away Home," "Ain't Got Time to Stay Here," "Go Down Moses in Egypt Land," "Swing Low, Sweet Chariot," "Way Down Yonder by Myself, I Couldn't Hear Nobody Pray."

These were songs of liberation, intelligence gathering, information spreading through the plantations telling us how to get away from the white man's oppression and getting dignity and respect—we were warriors then.

And I know what I'm saying. You don't like it. But I want you to get mad. Allowing yourselves to be misled, you have no strength to stand up to nobody. All you do is moan and groan, and burden God to death. You wake up in the morning with a reasonable amount of health and strength, and this is the provision God has given you to help yourself.

We are the only race of people on this earth that believes our only salvation is to stay on our knees and pray, and everything will be all right. Does that sound like a warrior? Does that sound like a people with strength? No—that sounds like—fools! Everybody has risen above us, and we're still saying "Wait, and one day it's gonna be all right." The Chinese, the Vietnamese, the Latinos, the Japanese, the Cubans, the Jews, the Russians—everybody—even the immigrant workers that came as wetbacks from Mexico are coming here with more dignity than we have.... And we're still saying—let's wait—be patient—there's a better day ahead—something gotta happen."

Don't get me wrong—nothing wrong with praying. But it's how you pray. You pray to God for strength and pray to God to give you knowledge of self. And once this knowledge of self is acquired, you get up off your knees. Don't bend your back cause when your back is bent, the white man ride you. Keep your head up. Move with dignity. Demand respect. Don't worry about whether he like you or not. You not here for nobody to love you. You have to be respected as a human being with dignity.

You have the power that no other race on earth has, but the problem is you don't trust each other. Money is power! You got the money because you made it and you spend everything you make.

Frederick Douglass, revolutionist of the nineteenth century, believed in self-determination. This is what we, a deprived people, must stir and awaken within ourselves: self-determination. Douglass said, and I quote: 'Our destiny is largely in our hands.'[1]

[George went on to explain that in order to succeed in life, black people would have to take the initiative "by our own energies and exertions" to fulfill any dreams that they might have. They would have to seek their own wisdom, to avoid foolishness, to gain their own wealth, to achieve their own economy—or be left behind in disgrace.]

Ladies and gentlemen—your time has come. Let it begin with you. You can't stop progress, you can only detain it! Thank you.[2]

George delivered a popular speech punctuated by his famous, "That's broke. Fix it" line in January 1991:

Dr. Martin Luther King's Birthday — "That's Broke. Fix It."

I am G. Washington Eames, Jr., president of the Baton Rouge branch of the NAACP. On behalf of this great civil rights organization, I extend warmest greetings to all of you on this national holiday, the birthday of our resolute leader, Dr. Martin Luther King Jr. All of us here, white and black, young and old, all who care about the future of our community and nation, have come to celebrate, remember, and renew a dream and the memory of a great man.

It is time, you know. Time to live by choice, not chance. It is time to act, not be acted upon.

Long ago when blacks were delivered to the shores of this country on the hated slave ships and sold into the interior of this land to spill their blood, sweat, and tears on a foreign continent, American society said: "These creatures are irresponsible savages. Slavery is good for them. Much time must pass before they could even begin to handle freedom."

But a woman called Harriet Tubman could not wait. She didn't have the time. In peril of her life, she raided the plantations again and again to bring her black brothers and sisters to freedom. Harriet knew it was time. She did not wait for the slave master to give up the whip.

American society said: "These blacks are not very intelligent; they need no schools because they can't learn. Much time must pass before the black race can achieve the scholastic accomplishments of the European peoples."

But Mary McCloud Bethune could not wait. She didn't have time. She refused to allow poverty's oppression to stop her from founding a college for blacks. She made those times her times.

American society said: "Blacks cannot play sports which require strategy, cunning, and coordination. Much time will be required if blacks are ever to equal the achievements of our national sports heroes."

But Jackie Robinson could not wait. He didn't have the time. Born on a sharecropper's farm in Georgia, he went on to become the first black to play major league baseball. He made time move at his pace.

Dr. Martin Luther King, Jr. in our own times knew when to speak and when to be silent. When all he could see around him was the nightmare of political disparity, human indignity and shame, the nightmare of brutal beatings and painful marches, he stood in a national pulpit to announce, "I have a dream." It was not the time to dream, but Martin didn't have time, so he dreamed anyway.

It is time for us. It is time to live by choice, not by chance. It is time to act, not to be acted upon. Time to make our time, to make time move to our beat, our requirements. Like Harriet, Mary McCloud, Jackie and Martin, we don't have time to wait for the society around us to recognize our need. We know what has to be done.

If you see politicians in the political arena not doing the things you sent them to do, that's broke. Fix it.

If you see young black teenagers with gold in their mouths, tattoos on their hands, streaks in their hair, and ears full of earrings, that's broke. Fix it.

If you see young black men and women selling dope in your community, terrorizing the old people who have been living there all their lives, that's broke. Fix it.

If you see young black teenagers refusing to pay attention to their instructors in the classrooms, intimidating other students who are there to learn, that's broke. Fix it.

When you see black residential areas, churches, schools, and playgrounds surrounded by nightclubs, liquor stores, and grocery stores where alcohol can be purchased, that's broke. Fix it.

When you see crack cocaine babies being born to young black teenagers, and drive-by shootings by young black males, this is a waste of human resources. That's broke. Fix it.

In our school systems around this country, and especially in East Baton Rouge Parish, we must teach and learn to respect the achievements of African Americans by teaching black history every day and in every way. And if we don't, that's broke. Fix it.

The NAACP is the oldest civil rights organization in America. It's been in existence for eighty years and has given black people and white people the right to learn and respect each other's culture. If you are not a member of the NAACP, that's broke. Fix it.

Ladies and gentlemen, young and old, let's do the right thing![3]

In January 1992 I entered the local NAACP celebration for Dr. Martin Luther King, Jr. "Echoes," as an active participant. The program that year presented varied heroes and heroines in the struggle for civil rights.

I performed a monologue dramatizing Viola Liuzzo for our young audience. A civil rights activist from Michigan, she was murdered by the KKK after the 1965 Selma to Montgomery marches in Alabama.

In the 1993 celebration "Save the Children: Victory through His Vision," I paid tribute to the late Dr. Valerian Smith. A line in one of George's speeches: "We need more warriors in our race," stimulated my thoughts on this wonderful man for a piece I wrote. Valerian Smith was a local African American music writer and musician, dentist, and father—much loved by our community. I honored him with several tributes, during the celebration honoring Dr. King, at his funeral, and at another service honoring him at the Unitarian Universalist church. Dr. Smith was also the late father of the famous African American actress from Baton Rouge, Lynn Whitfield—the granddaughter of Dr. Leo S. Butler of the famous Butler family of Baton Rouge, a family with whom we have been friends for decades.

A Tribute To Dr. Valerian E. Smith
Written and delivered by Kathy Andre-Eames

Years ago, G. Washington Eames, President of the Baton Rouge Branch of the NAACP gave a speech in which he lamented: "We need more warriors in our race."

Dr. Valerian E. Smith was such a warrior. His weapon was the lyric, his munitions, the words of song. Stark revolution. It was Valerian who told us:

"Black child, he ain't gon' wait" and
"We won't be satisfied
Till justice flows like water" and
"How many more must die?" and
"I'm gonna join his journey, marching with the king," and
"One thing I ask, one simple task, Spread love to one and all."

As he smiled, disarming the enemy, he made thrusts—not to the jugular—but to the heart. His aim was deadly and sure; rather than destroy the enemy, he recruited him. Valerian was a good soldier. He marched without weariness. When struck, he paid no attention to the wounds. When his companions fell, he lifted them.

Smiling in the teeth of danger, he moved with hope, with grace, and with dignity. He would not go down easy. Following his leaders with abandon and devotion, Valerian secured many victories for his people. His cause was one. The desires of his heart were universal: he believed in the future of children and fought that they might have a future.

Valerian gave us songs that were dreams, songs that were visions. His songs were songs of revolution, hope, songs vital and pregnant with life, tenderness, and caring. His songs wounded us in the heart, stirring our passion for civil rights, human rights, children's rights. He has gone down fighting the valiant fight, this warrior with a song for every season, our warrior of the Purple Heart that will continue to sing as long as we live:

"The children of the world cry out,
And you must hear their call.
One thing, I ask, one simple task,
Spread love for one and all...."

Is it enough to have known this man? To have shared his strength, enjoyed his smile, his magnetism, his friendship? No. Personal joy, personal grief is never enough when we say goodbye to a great man. It wasn't enough when the world bade goodbye to Jesus Christ. It wasn't enough when we followed the lonely stallion and casket of John F. Kennedy through the streets of Washington, DC. It wasn't enough when the nation mourned its bitter loss in the deaths of Dr. Martin Luther King, Jr. and Malcolm X.

What then? We must bury the pieces of our grief, and aim our remembrances like beacons of light to walk where they walked, talk what they talked, think what they thought, and dream what they dreamed. Before the ink has had a chance to dry on the last songs that Valerian put into our mouths, we must pick up the pen and write greater songs. We must sing of a time, join the journey, and hear the call, which is ever the call of a child who will not be quieted unless we ourselves sing to him. I give you this in the spirit of Valerian:

What Shall I Call You?
By Kathy Andre-Eames
Who are you, child,
Black child, black child?
What shall I call you,
Child of my soul?

I am the Dark Night
Startled by Starlight,
A Velvet-Eyed Panther
Dreaming of Snow.

Who are you, child,
White child, white child?
What shall I call you,
Child of my heart?

I am the Tail
of the Falling Comet,
Daisies and Diamonds
Streaming Below.

Who are you, child,
Red child, red child?
What shall I call you,
Child of my hand?

I am a Small Fox
Flushed from the Canyon,
Copper and Quicksilver,
Sprinkled with Sand.

Who are you, child,
Yellow child, yellow child?
What shall I call you,
Child of my spirit?

 I am the Dawn,
A Lost Lagoon Glowing,
Streak of a Tawny Fish,
Shimmering, Gone.

Call me My Loved One,
Blessed and Manly,
Warrior Rose,
Noble, Well-born,

Dark One Clearing,
Bright Fame Wandering,
Sunshine Linnet,
Lion and Dove.

Great Hill of Autumn,
White Brow of Summer,
Bright Circle Cheerful,
Vision of All,

Little Fire Faithful,
Golden Light Lady,
Rainbow of Heather,
Victory Fine,

Fullness of Pleasure,
Incense of Palm Tree,
Antelope Journey,
Cassia Queen.

Darkness Esteemed,

Mountain's Rough Island,
Son of the Ash Wood.
Heart-Brave and Free,

Home-Ruler, Watchful,
Cliff-Dweller, Guardian,
World-Mighty Dark Blue,
Counselor Bold.

Call me My Loved One,
Blessed and Manly,
Call me forever,
Child of Your Soul.

How far I had journeyed from Daddy's comment, "A black woman can't be a lady." I remembered Kunta Kinte in Alex Haley's *Roots*; I could always see in my mind's eye, the awed Kinte lifting his child to the heavens, "Behold, the only thing greater than yourself." It is the child, always, that we should lift up to a heaven full of stars.

I had learned by now that beauty, breathtaking and invincible, lay everywhere you looked —or didn't look. In every place, among every people and race, in nature; when I stumbled upon it, I claimed it for myself. I knew that no one could keep it for self alone, for it was universal. What I claimed, I absorbed until it became a veritable part of my soul. When I met George, all that was beautiful and memorable of black people, I embraced until it was mine. How I wanted this for all children! At some point, also, I tried to express this idea to a lovely young girl whom George and I met:

Take This, Towanda
By Kathy-Andre-Eames
I give you this seed for all time,
from this night of failing starlight
to whatever daybreak falls on your peerless eyes.

"You are a child of the universe,
no less than the trees and the stars,
you have a right to be here."[4]

A right to any gift at any price,

whatever mankind owns at any time
is yours, your birthright.

Take the Greek islands, ocean spray,
green lichens blessing the porous rock,
the harbor fleets of sweet anemone.

Take the shamrocks, sturdy Gaelic heather,
the fogs and drifts along the mountain tarns,
the highland ways of cloven-footed sheep.

Steep your soul in the keeps of Himalaya,
the cedar tendrils of India's deodar,
a lace of sunlight leaping on the slopes.

Cherish the fox, possum, and the coon
lifting his tender hand from the stream passing,
the washing trout, the mackerel, salmon lift.

Your brown face is the face of all women
ravishing in equatorial red,
combing down the ebony with rose.

Drift in your southern dreams along the Niger,
girl of the sampan, child of the heedless flood.
Follow the bloodline wheresoever she flows.

Chapter 12

Rivers

On June 10, 1992, George and I drove to California. It was a trip to explore the West that we loved and to see old friends. Travel inspired my writing.

Back in August 1983 we had spent two weeks driving and camping in the Garden of the Gods, a campground near Colorado Springs, Colorado. On the earlier trip our son Wardell, now known as Andre, and I had slept in a large tent, cooking in an electric skillet. George slept on the bed that he had built in his long blue Ford van. But on this 1992 trip, our plans didn't include our son, who was now nineteen years old.

We were longtime fans of western film, so we were eager to see more of the West for ourselves. We had originally planned to leave for California on June 3 or so, but George kept working on the thirty-eight baseball teams. Also, we were still working on the money. I wanted over $2000 before leaving because we would be gone for twenty days. We allowed $100 a day for everything: gas, food, lodgings and all other expenses. We would sleep in the van and stay at KOA and other campgrounds along the way, the only way we could afford this trip.

In Los Angeles we would stay with Terry and Cynthia Robiskie about three days. Originally, I planned only a day at a time. We didn't know except in a general way where we wanted to go but we'd see desert, Indian reservations, and we definitely wanted to see the Grand Canyon and Painted Desert. We drove Route 66, stopping at many small towns; camping in Santa Rosa, New Mexico; investigating varied cacti; and visiting Indian reservations and Tombstone, Arizona, where we drank sarsaparilla in the old bar there and paced out the OK Corral. Along the way, George called Baton Rouge every day to check on his beloved baseball program.

When we pulled into Terry's driveway in Sherman Oaks, he

insisted that we enjoy a drink and a long soak in their hot tub in the backyard, which overlooked the city lights. George was incredulous. How in the world could he even get in it! Not a problem—as he did with everything else, Terry just picked him up and placed George in the tub. I'll never forget the look of delight on George's face as he laughed and grinned at me, enjoying every second of it.

Terry had always wanted George to enjoy whatever he enjoyed. He had tried to persuade him for years to get into his boat. George had been with him when he bought it in Denham Springs, Louisiana. Terry had told him then, "George, you stay here and be quiet. These white folks might not sell me the boat if they see you here with me!"

Terry drove George to Watts to see the damage caused by the riots there, while I took a long walk through Sherman Oaks. We went to the Raiders headquarters to see Terry's office and to buy Raiders gear.

George also insisted on cooking a big spaghetti for the family, and he delighted in throwing a football to four-year-old Bryan and his baby brother in their backyard.

The trip itself inspired me in many ways. As George and I observed the terrain along the way, we noticed the dryness. In the desert, we expected this.

When I studied the map along the way, I anticipated seeing the rivers in the West. George and I had lived most of our lives a few miles or even closer to the mighty Mississippi. In Chatawa, Mississippi, my friends and I had walked to the Tangipahoa River, especially on our long Sunday walks after dinner.

As a religious sister in Dallas, I often walked with other young sisters to the Trinity River near the convent and university. To our shock, the rivers out West were pitiful things—narrow, pinched, spare. I began reading through the map of the entire United States, immediately struck by the sheer numbers of rivers in our country, and by their unusual, beautiful, varied names. This experience led me to write a poem, "Rivers," which would be followed by an essay. At the Fest For All in Baton Rouge on May 18, 1996, when I read the poem on the Poetry Stage (located in a downtown building) several members of the audience actually following me out into the street, pleading with me to read it again.

Rivers
By Kathy Andre-Eames
Rivers, visible torrents of the soul,
portraits of our depths, obscure or clear,
I call your name, brothers East and West:
Mississippi, Pecos, Trinity,
Colorado, Bighorn, Arkansas,
Rio Grande, Middle Fork, Flint,
White, Red, Hudson, Cumberland,
Merrimack, Platte, Delaware,
Dirty Devil, Sweetwater, Snake.

I call your name, sisters North and South:
Atchafalaya, Gila, Tallapoosa,
Cottonwood, Walnut, Marshyhope,
Stillwater, Crooked, Alleghany,
Sewanee, Wolf, Missouri, Chippewa,
Powder, Otter, Pigeon, Shenandoah,
Beaver, Wailuku, Kaskaskia.

Where are you born, our rivers great and small,
tumbling from the lip of a smooth stone?
Like a tear from the pointed juniper
you arrive purer than clay, as swift as sky,
more whole than the fragrance of light caught in bone.

Softly you run, like the footpads of wolves.
You chirp like the throats of mountain wrens
or stir the earth with the violence of moans
till even the bridges tremble at the sounds.

Rivers of soul, let us flow with you,
a brace of waters through gulches, dry arroyos,
a rill of ripples through dens of infested swamp,
fragile with power, fluid with silty life,
trickster or demon, guardian or friend,
pouring ourselves to feather, fur, and fin.

The rivers are one, for water is only one.
Let us stand in the center. We can never wander far.
River is blood in land that is our flesh.
Our bond, our song, plays ever in water tones.

*****

George and I lived on the Mississippi River, so our entire social and personal history was deeply touched by this mighty river.

The ferry which connected Port Allen and Baton Rouge since the early 1800s, thrilled me every time I boarded it. It was on the ferry that Daddy had tried to defend the black woman who was being stabbed when I was a young girl. In the summers, when I spent several days with my cousins in Port Allen, we often took our quarters and rode the ferry back and forth just for fun.

Mama grew up in a house near the levee in Port Allen, on the west side of the river. I grew up hearing about the great flood of 1927. Mama remembered that her father—my Paw Paw Altazan, an excellent swimmer—used to rope off a section of the river where he and his family of eleven children could safely swim.

Most intriguing of all, Mama told me of the family miracle that had happened on the levee. As a small boy, her father used to play with his brothers on the banks of the river. One day, he had climbed on a log that slipped into the muddy current. As the log floated further into the river with young Achille on it, his frightened brothers raced home to "Mon" (my great-grandmother, Marie-Lisette Druilhat, the midwife).

She came running with a couple of the neighbors. She saw her young son being swept downstream. She sank to her knees on the top of the levee and began pleading to Our Lady of Prompt Succor to rescue her son. None of the women there could do anything to help him.

Unbelievably, the log began moving back, against the current, returning to the place where it had entered the water. The boy was safe.

I have no reason to doubt the veracity of my family; several adults and children witnessed this phenomenon. In my mind's eye, I see women and children raising their arms to heaven, rejoicing and praising God.

Chapter 13

We Force the Spring

Mama called me to explain that Daddy was in the hospital, likely in 1992.

"I think that Daddy may be ready to see you," Mama said.

"You know what. It's time to bury this old hatchet," I told George. "Come with me. Let's both go to see him."

We did. As George wheeled into his room, I walked in.

"Hello, Daddy." He was quiet, but talked with us. He called George "Podnuh." "Podnuh" this and "Podnuh" that.

I was happy that Daddy had finally come to some resolution with our long estrangement.

George was happy for me—and with me.

A day later, my sister-in-law called to chew me out for daring to "bring that nigger to the hospital when your Daddy is so sick!"

What an old phony Daddy was! Pretending to be halfway happy to see us, to talk to us, and when our backs were turned, to complain to his daughter-in-law about it.

*****

George's sister, Joy Mae, died soon after we returned from our western trip in August 1992. She had cancer.

Hurricane Andrew had knocked out power all over the city. We held the funeral in a darkened church.

Joy Mae had no life insurance or burial insurance. At that time her daughter Debra was going to law school. I did not want to trouble the family. I took $6000 from my savings to pay for her funeral with no expectation that anyone could ever pay back the money.

1993—My mother, Emily Andre, and my father, Roy Andre, shortly before their deaths, six weeks apart in February. 1994

*****

On Oct. 17, 1992 George became embroiled in an international incident: the shooting of a Japanese exchange student, Yoshihiro Hattori, age seventeen.

George wanted a federal investigation. George and I drafted a letter to US Attorney Raymond Lamonica requesting a federal investigation of the incident to determine if Yoshi's civil rights had been violated. Included in the letter were statements alleging that a federal probe was necessary because local grand juries had shown indifference when a minority was the victim and the defendant was white.

We also drafted a letter to the young man's parents outlining the organization's course of action and expressing our deepest sympathy. George and I joined community to protest this needless death.

I included in the letter to the Hattori family the poem which I had written honoring this wonderful young man.

Yoshi
By Kathy Andre-Eames

I thought his smile spoke English rather well.
Sweeping as wide as a rainbow, it carried him
with those glad eyes of his, across the world.
His smile rode high above the water line,
a water dance of sky light and mist.
He entered as the sun might enter sand,
breached no man's life, but only as a boy might do,
sailed in on a wave of great good joy.
Only his hair came near his smile for shine,
as straight and clean as the light of life that grew it.
I knew him from merest glimpses of the news:
his dark head more pleasing than a story,
the gun that found him out while the man did not.
His smile remains, the deepest part of him.
It carried him so far; it keeps him still.

*****

Later that fall George ran again for president of the local branch of the NAACP. He was elected in December 1992.

*****

George was arrested one week later, on December 24.

I was out shopping. Police officers came to our home with search warrants for the house and for his van. They confiscated items in the van.

They arrested George for molestation of a juvenile and contributing to the delinquency of a juvenile.

Officers agreed, because it was Christmas Eve, to permit him to turn himself in after the holidays.

I have no idea how he kept this to himself. He said he refused to tell me because he didn't want to ruin my Christmas.

A few days later one of the most painful parts of our lives began.

We never hesitated in our many projects—despite the arrest, the defense, the pending trial, the interruption in his work with legal concerns and fund-raising. I supported him completely.

*****

This would be George's last celebration as NAACP branch president.

As he had done with other projects in the past, he always sought the most intelligent, socially conscious, talented, and inspiring individuals he could find to assist him. He wanted the best for his people, especially for the young. His passion was to lead, guide, and inspire the young with truly worthy role models, including their own successful peers. Wonderful, dedicated people—black and white, from all walks of life, from all classes—entirely too many people for me to name or to remember. They all walked with us, constantly supporting and assisting us.

As anyone will tell you if they knew George, when he needed you, he refused to take "no" for an answer. That included his wife, especially!

*****

George continued to serve as branch president. His installation, along with that of his board, took place on January 26, 1993. Judge

Freddie Pitcher swore in him and the board.

George asked me to write and deliver a tribute to Chief Justice Thurgood Marshall. He had died on January 24, and George, having worked with him personally when he was young, loved the great civil rights leader dearly.

A Tribute to Retired Chief Justice Thurgood Marshall on the Occasion of Installation of Officers of the Baton Rouge Branch of the NAACP
January 26, 1993
By Kathy Andre-Eames
Poet that I am, I live for words
the way some folks live for mustard greens and cornbread.
I chew them up slowly,
make them last a long time.
I swallow them.
I make them a part of me.
I did not sleep during
President Bill Clinton's inaugural address.
He had a word for me,
and when I reflected on Thurgood Marshall's death,
President Clinton's words came back
to make Thurgood's death take root in me
the way his life has taken root in all of us.

On January 20 we heard these few words
mark the beginnings of President Clinton's
service as the forty-second president of the United States:
"Today we celebrate the mystery of American renewal.
This ceremony is held in the depth of winter,
But by the words we speak
And the faces we show the world,
We force the spring."

What does that mean?
And what in the world
does that have to do with Thurgood Marshall?
Simply this.
When the racial climate was marked by frigidity,
when the ground for equal education
and human dignity was frozen

harder than the hearts of men,
Thurgood forced the spring.

Wherever the snow grew the least bit thin,
he shoveled back the cold crystals,
bared the fruitful ground,
and poured on good seed.
When winter fought back,
he held on, immoveable,
determined to have his way for his people.

The seed would have to sprout.
The ground would have to yield.
The black child would have to reap.
The snow would have to melt.
The ice would have to give.
The storm would have to recede.

Facing the blizzard is never easy for fragile men.
Yet Thurgood knew
the sun would have to break,
light would have to strengthen,
and someday,
children who walked in darkness would see great light.

Thank you, Thurgood
for forcing the spring.
Today, we celebrate the mystery of a man
who served the times in which he lived.
He lived in the depth of winter.
But by the words he spoke
and the face he showed the world
he forced the spring.

Chapter 14

We Find Our Roots

George and I drove east in July 1993 for a civil rights pilgrimage from July 16 through July 28. We planned again to sleep in the van and camp our way. We had not expected one of the hottest summers on record, with temperatures nearing 100 degrees almost daily. We endured. We visited Dr. King's church on Dexter Ave., in Montgomery, Alabama; the Southern Poverty Law Center; and the Civil Rights Memorial. We saw George Washington Carver's home at Tuskegee as we drove through the campus, visited the Atlanta Zoo, then headed for the NAACP office downtown.

We went on to Ebenezer Baptist Church and Dr. King's Memorial and tomb there. Coretta Scott King and Andrew Young were conducting a press conference. George posed joyfully for a photo with Andrew Young. We went to the home where Dr. King was born and to the Southern Christian Leadership Conference office.

In Macon we spent time in the Tubman African American Museum. Leaving Macon, we drove to Savannah, determined to find the cottage where walking tours of the Black Heritage Trail began. We viewed one of the oldest Baptist churches in the country there, the First African Baptist Church of Savannah, founded by members in 1773. As always, George wanted to see the poorer areas, and we also drove through rural parts of South Carolina. We saw dope peddlers who seemed upset that we were looking at them till they realized we were tourists, and we bought supper from a Black Muslim restaurant. While waiting on our food, I noticed a little framed quotation on the wall. After reading it, I pulled out a pen and jotted it down on a napkin for George. I knew it was just the sort of quotation he relished:

> "I am only one, but I am one.
> I cannot do everything, but I can do something.
> And because I cannot do everything,

I will not refuse to do the something that I can do.
What I can do, I should do.
And that I should do, by the grace of God, I will do."[1]

I delighted in camping on beautiful St. James Island where the Gullah people are located. One little black officer told us when we asked directions, "Don't worry, I wouldn't lost you!"

We spent the day on the grounds of Boone Hall Plantation where Alex Haley's *Queen* was filmed. There we saw original slave cabins, even a one-room schoolhouse where the slaves were taught to read and write—a first in the state. At twilight, worn out with sightseeing, we napped in the van on the plantation. We drove to the coastal beach where I had the opportunity to walk in the Atlantic Ocean. Later on St. John's Island we admired the 1400 year-old-oak tree that is believed to be the oldest living thing east of the Mississippi River.

As much as we enjoyed this historical pilgrimage, we suffered from the closeness of the van and the terrible heat and humidity.

Later, when George was in prison, he remarked: "Kathy, you know what? All that camping that we did prepared me for prison. It seasoned me and prepared me physically to deal with it."

No air conditioning in prison, either, no matter the heat of long Louisiana summers. If we were tough, it was because everything we did conspired to toughen us.

✶✶✶✶✶

We returned to our beloved West in 1994, spending most of our time in Santa Fe, which we loved.

It was in Santa Fe that I noticed that a small wound had opened on George's tailbone. It would never heal, draining constantly. It grew larger as the years passed, eventually becoming increasingly infected, until the infection entered the bone.

George felt constant discomfort and pain, yet he never complained as he shifted position often, trying to find some relief.

Throughout his life, I tended all of George's health needs as best I could.

He persisted in his work and would remain faithful to his purpose till his death.

When George was in prison, we talked about that trip on one of our visits, and he promised me, "When I'm released, I'm going to bring you back to Santa Fe." He did. We vacationed there again in 1999. Our trip in 1994 fed a deep need which the two of us had long felt.

✶✶✶✶✶

I left the church in 1994. My religion foundered, though my faith did not—at least, not at first.

I had learned a deep and abiding distrust of people, however, and turned elsewhere for the sustenance I needed to go on for the duration.

One sharp image of a photo in a book I had read filled my heart. It was from research I had done, believe it or not, in the fourth or fifth grade as I worked on a Native American project. I wanted to reconstruct this wholesome talisman for myself. Being a poet, I wrote:

Hopi Woman
By Kathy Andre-Eames
Like a shock of corn greening summer fields,
you stand fresh, Hopi woman, in my soul.
For thirty years your squash blossom hair
has coiled black above a grinding bowl.

Turquoise buds, bits of coral shell,
sterling blooms dance sierra down.
Light of the hogans, the full blaze of your skirts
bell in the wind, swinging wide and brown.

Thankful woman of pinto beans and corn,
clay baskets, yards and yards of sky,
your blue fire curls in smoke against the cliffs.
Like steaming prayers, the roiling clouds blow by.

Hopi woman, I remember Hopi:
the corn baked bread, a woman breaking gold.
From the fifth grade I remember Hopi;
For 30 years your wholeness fills my soul.

One reason this fifth grade work had meant much to me was that I knew that my paternal great-grandmother was a full-blooded Indian woman.

When R. J. and I had played cowboys and Indians, we both wanted to be the Indian.

My sense of justice was strong even though at that time I had precious little sense of the saga of genocide and oppression of entire nations of people. All I knew is that I identified with them in my soul. For this reason also, when a Native American family moved into Brusly, my childhood home, I sympathized with Margaret and Mike, the two children who attended Brusly Elementary. I was kind to them. My classmates generally seemed to despise them from afar, keeping them at a distance. I was too shy then to overcome this divide and become close friends with them, but I observed the prejudice and it bothered me.

In 1990 or so, I had already written a poem lamenting the loss of my roots. I didn't know my great-grandmother's tribe or name. So much was irretrievably lost. I was thrilled to have this poem published in a little booklet *Teepees Are Folded* by the Council of Indian Education in Billings, Montana. The poem expressed well for me what I felt and what other Native American people also felt:

Winding Fingers
By Kathy Andre-Eames
Grandmother,
what shall I do?
I have lost the thread.
What help is there for me?
You have gone before
and taken the spool with you.
You wrapped it tight,
and it sits in your pocket
forgotten where you fell.
What help is there for me?
The stories you weaved
as you twisted the fibers
are cut off now.
The old cloth is tied
on all four corners.
The red line has ended
in a hard white knot.

What help is there for me?
My hands are lost.
My dress is frayed.
Grandmother,
what shall I do?
I have lost the thread.[2]

Alex Haley published *Roots* in 1976, and the mini-series came to television (the next year, the year we were married). Not only did I take note, but George and I watched the series with great intensity. I bought the book, devouring it from cover to cover. Alex telling his story, was revealing the great hole in the heart of many African Americans and probably Native Americans as well—certainly me— and healing that deprivation with many images of suffering and triumph. Out of my spiritual loss, I gained ground as I pursued the history of Native Americans—especially gravitating to their spiritual heritage—and the prevailing devotion to the Great Spirit, to which I clung like a drowning man clinging to a branch.

To illustrate how this experience affected me, in 2009 shortly after I created George's Web site, I created my own Web site, Louisiana Visions. Though I had never been able to finish it because of George's health problems, I included some of my Native American material. In the little section on Native Americans, I wrote:

The Native American expression, "All My Relatives" [*Mitakuye Oyasin*] is at once a prayer, an act of faith, a blessing, a confirmation, a hope, a declaration of a sacred tradition. "All My Relatives" is an affirmation of the circle of life, the unity of all life: the winged creatures, the stone people, the green creatures or plant life, the four-leggeds, the two-leggeds, and all that swim the waters.

"Ute Lake" [New Mexico] is one of my sacred places, a place where I feel connected to "All My Relatives" of all time. It is a place which sacramentally enables me to tap into the fullness of our Native American spiritual tradition.

Ute Lake
By Kathy Andre-Eames
Its border tucked by stones smooth and flat,
the lake shows a clean face to the sun.
The same sun that has warmed its great heart

two hundred years, four hundred years and more
finds me drowsy here, my skin hot to touch,
near the steep pool at the edges of the drop.
Who stopped here to drink long ago?
Did a Ute woman crouch at its lip?
Or did Kiowa lead their horses here,
feathery tails glinting in the heat?
These old waters are gathering like peace
in the dry bones of All My Relatives:
runts of cactus, thorns of scrub mesquite,
the horns of survivors, remnants of ancient bloods.
These old waters are me, and all I find
I find to be true, here, now and forever:
this roadrunner that runs the identical trail,
this prairie dog, the child of a prairie dog.
The Great One again is the presence of this sky
and the Wind that has always been to blow my hair.[3]

Later, when George was in prison, I gained strength from this
meditation on the bison or buffalo:

Snow Bison
By Kathy Andre-Eames
Let me stand the snow like them,
rooted to the storm ground, unchanged,
my halo, a freeze of breath and pitiless sky,
my massive shoulders pushed against the wind.

Let me stand the snow like them,
my head still, a blaze of sleeting light,
my head hard as a mountain, hooves of rock,
my horns pointed north until the thaw.

Let me stand the snow like them,
my sinews and tendons married to the cold,
my eyes used to unbearable, blinding white,
as vast as the prairie itself, as undisturbed.

Under so much snow, who would believe the grass?
Under so much pain, who could believe the green?
Let me stand the snow like them, and with them
move on as the prairie itself goes on.

If I was tough, it was a toughness handed down to me from generations, a toughness which I consciously nurtured. If I felt any peace, it was a peace which came to me from "All my relatives." Furthermore, I would try to give my vision to George. When we went to Santa Fe, New Mexico, in 1994, especially, I dug deeply into this tradition and devoured the natural environment with George by my side. When we visited the Painted Desert, I was ecstatic to see the kiva. I marveled at it. George could not see the site. It was not handicapped-accessible.

Not only did this wonderful sojourn influence my spirituality and thinking, but it deeply influenced my writing style. Another poem that I wrote at this time, derived from the Navajo tradition, sums up well the peace I gained from this heritage of mine:

Navajo
By Kathy Andre-Eames
Snow is warm
melting in the sun's corner,
pressed to life by the squirrel's foot.
Snow, the hawk's circling eye.
Snow, the eagle's neck ring.
Let us speak, snow. Let us be peace.
Peace behind me Peace before me
Peace above me Peace below me
Peace the snow dust. Peace the snow cloud.

In addition to this sojourn, I delved deeply into Eastern traditions of spirituality. I never actually became a Buddhist or Taoist, but these traditions comforted me and shaped my spirituality. The Buddhist tradition of cherishing all life, never to kill or injure any living thing was a mirror image to the "All My Relatives" tradition of the Native Americans. What I loved most of the Taoist tradition was the concept of flowing with life. In a synthesis of all these traditions, I wrote during this time also, speaking for God:

Be Where You Are
By Kathy Andre-Eames
Be where you are
like a stone on a mountainside.
You are already a pebble to my granite,
cracked or smooth, sliding to a gulf,

bumping along the creek's bottom sands
or dry on the bony floor of a fox's lair,
entrance to den of cougar or black bear.

Be where you are. However your jade lies,
your markings are clear as an ancient polished jar
pouring its stream of green temple tea.
In construction or repose you are there,
in destruction, out of love, or in the fire
emerging or descending, on the rise,
you cannot be where I am not.
Always you will sleep in my broad arms,
always to emerge born of my warm breast
a sacred word, spoken unique again,
now with feathers, now with scales or fur,
remarkable eyes, agile fingers and tongue,
child of your mother and new under the sun.

When George was in prison I would remember this wisdom, "Be where you are. Go with the flow." This had become a part of who I was. How natural and reaffirming to read Stuart Wilde's: "When you are up to your eyeballs in muck and bullets, do muck and then do bullets."[4]

On January 17, 1994, increasingly concerned by the level of violence we were observing in our community, we created a new celebration for the birthday of Dr. Martin Luther King, Jr.: "Time to Stop Crying: Start the Healing and Building." In one part of the program in the Centroplex, I read the poem which I had written in November 1993, "Trying Not to Cry," which gave the theme. George loved the poem because it was simple; he felt the children would be able to understand it.

Chapter 15

Family Crisis and a Final Tribute

Throughout our preparation for the Martin Luther King Celebration, through the fall of 1993, I had been helping to care for my parents.

Daddy had a series of strokes after Mama was diagnosed with an aggressive blastoma, brain cancer. My brother and his wife stayed overnight with them during the week, and I spent weekends.

The tumor was playing games with Mama's brain—she often forgot that Daddy had died. As he lay on his deathbed, she kept telling us, "You better wake him up. If he naps too long, he won't sleep a wink tonight."

Daddy died in January and Mama died on Feb. 8, 1994, about six weeks later.

She knew that what would follow would be nothing but trouble.

R. J. was closest to Daddy, so he and Mama planned his funeral.

I attended Daddy's wake and funeral by myself, without George.

However, when Mama died, R. J., Kathleen, and I had to plan her funeral. All went well in the funeral home. We agreed on a casket and gave the obituary.

Once outside on the sidewalk, however, R. J. warned me, "I'm telling you right now, if George tries to come to the wake, I'll have him arrested for disturbing the peace."

I'm sure my mouth hung open in dismay. I didn't even try to answer him. He turned away, not caring. Not only would R. J. do it, but because our first cousin Randall Andre was sheriff of West Baton Rouge at that time, he could do it.

I returned home and told George what had happened.

"It doesn't matter. I don't need to be there."

I was outraged. "If you aren't welcome, I'm not going either."

"But that's your mama," George said quietly. "You should go."

"I'm not. I'll go to the funeral, but I can't go to the wake. I can't take a chance on your being arrested, and I certainly don't want a big scene. I'm going to walk around University Lake instead." I did.

At the wake, numerous cousins approached R. J. and Kathleen wanting to know where I was.

"We have no idea," they said. "She just didn't show up."

Knowing how close I had been to Mama, my cousins called the house. George answered because I was walking around University Lake. I was crying and talking to Mama, telling her, "Well, you knew what would happen, didn't you? If anybody understands, I guess you do."

My cousins were incensed and vowed to sit with us at the funeral. In the meantime, Mama's elderly brothers—Milton, Gerald, Uncle Curly, Uncle James (her sister Faye's husband)—approached R. J., telling him, "What you are doing is not right. Kathy has the right to bring George to the funeral. He is her husband. Leave them alone."

In addition to this intervention, I had called Lenny and Barbara, my father's nephew and wife. Lenny and his brother, Roger, had been like brothers to me when I was growing up. We played with them in Erwinville every Sunday when we visited my paternal grandparents. Telling Lenny what R. J. had done, I asked him and Barbara to meet us at the church and go in with us.

The funeral was such a disaster. Lenny and Barbara met us at the ramp on the right side of the church and about ten of my cousins sat all around us. While we entered the right side of the church up front, R. J. and those who clearly disapproved of us sat on the left, in the middle pews.

Tension was palpable. As the funeral began, I realized that planning had not been completed for Mama's funeral. No music, no special words or remembrances—only tension. I had thought that R. J. and Kathleen would complete the arrangement since I was not there; nothing had been done. I was hurt, but nothing could be done now.

More hurtful was the line of faithful going to communion. Some sympathetically patted our hands as they passed our front pew. Others deliberately lifted their noses into the air refusing even to acknowledge our presence.

After this fiasco, I left the church for fifteen years.

I finally returned to my beloved St. Paul the Apostle Church in 2009. A black Catholic church.

Despite the way R. J. and Kathleen acted at that time, Mama and

Daddy had named my brother executor of their estate, a role he fulfilled with fairness and complete fidelity to my parents' wishes. Although Daddy's first desires were to deny me as his daughter, he had eventually relented, and I had inherited my full share along with my brothers. We peacefully settled my family's estate and belongings, sharing them satisfactorily among ourselves.

R. J. has not spoken to me since.

*****

George's trial was scheduled for March 1995. Nevertheless, on Monday, January 16, 1995, we planned and held our annual celebration honoring Dr. King, a holiday he had fought for on behalf of all the school children.

Herman Brister, Sr., Deputy Superintendent and Dr. Bernard Weiss, Superintendent, had arranged for all interested students from elementary, middle and high schools to be picked up by a school bus. As usual, they were brought to McKinley Middle School, near the Centroplex.

Beginning with music and workshops, after a bag lunch for all

1991—After successfully winning a school holiday for Dr. Martin Luther King's birthday, George and the local branch of the NAACP organize a full day of activities for students, including this Freedom March in 1991.

participating adults and children, we created our own little freedom march. We walked to the Centroplex Theater of the Performing Arts, for the dignified and more formal celebration: "The Legacy Continues as We Build on the Dream."

Several offered greetings: attorney Alvin Washington; Dr. Dolores Spikes, President of Southern University system; Greg Brown from the mayor's office, and Rev. T. J. Jemison of Mt. Zion.

Music included *Heritage*, led by Clarence Jones, and the McKinley High School Jazz Band. Torri Virdure, Trey Virdure, Tina Mitchell, and Tony Mitchell also performed *Truth*.

Michael Harrell presented a puppet show; dances were performed by Kristi Vincent and Cortni Hall of Scotlandville Magnet High School and also by Belfair Visual/Performing Arts and Extended Day Academy led by Linda Harris; Miss Southern also appeared.

Rev. James Stovall, Louisiana Coalition against Nazism and Racism, led the Benediction. Then I read the poem honoring Dr. King which I had prepared for the occasion:

The Elements He Knew:
To Dr. Martin Luther King
By Kathy Andre-Eames
The elements he knew were far more kind
than the people who ruled the parishes and counties,
as kind as the grit and toil down Selma road.
After billy clubs and prods, Martin knew God.
In the heat of flares, he knew water like a well.
Like a bell his cistern rang, ringing it down,
till Justice rolled like a flood in a parched land.

The elements at their worst were far more kind.
As tired as the blues, he got hungry when he fasted,
beaten by stones, soiled by the red mud,
Alabama on his hands and in his shoes.
Blisters rubbed him raw, sun cut his eyes,
abrasive winds wore him to the bone.
But the purposes and accidents of nature
Martin found acceptable, every one.

Man alone denied his humanity:
denied him a seat, a vote, a piece of bread,

denied him a sip of water, a home address,
denied him a smile, a job, a ride on the bus,
denied his children a playground, an ice cream cone,
a ride on the horsey on the merry-go-round,
a potty break for the urgent two year old,
or a peaceful Sunday morning without a bomb.

The elements at their worst were far more kind
perhaps because they seemed accidental,
or at least treated everyone the same.
It was the unjust act permitted by law,
the incident that maimed the innocent,
inequality gained by purpose or design,
that Martin condemned and found unacceptable.

Denied a seat, he would walk a hundred miles.
Kept from motels, he would spend the nights in jails.
Prevented from playgrounds, swimming pools, and parks,
his children would open entries to the schools,
past bristling dogs and mobs and principals.
The elements at their worst were far more kind.

After billy clubs and prods, Martin knew God.
In the heat of flares, he knew water like a well.
Like a bell his cistern rang, ringing it down,
till Justice rolled like a flood in a parched land.

1988—Judge Freddie Pitcher installs new president G. Washington Eames, Jr., and his new board for the local NAACP branch. In 1983, Judge Pitcher, one of George's cousins, was elected citywide as the first African American city court judge in the history of Baton Rouge. Four years later, in 1987, he ran a successful citywide election for the Nineteenth Judicial District. He was the first African American elected to this position.

1988—Judge Freddie Pitcher with George and another cousin with whom we were close for years, attorney Robert Judge Eames, one of NAACP branch attorneys. He worked tirelessly on the school desegregation case and other legal matters.

Chapter 16

George Fights His Accuser and Loses

We struggled during all of 1993 and 1994 through the early spring of 1995 to raise money and to plan George's defense for the molestation defense.

George was firm on one tactic: in no way would he put our home in jeopardy. We would not mortgage it or use it in any way to gain a defense. He was adamant. As far as he was concerned, this was Kathy's house; and fund-raising would have to be done in other ways.

Joe Delpit worked tirelessly for George's defense fund, literally going door to door. "We must help him," he insisted. Though George and Joe were at odds at different points during the years, they were truly close much of the time. I believe we probably have Joe to thank for saving our home.

Then too, we had asked Joe and Precious to be our son Andre's godparents, and they had done much to help him also, giving him a job at the Chicken Shack.

✳✳✳✳✳

In the beginning, George had no idea who the girl was who had made the accusations against him.

Eventually, George realized that months before, the girl's mother had called him to ask him to talk to her daughter because she was having trouble with her.

During the three years preceding the trial, we learned disturbing information about her from our attorney Michele Fournet. Two events which Michele told us about her had happened prior to the alleged molestation in the summer of 1992.

In the spring of 1992 this same young woman had stabbed her stepfather with a pair of scissors, according to our attorney.

That same year she traded her mother's car for crack, according to our attorney.

And that when she disappeared for a couple of days in the middle of the trial, she was in a crack house, according to our attorney.

Nothing of this could be used in the trial.

"How could anyone think I could mess with an ugly little twig like her when I have a beautiful wife like you?" George told me during the trial.

A woman called George with a suggestion about the motivation of the young accuser. During this time one of the accusing family's neighbors, an elderly white woman, called and said that she knew why the girl was doing this. The girl wanted money and figured we had lots of money. The girl had even told the neighbor that "if this doesn't work, I know another old man I can accuse."

George remembered the accusing girl admiring his van, especially because it had a bed in it; we knew she wanted it.

As young as she was, we had heard from that same neighbor that the girl was already engaging in prostitution for drugs.

I read in the newspaper in 2000 that she had been arrested, tried, and found guilty of simple burglary, serving 13 months.[1]

As we struggled with our defense, Michele Fournet told him frankly, "Mr. Eames, there's a whole lot of people out there who hate you. They want to send you to prison. And I just don't know if I can keep you out. But you don't have to go to prison, Mr. Eames. The DA is offering a suspended sentence for you if you want to plead guilty. I recommend that you take this deal."

"But if I plead guilty, I would be admitting to something I didn't do!" George said.

"Well, Mr. Eames, that's what we have to do sometimes!" Michele said.

"I don't like it. If I plead guilty, I would have no reputation for the rest of my life in this city, and I wouldn't be able to work with the NAACP or with the baseball program. Kathy, what do you think?" George asked, turning to me.

"I wouldn't do it, George," I said. "I would never admit to doing something that I didn't do; they could throw me in jail or kill me. I just wouldn't do something like that."

"I agree," George told Michele. "I won't take any deals. I want justice, and I'll take my chances with a trial. If they find me guilty, I'll just have to take the consequences. But I can't say I'm guilty when I'm not."

I can't begin to recap all the details and what evidence we found for this young girl's accusations.

Twenty years have passed. George and I moved on. We threw out much of this material.

I just want to state simply what our viewpoint was in all this—this travesty of justice.

We felt we were forced to fight with our hands tied behind our backs.

What hurt the most was the crime for which he was accused. Could there be leveled against any man more shameful behavior than assaulting a child?

To this day, I believe wholeheartedly that George was completely innocent.

The girl saw an opportunity to use us—and she did, with the public's help.

We felt throughout this ordeal that the charges had been initiated through a conspiracy to unseat George as president of the NAACP branch. Yet without appropriate evidence, how could we prove his innocence?

George Resigns as President of NAACP Branch

As soon as George was found guilty, he drafted a letter resigning his presidency.

In our front yard, George tendered his resignation as president of the local branch of the NAACP just five days after his conviction in March 1995.

As I usually did, I helped him to draft the letter. It was reported in an article in the *Advocate* on March 24, 1995.

George declared simply that he had served the civil rights organization faithfully throughout many years. He had no wish to burden the NAACP with his legal problems. Due to his conviction, national policy required that he resign. When he said, "I hereby tender my resignation," George choked up, close to tears.

He wished only that the local branch carry on strongly, continuing to address problems in the black community.

Rev. James Stovall expressed appreciation for all George had accomplished throughout the many years he had served so well, and commented that George had enjoyed the backing and general support of the public.[2]

George was sentenced on June 28, 1995 to three and a half years of hard labor. I made a last-ditch effort to help him. On June 16, 1995 I wrote a lengthy letter to the US Attorney requesting his help in protecting George's civil rights and detailing the conspiracy theory.

I then wrote a press release summarizing the letter. I no longer have the letter, but I do have the press release. I do not now remember what response I received—or if I indeed received a response to either one.

PRESS RELEASE

On June 16, 1995 I submitted a formal complaint including an outline and pertinent documentation to US Attorney L.J. Hymel on behalf of my husband, G. Washington Eames, Jr., former president of the Baton Rouge Branch of the NAACP

In that letter I requested: "...that the US Attorney's office, under your auspices [L. J. Hymel], investigate...allegations and complaints that G. Washington Eames' human and civil rights have been, repeatedly and viciously violated in East Baton Rouge Parish."

The role of the press: The outline reveals how the *State Times* and *Advocate* created misconceptions about Eames' character at the time he was shot and paralyzed in 1956. Documentation sent from the DA's office to the Veterans Administration in 1958 reveal that he was not engaged in wrongdoing at the time he was shot. Yet that documentation was concealed from Eames by the Veterans Administration which denied him a pension based on the fact that he was "engaged in wrongdoing" at the time of the shooting.

Conspiracy based on a personal vendetta and allegations of attempted bribery: I asked the US Attorney's office to investigate a conspiracy which had as its sole purpose to destroy by any means necessary the good name of G. Washington Eames and to remove him from any position of leadership in the community.

As early as spring 1991, individuals who resented George and local

NAACP policies began probing for any kind of material that could be used to discredit Mr. Eames' character and reputation, including interviews with community leaders, leaders in the community at large and leaders in the NAACP. These individuals researched the shooting of 1956, [at which time George was paralyzed] and used channels within the NAACP itself in an attempt to unseat the president. With each local election, complaints were lodged with the national office which conducted its own hearings and investigations into the local branch.

Complaints ranged from irregularities in election procedures to charges that Eames was overcharging teenagers for memberships. In 1991 came the first suggestion that Eames was guilty of sexual harassment: a woman testified that instead of Eames trying to help her with her civil rights problem, Eames had tried to "go with me," or made an inappropriate pass at her.

In 1991, a local group held a town meeting to decide "what to do about GWE."

In 1991 on WXOK radio in a public forum, one individual claimed to have "stacks of allegations" against Eames from persons in the community.

In the fall of 1992, before the 1992 election, we heard that someone had attempted to bribe a member of the local branch with $1000 to run against Eames for NAACP president. We heard that it had been made clear to this individual that Eames "has got to go," that money was no problem, and that a woman known to this group was nearly convinced to bring charges against Eames.

Eames was re-elected president on Dec. 19, 1992. Less than a week later, charges were filed and he was subsequently arrested.

Secondary indications of conspiracy to extort, to defame, and to influence sentencing of GWE: I further requested the US Attorney to investigate the following:

In the fall of 1993 a couple contacted Eames to warn him that unless he came up with $350 within twenty-four hours or less, they would file charges on behalf of their daughters for molestations which occurred, [they alleged] in March-April 1993 [three months after GWE's arrest in Dec. 1992].

The DA's office was immediately notified. The DA's office refused to investigate though documentation [taped conversations] was available. Yet the so called allegations of the extortionists have been presented to the judge for his consideration with respect to sentencing on June 28, 1995.

Signed, T. K. Andre-Eames

Why Did the Group Conspire against George?

What could have been this group's motive in conspiring to remove George from the NAACP office? As simple as this: George and his board had voted in April 1991 to press the city to rename Florida Blvd., the main business artery in the city, after Dr. Martin Luther King. George presented a slideshow documenting the shortcomings of Acadian Thruway, rundown businesses, night clubs, and the like—all of which, he felt would dishonor Dr. King's name.

This civic group opposed the position of the NAACP and were determined to unseat George at any cost.

Also in June 1995, immediately after George was imprisoned, I wrote a narrative, [parts of which follow], detailing something of what we had endured:

"I hurt deeply that this generous and kind man who is a paraplegic, who has put his life on the line and sacrificed so much personally for the black community, has been unjustly treated in the last few weeks. It breaks my heart and disappoints me to see such a severe miscarriage of justice. I will never abandon him. I will never stop trying to see justice done—whatever we have to do to turn this parody around.

This whole scene feels like a nightmare. How could so much good have spawned so much evil? At the same time, look how many civil rights leaders have been assassinated, bombed out, and burned. To work in the civil rights arena has ever meant to put your life on the line. It seems we've made little progress in the last forty years.

We look to justice from God. It may be the only place we will ever find it."

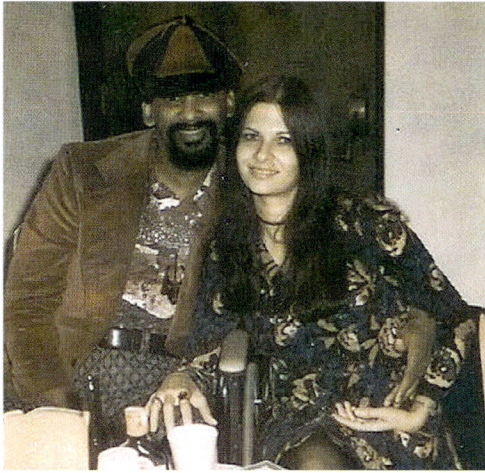

1971—This is the first picture taken of George Eames, Jr. and the author.

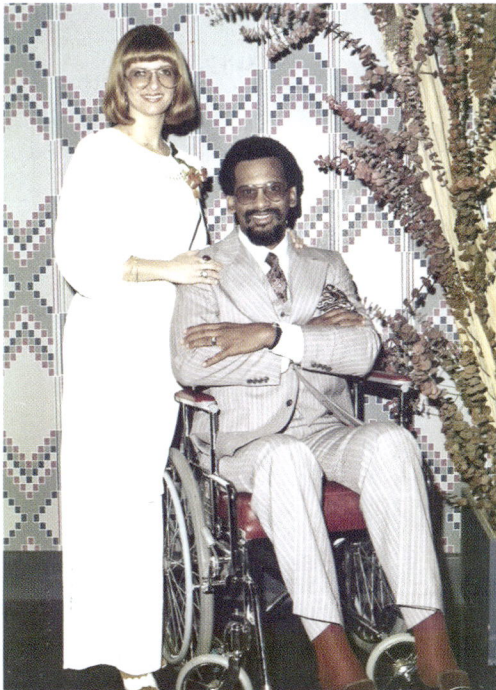

1977—The author and George attend a public function just one week prior to our wedding on Nov. 21, 1977.

1978—Wardell, our son, in one of the first photos taken of him during the first week he came to live with us. He's proud of LSU!

1982—A family portrait: George, Kathy, and Wardell

1983—The author, during her 15-year career as a retail manager with Sears

1980—Wardell meets George's two sisters: Gloria E. Moore, and Joy Mae Eames.

1988—George and Wardell, now 15, exchange a hug.

2000—Our "Square Table" group: top from left to right Fannie Godwin, Alice Stovall, Kathy Eames, Dr. Bernard Weiss; bottom, George and Marie Weiss. Not shown is Rev. Jimmie Stovall, who is taking the picture.

1988—George and the author attend the Super Bowl XXIII in New Orleans.

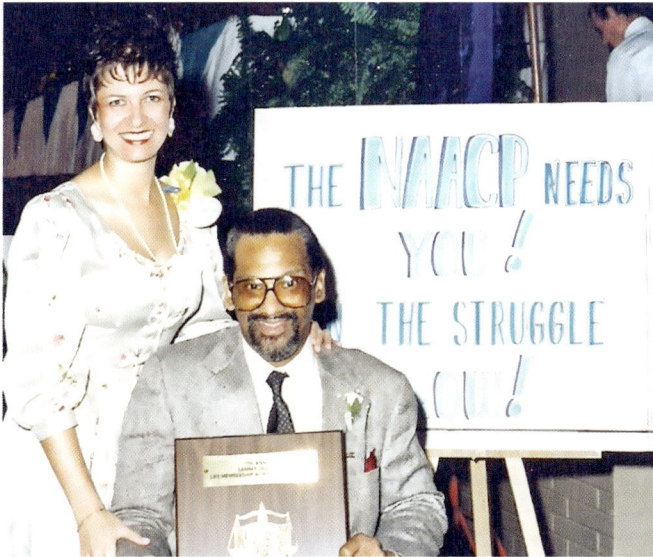

1987—George Eames and Kathy attend the annual Freedom Fund Banquet.

1974—Christmas, George and the author

1978—A professional portrait of George

1987—Then-Gov. Edwin Edwards delivers greetings at the Freedom Fund Banquet. He is flanked by the first black woman in Louisiana to run for the US House of Representatives, Faye Williams from Alexandria. They are greeted by George Eames and the author.

1998—Upon his return from prison, George worked to reorganize a new baseball program. Here is the staff: Rev. Leo Cyrus, President of the Fourth District Baptist Association; W. E. Tucker, realtor and Baton Rouge businessman; Skip Bertman, head baseball coach of LSU; Robert J. Williams, Jr., Zachary, East Baton Rouge Parish schools administrator; and Herman Brister, Sr., EBR Parish schools administrator.

2010—George meets with his cousin, student minister Rashid Muhammad, at a banquet held in Rashid's honor.

2010—Kathy and George are at the banquet honoring student minister Rashid Muhammad, George's cousin, who worked with us in the civil rights struggle in Baton Rouge.

Chapter 17

Prison For Two

When the judge pronounced sentence, the numerous deputies lining the walls of the courtroom rushed George to the ambulance waiting to carry him to Parish Prison. They did this so swiftly and abruptly that they allowed us not even a minute to say goodbye or exchange a hurried kiss.

I had grave concerns about his health. The wound on the tailbone was beginning to trouble him greatly by this time. Also, as a paraplegic, George had to catheterize himself in order to relieve his bladder. He had nothing with him to care for himself; I hurried home and put together a bag of clean underwear and his other personal items. The parish deputies were kind and promised to give him the necessary articles, including his Bible.

Though prisoners bound for state prisons are normally held for several weeks or so, less than three days later at about 4:00 in the morning George was awakened for transport to Hunt Correctional Institute.

He was not told where he was going for "security" reasons. Again they transported him in an ambulance. When he arrived, he was told, "Man, we been waiting for you!" He was put into solitary and given no phone calls for thirty days while they were "processing" him.

I had no idea where he was or what had happened.

When he did call me, he said that he had not been able to take anything but the medical items. His Bible, watch, and ring, I was able to recover from Parish Prison, but the underwear and other personal items had disappeared.

When we finally had a chance to visit face-to-face, George narrated a strange experience he had three and a half months after he entered prison. It was the day of the Million Man March on Washington on Oct. 16, 1995.

George was hustled from place to place by guards, each one watching him carefully.

Finally, he asked one of them, "What's going on?"

The guard replied quietly, "We heard that someone was going to break you out of here for the march. They are watching for the helicopter that they will be sending for you."

George laughed and laughed.

"Man, how in the world could I even reach a helicopter if one did come? How in the world could I roll through the field to it? Who do they think I am? What kind of power do they think I have?"

The prison staff watched him warily for a long time, calling him "Eames." Guards told him that nobody was called "Mister" in this place. The irony was that by the time he left, inmates were calling him "Mr. President"—and the staff, including the warden, called him "Mr. Eames."

Even though guards protested he was just another inmate, George gained their respect as they realized the kind of man he actually was.

He eventually began to fight for the rights of the handicapped inmates for shower chairs, safety issues and such. The staff began to ask him, "When are you leaving?"

Thankfully for me, Hunt was in St. Gabriel, not too far from Baton Rouge. As soon as he was permitted, I began to visit on the allowed days—about every two weeks—provided George had not committed any infractions.

Rules are numerous in prison. George was accused of many transgressions for the first few months. For example, he was put in solitary and not allowed visitors one time because he had been accused of "strong-arming the TV,"—apparently hogging it for himself. Ridiculous.

His punishment for some of these "infractions" was sometimes solitary confinement. Confined to a solitary cell, he was deprived of normal "comforts," which worried the heck out of me. For example, instead of a cot or bed, he had only a low concrete platform about twenty inches from the floor. It was difficult for him to access it. And without bedding, his wound could only worsen. His only choice was to sit in his chair for hours at a time or to recline on concrete, making retrieval of his meals impossible if he were lying down when they brought them. They would not wait for him to get up to reach his tray.

He did not have adequate bathing facilities. The prison had only showers and no shower wheelchairs provided for prisoners. George had to roll into the shower with his normal wheelchair, repeatedly wetting it. All he could do to prevent the back and seat from getting wet was to cover the wheelchair with plastic bags.

George Pleads: "Get Me Out of Here."

Early on, when George called, he pleaded, "Get me out of here."
I felt helpless. I was angry for months, but I had little recourse.

The first year that George was incarcerated was the most difficult because our circumstances were new. I had no idea what to expect. As difficulties arose for both of us, neither of us was sure how to cope. I alternately wept and fumed, angrier than anything else.

I designed a poster showing the logo of a wheelchair behind bars, pleading "Please help!" and posted it on our front door. I have no idea now what I intended that poster to do to help us, but I wanted everyone who passed by to know that we were in trouble. Neighbors and friends called to give comfort.

One of the most meaningful gestures was a card placed in our mailbox by children of our neighborhood. On the cover, a little rabbit peeked over a gate surmounted by the opening script: "Without your friendly, smiling face..." Inside, the script completed the thought: "...it's not the same old place. Miss you!" The inside of the card was filled with names of children, more than seventy of them, in their own handwriting or print. What a tribute to the man who had been accused of molesting children! I knew why they had done this. Children passed by our home on the way to-and-from the store, and to-and-from school because we lived in the second house on the street entering our subdivision. Never a stranger, George had gotten to know them. Whenever he was in our yard, George would greet the children, ask them what grade they were in, would ask how they were doing in school, and would encourage them to excel. Some we had seen grow up, entering high school, and then college. It was not me they knew; I was usually at work. But George was that friendly, smiling face whom they trusted and liked.

✳✳✳✳✳

In the summer of 1995, George had just been incarcerated in Hunt Correctional Center Institute. Wardell, now twenty-two, was referring to himself as Andre, one of his middle names. Though I immediately tried to call him Andre, per his request, George had a hard time doing this. George called him Wardell till the day he died. The state originally sent Andre to Hunt; but when prison authorities became aware that they had both father and son, they quickly moved Andre to Dixon Correctional.

I had both husband and son in prison at the same time. I used to joke, "How did I, a good Catholic girl, manage to end up in this situation?"

When Andre went into state care, later going to prison, I was torn. My heart full of anguish, I felt that he was lost.

Then I was struck by this thought, "How can you dare to think such a thing? Don't you realize that he never has been in your hand, that you never were able to do anything for him? He is in God's hand, and God will deal with him as only he can." After that, I felt peace.

I felt like I had been cut in half. I kept saying to myself: "I can't wait till all this mess is over and I can return to my life!"

Enlightenment suddenly came to me, "Kathy, this is your life!" It seemed like I had been knocking my head against the wall.

I stopped.

My attitude changed. Instead of resisting, though I fought just as hard to protect George as I could, I began to submit and go with the flow rather than fight every second.

Gov. Edwin Edwards: "George Is Such a Hot Potato. I Just Can't Touch This."

I was infuriated with the way George was being treated. I finally devised a plan to protect him.

This plan involved attorney Alvin Washington who had become chapter president after George resigned. I got a lot of law firm envelopes from him. Since attorney-client privilege was sacrosanct, even in prison, I began a siege of complaints to the Hunt Correctional warden. With a stub of a pencil, George conveyed details of unjust actions which had been leveled against him. I typed up formal complaints and mailed them to the warden in the attorney-privileged envelopes. Every complaint had to be investigated, and if reprisal against the prisoner had been unjust, the guard was fined. Soon they left George alone.

In 1996 I began a vigorous campaign to secure a pardon from Gov. Edwin Edwards who had known George personally. I began by securing letters pleading clemency based on the many contributions which George had made to the community over the years. I asked for letters from Coach Dale Brown, Rev. Jimmy Stovall, Dr. Bernard Weiss, Terry Robiskie (former running back at LSU), and others.

I made an appointment with the governor. Edwards met me cordially and sympathetically.

"George is such a hot potato. I just can't touch this." He wrung his hands. In his last days as governor, Edwards attempted to pardon several prisoners—among them George—but was effectually blocked because he had delayed his efforts. Pardon was no longer feasible.

George's sentence included "hard labor." Doctor's orders exempted George from it, and he was assigned light dusting and such. When he tired of sitting in the wheelchair, he was free to go to his narrow cot and ease his backside—provided he was not in solitary.

The prison food was terrible, but George had money from me to go to the commissary for snacks, which he enjoyed more than his meals.

His sister Gloria and I visited George every two weeks. Thankfully, other close friends visited. They included Bernie and Marie, Herman Brister, Sr., Rev. Jimmy Stovall, Alvin Washington, Coach Dale Brown, and others.

Eventually our son Andre was released from Dixon Correctional. He came with me to see his father.

Finally, George earned picnic visits as a reward for good behavior. I was overjoyed with his sister to bring him home-cooked foods, which he enjoyed immensely.

In the winter months, picnics were near impossible because we froze outside—the only place we could have them. Other prisoners who had no picnic privileges sat with their guests in the visiting room; we had to go outside. In truly cold, rainy weather, we had to skip the picnics.

One Christmas day occurred on a visiting day. George had told me on the phone, "Bring me some pralines." George loved these candies above all treats.

Pralines are a special kind of Southern pecan candy—I excel at making them. As a matter of fact, for years, pralines were the only gifts we gave our friends. I made dozens of pralines, packing them in decorative tins.

But this was not a picnic visit, and I would not be allowed to bring pralines into the prison. If George were caught receiving pralines, they would be considered "contraband"—and he could be sent to solitary.

I reminded him of all this.

"Kathy, without your pralines, there isn't any Christmas," he said.

I wrapped two large pralines in tinfoil, and tucked them into my bra. Once in the visiting room, I went to the ladies' room, retrieved them, and slipped them to him under the table. He stashed them under his seat in the wheelchair.

George was not caught and enjoyed his secret stash in his bed that night. That simple treat made Christmas a delight for him.

✳✳✳✳✳

During those three years, I didn't want to go anywhere in the evenings. If George was in prison, I would be in prison too.

My friends from school invited me out. Especially Sharon Gautreau, Barbara Stockner, Jeannine Johnson, Sarah Campbell, Chip Cappel, and others. They invited me to parties, to the movies, just to hang out. If it was after 5:00 p.m. I usually declined. George called me once a day in the evening, from Hunt, and I could not disappoint him by not being home for the call. That call was our best link—our only real link—except for the visit every two weeks. I would not miss the call.

The year before George was sentenced, we had started a garden in our front yard. George hired a man to put in a small fishpond; he also planted two palm trees and moved the nandina bushes my mother had bought for us years ago. George had another man pour an outdoor aggregate patio, and we moved the wrought iron chairs and table which had been on the backyard patio.

Here George and I had spent many pleasant days just before his incarceration. He drank up as much of this natural beauty as he could in anticipation of being locked up. We ate boiled seafood out there, barbecued, and sliced sweet watermelons. We didn't entertain, but did this, just the two of us, cherishing this time together. We grew close, and spent more time together than we had had in years.

George had resigned his presidency in March 1995. He would be sentenced at the end of June. This entire period was ours. We knew he would be going to prison, and we determined not to lose a moment that we could be together. Through our long conversations, we grew our spirituality.

On June 28, our separation crashed down on us like a cleaver, causing us grievous pain.

On holidays and during the second summer of his incarceration, I continued to improve the garden. The labor provided intense therapy. I hired an ironworks company to install a wrought iron fence around the garden and planted Carolina jasmine along the fence. Haunting garden shops, I began potting varied green and flowering plants, and installed little critters: an owl, bunny, ducks, and a cement pig snoozing beneath a large pot. Even a two-foot tall crouching child cradling a small bird. That spring I bought a wire deer, the type used to create lighted lawn ornaments at Christmas, stuffed it with moss, covered it with screen, and slathered it with cement that I mixed myself. I created a large centerpiece in front of our living room window in the garden. Then I painted it mahogany red.

When George came home, he would return to a private oasis of natural beauty that could only grow lushly in our damp Louisiana climate. After three years of deprivation, what could have been more healing?

The next summer I remodeled the bathroom. When he returned, George might not be able to lower himself into the deep, old-fashioned tub in our main bathroom.

When I told him my plan, he pleaded, "Wait till I come home." He didn't think I could accomplish such a project without his help.

"That would be too late; I need to do this while you are gone. When you come home, if we do it then, you would have no bathroom to use while the project is going on."

I planned to take down the wall between the old bath and the adjoining bedroom, removing the tub, and moving the closet, and the main entrance. Plotting the new bathroom to scale, I sent the detailed layout in the mail to George, attaching snippets of color to indicate my plans.

"Kathy, when I received all those plans from you, they called me in and interrogated me. They thought you were plotting a scenario to break me out of prison!" he told me later.

I hired a carpenter, electrician, plumber, and tile installer, purchased all fixtures and completed the project. They built a huge shower that George could simply roll into with his new shower wheelchair. I painted the bathroom and stained and varnished all the hardwood and furniture there. Large, airy, and gorgeous, it was ready for George when he returned.

Everything that I had done, garden and bath, was completely paid for, as I used money from my inheritance.

How George Helps Young Prisoners

Throughout his three years in Hunt George gravitated to the young prisoners. He tried to reach them, and to mentor them as best he could. He had endless conversations with them.

He told me this story about a young man and a lot of drug money.

George wanted to convince him that huge amounts of cash gained from selling drugs was not the best option in life.

He asked one young man, "OK, you got a million dollars. What are you gonna do with it?"

The prisoner thought a minute, "First of all I would buy me some fine wheels. A Lexus."

"You have $960,000 left. What else?"

"I need a house—not too big now, just big enough. I wouldn't spend more than $60,000."

"You have $900,000 left. What else would you buy?"

"Some clothes. At least $1,000!" the young man exclaimed.

"You have $899,000 left."

Thinking hard now, the young man answered: "I want some Nikes and a stereo."

"You still have $898,500 left. What are you going to buy with the rest?"

"Shit, Mr. Eames, you give me too much money!"

✳✳✳✳✳

In the beginning of his incarceration, the other prisoners harassed him, "Well, Mr. President, you ain't nobody no more; you got a DOC number just like us!"

"There's a big difference between us," George said.

"What's that?"

"You live here. I'm just visiting." They howled in protest.

The guards also harassed George. One guard in particular delighted in tormenting him in any way that he could. Finally one day George said to him, "How long you been doing this?"

"How long I been doing what?"

"This job. Locking and unlocking doors. Watching prisoners," George said.

"I been here about 25 years," the guard answered. "What of it?"

George appeared lost in thought.

"I said, 'What of it?'" the guard demanded.

"A trained monkey could do what you do," George said.

"You calling me a trained monkey?" the guard asked.

"No," George calmly said, "I'm just saying that monkeys can be trained to give people a glass of water, hand people a phone, unlock or lock a door and open and close it."

Unable to respond, the guard left in a huff.

At home, as soon as he had begun to gray, George began coloring his hair. In prison, he was no longer able to color it. He quickly grew completely gray. At that point, the younger inmates began calling him "Pops." Although irritated at first—George was sometimes vain to a fault—he soon began seeing the humor in it. He had a wonderful sense of humor and loved having fun, especially verbal repartees.

Doctor: "Boy, You Got an Aneurysm."

In 1997, the old doctor who was treating George in prison, felt a pulse in his abdomen. "Boy, you got an aneurysm."

"A what ?" George asked.

"Aneurysm. We got to send you to the Charity and get this thing checked out."

Rising at 4:00 in the morning, George began a series of trips to the prison ward at Charity Hospital in New Orleans.

The doctors determined that this aneurysm on his abdominal aorta was life-threatening.

George made several visits, chains on his ankles and wrists, often riding in the van with the folded wheelchair on his lap when there wasn't enough room. I was horrified later when I learned of this callous treatment—putting a wheelchair in the lap of a man with an abdominal aneurysm seemed the height of insanity.

The doctors and prison officials insisted that surgery be performed immediately. They brought papers for George to approve the surgery.

"I ain't signing nothing till I talk to my wife!"

"You have to sign it!" they insisted.

"Man, you don't understand! I ain't no throwaway. I got a wife, we love each other, and we don't do nothing without talking about it. I have to call my wife!"

They gave him permission to call me. We discussed it.

George was hospitalized for numerous tests to determine the feasibility of surgery.

They had estimated that he had less than a 50-50 chance of survival.

Once I learned this, I called the warden and demanded to see George daily. I insisted that my husband was in imminent danger of death, and that I had the right.

The warden gave me permission to visit George for fifteen minutes a day in the Charity prison ward in New Orleans.

At first, I stayed in a motel overnight for three or four days, then realized I could not afford to do this every day.

I drove eighty miles there and eighty miles back after school on a daily basis to see George for that fifteen minutes. Fifteen minutes was short!

I was disturbed that George was handcuffed to the hospital bed, but could do nothing about it. I could see his doctors, and I talked to them at length about the risks of surgery. We learned that the infection in the wound on his tailbone was actually in the bone. If any infection entered George's bloodstream, it would mean death.

His doctors marveled at me; I had done my medical research, and could talk to them in their own jargon on a level they had never before experienced from a patient or patient's family.

George had to make a decision: surgery or not.

George asked his surgeon, "Doc, if it was you, what would you do?"

"I'd have the surgery," the doctor said.

"Then I'll have the surgery," George said.

I was in the waiting room during the surgery. They allowed me in intensive care later. I saw that most of George's cover, just a sheet, left his shoulders exposed. I told the nurses immediately to bring him a blanket. I pulled the sheet and blanket over his shoulders, tucking them in. With poor circulation, George was always cold, and the hospital was freezing.

Then, looking up at me, George smiled. He saw the monitor high on the wall which showed his vitals. "Can't you find a better station? Find me the news," he said.

*****

During his entire incarceration, I wrote George many cards and letters—anything that might boost his morale. What he loved more than anything else that I sent was a poem by Clarissa Pinkola Estes. He put it in his Bible and read it every day, "A Prayer." Every time I read it, I thought of him. This little poem epitomized George's spirit and character so well, beginning "Refuse to fall down." The poem continues with line by line admonitions to resist your own destruction in every possible way, till finally you have no other option but to lift your heart "to heaven" if you have no other way to resist.[1]

I Learn about Friendship and Loyalty

I learned about friendship and loyalty during my campaign to get George released. I had approached several close friends, and leaders in the community to write letters pleading clemency and a pardon for George during his incarceration. I solicited letters from both head basketball coach Dale Brown and baseball coach Skip Bertman.

Both had worked closely with George and knew his concern and dedication to youngsters. Both wrote the letters. Pressure commenced on them both from some LSU fans, LSU officials and the press. Dale, was probably as stubborn as George was on principle. Dale never yielded an inch.

Skip buckled to the pressure, retracting his plea on George's behalf. I felt deeply betrayed. George tossed it off, never holding it against Skip. When George was released from prison and wanted to revive the baseball program, he went immediately to Skip with no reservations.

Although George could grow extremely angry, and might stop talking or meeting with someone, he was never vindictive or vengeful. Unless he was ill and not himself, he forgave and went on from there. He understood pressure. What disappointed George more were the actions of Rev. Charles T. Smith in leading his churches to abandon baseball in favor of basketball.

Chapter 18

Finally Freedom

Finally, freedom came. At midnight at the end of June or early July 1998, I met George at the gates of Hunt Correctional Institute to bring him home.

How can I begin to describe his joy and relief as he toured what was to him an amazing home? It was renovated and designed for his comfort and healing.

George was released months early for his good behavior.

The only damper on his happiness was the requirement of his parole. We had to install in our front yard a sign displaying his name, address and offense. We balked at this; I pleaded, that as a teacher, I felt it most inappropriate for the criminal justice system to require this of me—this was my home too. But they were adamant.

I made the sign myself. About two weeks later, someone had lightly spray-painted it black, concealing its dire message. George's parole officer demanded that we replace it with a new sign. I complained again of the cost and difficulty. I pointed out that the perpetrator, whoever he or she was, would likely destroy the new sign as well. The sign remained as it was—a sign I could live with.

Years later I wondered whether George himself had slipped into the front yard one day and vandalized the sign. He never admitted it, never even hinted at it. It would have been so like him to do so.

George began telling his story to the media the month after he was paroled. A journalist from the *Urban Leader*, a small black paper edited by Dwayne Elliott called to ask for an interview.

George met the reporter in our garden. He wore his Capital City Baseball League Executive Director baseball cap and scrubs. They talked about controversial issues involving George during his years as NAACP branch president.

One such controversy was a school holiday honoring Dr. Martin

Luther King, Jr. George insisted that he would disrupt the dialogue needed to advance the desegregation lawsuit against East Baton Rouge Parish Schools if they did not adopt a school holiday. George had famously declared, "If you don't have the courtesy to honor and respect the name of MLK, we will not meet with you again in this life!"

Another hot topic they talked about was proposing MLK Boulevard. George and his board had suggested renaming Florida Boulevard, the main commercial artery of Baton Rouge, after Martin Luther King, Jr. This was a move that both the black and white communities had strongly resisted.

George shared his tough opinions about black youth with the reporter. He agreed with Judge Bonnie Jackson, when she insisted that young offenders "take the gold out of their mouths." George had been adamant about this for some time. He also supported school uniforms and the elimination of baggy, dragging pants on young black men. George felt these standards would improve discipline at home as well as in school.

When asked by the black reporter about the strategy of compromise, George looked at him skeptically, "I never have believed in compromise. Black folks practice compromise too much already. The Native Americans accepted compromise, and look where it got them!"[1]

The reporter learned quickly that George had not only survived prison—but survived it with his ideas and beliefs intact and unchanged. The story about George was published in the first edition of the paper, August 14, 1998, on page three.[1]

George Lives in Pain After Exercising

That month, August 1998, George broke his hip while exercising. We could find no doctor who would agree to do the surgery, given George's health history.

Finally a year later, in the summer of 1999, we did find Dr. Theodore Knatt. He was a young, black orthopedic doctor in Zachary, who determined to perform the surgery.

During the intervening year, George lived in pain from the broken hip and the surrounding inflammation. Yet he continued to pursue his interests. He tried to revive the baseball program, for example. Earl Thomas had his own health issues, and though Skip Bertman donated $10,000 to the cause, George returned the money because his attempts were futile.

During the year, George drove me to the Gulf Coast to one of our favorite casinos where we enjoyed playing the nickel machines.

I was concerned about his pain level, but he insisted.

"It doesn't matter. If I stay home, I'll hurt. If I go, I'll hurt. I may as well go. At least I'll have a distraction to take my mind off my pain." George Eames was the toughest man I have ever known. He would not take pain medication—not until he was dying with fourth stage lung cancer. By then he was in a coma, and I gave him morphine for the last four days of his life.

Recovery from the hip surgery was difficult. I had to take down his full size bed in his office and install a hospital bed. I cared for him by myself, turning him, bathing and facilitating his other needs. He was unable to use a bedpan, so these matters were complicated and always difficult.

✱✱✱✱✱

Eventually, after some months, George was well enough to travel and drive.

Our trip to Memphis was memorable in many ways. It was just in time to celebrate in Memphis with his "adopted daughters," Janis and Jamie. Jamie had already been married to Tic Price, now Memphis State college basketball coach. Janis had married Mabra Holeyfield, a Memphis businessman, in Las Vegas just before this visit. They were celebrating their wedding in a grand reception on Christmas Eve in a social room reserved in their condo on the Mississippi River.

Mabra owned a Best Western and Econolodge hotels downtown; we had a free room reserved for our use across the street from the Peabody Hotel, and drove to Memphis. We may have brought Joyce, the twins' mother with us that time; I don't remember. I do know that we did bring her with us on other visits in future years.

Janis wore her wedding gown as we danced and partied. We enjoyed meeting Mabra's family. Christmas Day found us at Jamie and Tic's home for dinner. Joyce, Janis and Mabra as well as Jamie and Tic enjoyed our wonderful reunion.

While in Memphis, George and I listened to some great music in the Jazz Club at the Best Western, watching the ducks do their thing at the Peabody Hotel across the street, and playing tourist on Beale St.. We spent a couple of hours in the Rum Boogie Cafe where we warmed ourselves before visiting the birthplace of W. C. Handy. We both loved music so it was fun to drink hot coffee in the Hard Rock Cafe and marvel over the many music mementos! Also on Beale St., George took pictures of a sign honoring the famous civil rights activist Ida B. Wells. The sign read:

"After moving to New York, she began an international speaking tour where she influenced the establishment of the British Anti-Lynching Society. She co-founded the NAACP in America and organized the first black women's political organization. A Chicago housing project is named in her honor. Ida B. Wells crusaded against lynchings in Memphis and the South. In 1892 while editor of the *Memphis Free Speech,* located in this vicinity, she wrote of the lynching of three black businessmen. As a result, her newspaper office was destroyed and her life threatened...."[2]

We spent a day visiting the Lorraine Hotel where Dr. King had been assassinated. It's now a civil rights museum.

✳✳✳✳✳

In the summer of 2000, George and I drove to New Roads, Louisiana for the Altazan family reunion—my mother's family. Here, for the first time in many cases, George met my cousins, aunts and uncles, many of whom had stood stalwartly with us at Mama's funeral.

We also took my cousin, Vee, with us to the casino campground in Bay St. Louis for a few days. That summer Joe Delpit and his sidekick, young "Peanut," now attorney Domoine Rutledge, came over for drinks. Rutledge was serving as parish attorney for the school system. We also invited Bernie and Marie over for dinner.

I Found the House Burned Again

A fire struck one day in 2004.

A student delivered an urgent message to me in my classroom:

"Come home. You are needed. No one is hurt, but come home now." What would anyone do? I worried all the way home.

I found the house burned again.

The story started when George had hired a young man to work on our floors, upon a friend's recommendation.

George was in his office at the time.

The young man proceeded to coat the floor with a toxic chemical that would remove the old finish. The area wasn't ventilated and we had insulated windows.

"Mr. Eames, your house is on fire!" The fumes had ignited from the pilot light in the hot water heater at the end of the hall.

After calling 911, George rolled to the hallway where the two grabbed rugs and anything else they could find to beat out the flames.

By the time the fire department arrived, the fire was out; the firemen could do nothing but insist that the two men go to the emergency room. Although they had breathed much toxic vapor and smoke, they refused, claiming that they were unhurt.

When I arrived, I was upset, but more horrified that George had been rolling in the fire. He could have been seriously injured or killed.

When he saw the fire, he said to himself, "I can't let that white woman's house burn up again!"

✳✳✳✳✳

In the decade beginning in 2000, George and I would begin to enjoy his retirement.

Above everything else, George loved his games: LSU and Southern football, basketball, track and field, baseball. He still received free tickets to football and basketball as well as parking permits. We bought the tickets for women's basketball and track and field; but without the free tickets, we would not have been able to attend these events.

Over the years, Bo Bahnsen became a close friend to both of us as he arranged the free tickets and parking at LSU. Always accommodating, Bo has served the university back to his undergraduate years. That's when George first met Bo and liked

2007—When famous Grambling football coach Eddie Robinson died, former LSU head basketball coach Dale Brown, George, and other notable fans went to Grambling for a service in Robinson's honor.

this warm and friendly student who served as manager of the LSU basketball team as an undergraduate at LSU. In 1982, he became the administrative assistant for the men's basketball team, where he worked for five years before moving into athletics administration as director of purchasing and travel for two years. In July 1987, he became administrative assistant to Athletics Director Joe Dean, overseeing the purchasing office and departmental travel operations until his promotion in 1989. In 1989, he was assigned his primary responsibility as NCAA compliance officer as assistant athletics director, and then was promoted to associate AD in 1996. In 2009, Bo served in the compliance office once more.[3]

How We Live on a Teacher's Salary

Sometimes there were rumors and perceptions that George Eames was waxing wealthy at NAACP expense.

The truth was that I supported our family on my teacher's salary while George did community service. All his time was unpaid—gratis.

George wasn't paid until he began driving around caring for the NAACP baseball program. Then he was reimbursed for gas money.

His income was small all the years I knew him and was married to him. From the sixties, his only income, except for the three years he was in prison, was a small Social Security disability check. When he died, it amounted to $647 or so a month.

Given the cost of tickets for college athletics, without support from friends, attending all those games would have impossible for us. Dale was kind to take George on some basketball trips out of town, and he solicited funds from other fans for George.

People who knew George were generous. Years before, as he was plunging into the thick of civil rights work and the baseball program, for several months, George had begun to tease me.

"The oil wells are pumping!"

I had no idea what he was talking about.

"I don't see any oil wells!" I answered.

Then I saw it. A new, extra-long, blue cargo van. It had been donated to him from civil rights supporters who felt he should have some kind of transportation. The fund-raising effort was led, more than likely, by Joe Delpit. Coach Dale Brown supplied the hand controls and power lift installation from his own pocket.

George was thrilled with the "Big Blue Machine" for years; it meant complete independence. He could come and go unassisted. He parked it under our carport, so he was protected from inclement weather.

In addition to sporting events, we occasionally visited the local casino where we played the penny, nickel, or perhaps quarter slots. We couldn't afford to lose much, so we limited ourselves to thirty dollars or less. When that was gone, we were done. For that small sum, we had a few drinks, a few laughs, and invariably George had great conversations with anyone sitting near him.

George Is Injured in an Accident near Southeastern

Anyone in a wheelchair is somewhat limited in the activities they can undertake for fun, especially as they begin to age.

The Mall of Louisiana in Baton Rouge offered diversions. We sometimes went there for lunch on Saturdays. Then I walked around, exercising and perhaps buying something we might need. George read his newspaper, watched people and had friendly conversations with strangers he met or with people he knew who happened to walk by.

We did virtually the same thing after I retired. On Wednesday or Thursday we spent a pleasant afternoon having lunch at Whole Foods in Baton Rouge, where George read his newspaper while I ran other errands. Coming back, we enjoyed a cookie and hot coffee in the winter, or gelato in the warm months. After buying our groceries, we would return home.

When Simone Augustus began playing women's basketball at LSU, we bought season tickets and went to as many of the men's and women's games as we could. One night, maybe 2005, George, his cousin Rashid Muhammad and another friend drove to Hammond to see her play. Somewhere on or near the Southeastern Louisiana University campus, a woman cut directly in front of him. To avoid hitting her, he swerved to his left, off the street, nearly hitting a tree. All the back seat passengers were thrown forward.

George violently hit the steering wheel. He suffered rotary cuff damage to both shoulders.

George managed to drive the van home. He had no alternative— it's not possible to fit a motorized wheelchair into anything but a customized van. Unfortunately, the van was totaled by the insurance company; we would later have to buy a new van and have it retrofitted with hand controls and lift.

Before that, however, George had surgery on the worsening rotary cuff injury.

A rotary cuff injury and surgery may be intolerable for the average person. For a paraplegic, it is far worse. Imagine a 200-pound man paralyzed from the mid- chest down who has lost the use of both arms. He could no longer use the commode unassisted, slip into or out of bed or into or out of his wheelchair. I had to help him brush his teeth, eat, bathe, and turn from side to side in the bed. When he needed the commode, I had to summon the help of a strong neighbor or call Rashid from across town. Even then, we were trying to move a dead weight. George could do nothing to help us. We swore we would never have the second rotary cuff injury repaired. Even with the surgery, the improvement was slight.

This remained even after George healed. He could no longer lift himself. How would he move about? I finally conceived of an ingenious plan. I screwed two huge eye screws through the paneling behind the bed, about a yard apart, running a rope through each one. Next I cut a three foot wide piece of vinyl backed with material long enough to hang down on either side of the bed about a foot. Sprayed with silicone, the vinyl became slippery enough that when he placed his legs perpendicular to the wall, George could pull himself into the bed using the ropes, sliding right in. On the slippery vinyl, he slid around facing the foot of the bed. We reversed the procedure when he wanted to access his wheelchair. Grabbing the top of his pants, I pulled him backwards on the vinyl into his chair. Instead of entering the bed from the side of the chair, he now took off the foot supports and eased the chair facing the bed, as close as he could put it. The only disadvantage now was that he often needed assistance getting out of bed, whereas before he had been able to do it independently.

Even after George left prison, when he wasn't hospitalized, he was often frustrated that he could do little civil rights work. Yet when an unjustifiable shooting occurred in a scuffle with police in February 2006, George requested that I work with him to draft a lengthy letter documenting in an outline such shootings that had occurred in Baton Rouge since 1969. Many of these shootings he had investigated in the past. Perhaps he empathized well with the victims and families because of his own unjustifiable shooting in 1956. Whatever the reason, these events always disturbed him greatly. Knowing his prison background might deter his message, especially since he was no longer the president of the local branch of the NAACP, George developed the letter as a message to US Attorney David Dugas from his pastor at that time, Rev. Leo Cyrus, requesting that Rev. Cyrus send the letter. I have no idea if Rev. Cyrus ever actually sent the missive, but this single action showed clearly to me that George did not act for self-aggrandizement, of which he was often accused, but out of sincere concern for people.

He would never be credited recognition for someone else's letter. The letter follows:

Letter to US Attorney David Dugas
US Attorney David Dugas
Middle District of the State of Louisiana
777 Florida St.
Baton Rouge, LA 70801
Feb. 27, 2006

Dear Attorney Dugas:

I'm writing you in reference to the incident on Greenwell Springs and Joor Road on or about Friday afternoon, Feb. 20, 2006. Before we get into this particular case, I would like to do a chronology of the history of the Baton Rouge police department from 1969 to this present day.

In 1969 the DA then was Sargeant Pitcher, Jr. In that time period Sargeant Pitcher, Jr. issued an edict to the police department to "shoot all fleeing felons." That directive caused at least eight to ten young black males to be shot while running from the police. One of the police officers who was a part of a homicide eventually became a police chief.

In 1972 on the Southern University campus, the students were staging a civil rights demonstration because of lack of facilities and because of the train's delaying students at the railroad crossing. At the last demonstration seven or eight sheriff's deputies stood in a line with shotguns and other weapons. After firing tear gas into the crowd, one or more of them fired their weapons with the result of killing Denver Smith and Leonard Brown. One of the deputies who was in that line eventually became a high profile person in East Baton Rouge Parish sheriff's department. I think the district attorney, at this junction, was the honorable Ossie Brown.

In 1983 or 1984 a Baton Rouge police officer by the name of Ernie Rhodes shot and killed an unarmed man leaving a laundromat approximately at 10:00 p.m. Ernie Rhodes claimed that he thought E.J. Mencer (the victim) had a gun. Rhodes fired his weapon twice, hitting E.J. Mencer in the chest. This is the only case in E.B.R. Parish in which a police officer was ever charged with killing a black man. The charge was a misdemeanor.

On or about 1984 or 1985, on Thomas Delpit Dr., in front of a cab stand near a little cafe, an unarmed black male was harassing the people in and outside the cafe. A police unit with one officer was passing by, and he asked the black man to come to him. The black man went into a karate stance. The officer shot him twice, killing him.

In 1985 or 1986 the chief of police was Pat Bonano The district attorney was Ossie Brown or Attorney Brian Bush.

On or about 1987, 1988, or 1989, a young black deranged male had a family altercation in the family residence. The police came, ordered everyone out of the house, and everybody else out of the neighborhood. The three police officers entered the house where the subject was in the kitchen, and their accounts of the incident were that the subject "lunged" at the black officer with some type of object. The white police officer shot the suspect and killed him. The NAACP asked then police Chief Pat Bonano why the officers didn't use tear gas. Bonano said that if the officers had used tear gas, the suspect might have hurt or killed himself and the police would have been charged with negligence. The next question the NAACP asked was why the officers didn't use mace. The answer was "We don't use mace." The next question was why didn't you shoot to wound the suspect. The answer was that when an officer draws his service revolver, he shoots to kill.

In 1992, on Gardere Lane, a 14-year-old black youngster was accused of some type of altercation in the neighborhood. E.B.R. Parish sheriff's deputies were called. When the deputies arrived, the young black male ran into a vacant apartment and hid in the closet. When the sheriff's deputies entered, one of them said later he saw a shadow that "looked like a gun," so he shot through the closet door, killing Chauncey Thomas.

On or about 1992, in Central, a white homeowner by the name of Pierce confronted a young Japanese student looking for a Halloween party. The homeowner said that his wife went to the door, saw someone with a mask outside on the carport, and called Pierce. Pierce said he went outside with his gun and told the young student, "Freeze!" which is a military term meaning "Don't move." The Japanese student did not understand the expression and he moved forward to ask for directions because the homeowner's address was similar to the address for the party. Standing in close proximity to the Japanese student was his classmate, Haymaker. For some reason, nothing happened to the white boy. Neither District Attorney Doug Moreau, nor Sheriff Elmer Litchfield thought there was a reason to arrest the homeowner for shooting and killing the Japanese student. The NAACP, according to my research, got in touch with the US Attorney Raymond Lamonica and asked him to thoroughly investigate the shooting in Central because, as far as the NAACP knew, no white man had ever been charged with murder, second degree murder, homicide, or negligent homicide of a person of color. After US Attorney Lamonica's investigation and finds, District Attorney Doug Moreau convened a grand jury, and the homeowner was indicted.

In 1993 a deranged black male had a toy gun down on 11000 Florida Blvd in the parking lot at Rabenhorst Funeral Home. A young white junior deputy along with other officers fired his gun two or three times and killed the young black man.

Around 1994 a black male in Eden Park was arrested by the police, hog-tied in the back of the police car, and died from choking on his own vomit.

On or about 1995, a young black male was running from the police on the corner of 14th St and North Blvd. near a recreation center. When the police spotted him, trying to get away again, he was killed.

On or about 1998, an old black man was living by himself in a rooming house on College Dr. The white police officers claimed that they were searching for drugs or other paraphernalia in the neighborhood. They kicked down his door; and when they entered the room, he had some kind of stick or bat in his hand. He had no idea what was going on. He was killed.

My question is, if an officer writes a ticket to a motorist, why should he want to pull the motorist from his vehicle? The question is what precipitated that? What also needs to be investigated are the phantom shots heard by Perry Stephens who seems to be using this excuse to enter the situation with "gun a blazing." According to my experience in watching CSI, crime scene investigation, how could the chief issue an order, without thorough investigation, that nobody still living would be arrested?

Now, in an article in the *Advocate* dated Feb. 11, 2006, another shooting occurred which was inadequately investigated. According to the article, Baton Rouge police did not plan to make an arrest in the shooting death of George Temple II. This 24-year-old man was shot by a witness, Perry Stephens, who thought Temple was attacking a Baton Rouge police officer. Stephens, who wore a neck brace and used a cane, heard the police officer call for help. Stephens demanded that Temple "get off" Officer Harrison, and when he did not respond, Stephens shot Temple in the chest four times. Warning the supine man again, when Temple failed to comply, Stephens shot Temple in the head, killing him. According to Phares, the scuffle occurred when

Officer Harrison attempted to remove Temple from his automobile.
Sincerely,
Rev. Leo D. Cyrus
Pastor of New Hope Baptist Church, Second Baptist Church and
President of Fourth District Baptist Association

George Solves Problems of All Sizes

Now that we had a new van and George could move about again, we embarked on our last great civil rights project. Since he could no longer work with children, and was no longer president of the NAACP, George wanted to take on violations of the ADA, Americans with Disabilities Act—here he would be at an advantage, and no one could question his right to challenge public businesses and institutions. He was, himself, disabled, and had felt for years the problems which handicapped people encountered every day.

As we warmed up, George and I pursued several small cases. One elderly white man called one day, "Mr. Eames, I sure hope you can help me. My wife is buried in Greenoaks Memorial Cemetery. She's buried on a kind of hill in there. You can reach it only by some cement stairs, about twelve of them—and because I use a walker now—I can't visit my wife's grave. Do you think you can convince them to build a ramp or something?"

Yes, we could and we did. George called the owner and manager, and talked in his inimitable way, convincing the owner to build a ramp to enable his disabled clients to visit their loved ones. Problem solved.

George approached his longtime friends, Joseph Delpit and Henry Baptist, urging them to bring the Chicken Shack into compliance with ADA guidelines. That they did. And so did Memorial Stadium, a beauty retail establishment on Florida Blvd, and Crifasi's Hi Nabor Supermarket on Winbourne Ave.

Although we started strong in the fall 2006, our project suffered a major setback in February 2007: George's failing health.

George called me at school, a rare thing, to ask me to come home right away; he was feeling weak. When I reached home, he told me he was so weak he couldn't even catheterize himself. I immediately took his blood pressure; I never could get a reading after several attempts. I called for an ambulance. The medical techs couldn't get a reading until they were enroute to the hospital: It was 60 over 30.

George did not seem worried. During that drive George told the ambulance attendants that he had to be back on Monday because he didn't want to miss the basketball game!

An MRI revealed that the stent which had repaired his abdominal aneurysm in 1997 was leaking, badly. George went into immediate surgery. A week later, George was released, having received a lot of blood.

We were home less than forty-eight hours when severe vomiting and diarrhea ensued. Back in the emergency room, we now found that George needed another surgery, a larger incision, and weeks to recover.

I Cook, Clean and Care for Us with One Arm

Knowing George was scheduled for release on a Saturday in March, I went home that Wednesday afternoon. I was determined to clean my much-neglected house, so it would be presentable when George came home from the hospital.

Disaster struck. Sweeping the back patio, I tripped backwards over a brick, falling on my back right side on the concrete. As soon as I hit the ground, I knew I had broken my right arm severely—a complete break.

The pain was excruciating. I gave myself first aid. I improvised a sling and took a couple of Tylenols. I called a friend to drive me to the emergency room. All the medics could do was to confirm the break, give me another temporary sling and advise me to see an orthopedist.

I called George, of course, and we were both confounded. How in the world would I be able to handle him with one good arm?

The next day I called a neighbor who drove me to the doctor's office. Because I had no standing appointment, I had to wait all day, six hours to see him. He advised me that surgery to insert steel pins had to be performed. I don't know what I would have done without the help of our neighbor, Leo Franklin, and George's niece, Mary Esther Bailey.

Friday I had the surgery, and George came home that Saturday.

With one arm I cooked, cleaned and cared for both of us

My students who were enrolled in the health magnet school program at Glen Oaks High School heard what our situation was; they urged their supervisor to let them help me. My students came two at a time each day of the week for a couple of weeks to help me with cleaning, washing dishes, washing clothes, and anything else that would be useful.

They did not touch George. He wouldn't let anyone but me do that, generally—and certainly not these little high school girls.

By the end of the summer, my cast had come off and I had completed my therapy, regaining the use of my arm.

I had retired in May, earlier than I had wanted, and money was tight; but we felt we could survive till my Social Security check started in a couple of years.

By the fall of 2007, we resumed our ADA projects. We were increasingly irritated by major obstacles to participating in the numerous festivals held downtown. These included Fourth of July Festival, Blues Festival, International Festival and others.

On some of these occasions we had actually been turned away, denied any place close to park, or actually advised to return home rather than participate. So we took on city-parish government.

George sought the help of US Attorneys. He began working closely with US Attorney James Nelson, who became simply "Jim" to both of us and his associate, US Attorney John Gaupp, who himself had a handicapped son.

We amassed letters, pictures, and other evidence to illustrate the ADA problems we were having. The federal government filed an ADA lawsuit against city-parish.

On his Web site, ADA page, I posted this introduction and letter, our first letter to Mayor Kip Holden which was never answered:

This complaint is of long duration, beginning in July 2008 with a letter that Kathy and I wrote after a frustrating Fourth of July Celebration downtown. I am attaching here the four letters which we mailed to the mayor, responses, the presentation which we eventually made before the Mayor's ADA Task Force, and the media response to that.

First Letter to Mayor: Fourth of July Celebration
July 15, 2008
Mayor-President Kip Holden
P. O. Box 1471, Baton Rouge, LA 70821

Dear Kip,

The new plans for downtown development are magnificent. I commend you for your foresight and ambition for Baton Rouge. Hopefully, the new physical layout will facilitate the already wonderful festivals, Live after Five, Fourth of July festivities, etc.

However, the city of Baton Rouge is in total violation of the American Disabilities Act. For example, when Kathy and I attempted to access the area of the Fourth of July festival, our first encounter was the barricade on River Road going south. The police officer on duty there told us that we could not proceed because there was no handicapped parking anywhere near the capitol or in the convention center area.

We proceeded to turn around to go to Fourth St. which took us to Ferdinand, and to Government St. down the hill to St. Phillip St. The police officer there with the barricade told us that we could not proceed, that there was no handicapped parking in that area because all of the parking had been taken up by the vendors and the entertainment aggregations.

So I asked him, "What should we do?" He just stared in disbelief. Then I said, "I guess we should go back home." He said, "I guess so." I took it upon myself to turn around and go down St. Philip St. When I got to the next corner, I stopped, looked down by the Sheraton and saw something that might serve as my parking spot behind the valet parking area (that was also barricaded). I proceeded to park in the red line area on the curb that was totally illegal.

Kip, this is ridiculous for a city of this size with all of the development and improvements that I see enhancing businesses, LSU, Perkins Rowe, Mall of Louisiana, etc., all of which are in total compliance with the American Disabilities Act. When I contacted Bill Palmer, the director of BREC last year, prior to the start of the high school Jamboree, about Memorial Stadium not being in compliance with the Americans with Disabilities Act, BREC promptly got the stadium, ramps inside, parking outside to the strict specifications with the Americans with Disabilities Act—in toto.

After all of that, I had to call Chief LeDuff to order his officers to enforce the parking facilities for the handicapped at the stadium. He did that forthwith.

So Kathy and I are requesting you and your agents of downtown development to promptly amend your plans to include Third St. N., St. Louis St. N., North Blvd. N., and S. River Rd. (north and south). Provide handicapped parking according to specifications of the Americans with Disabilities Act. Please note that a van that has been retrofitted (elevated to accommodate an electronic wheelchair) cannot fit in the parking garages with their present specifications because the ceiling is too low.

I would like to meet with the engineers or whoever's in charge of the project to make clear to them what needs to be done to accommodate the handicapped. Also, I'd like to mention something that we observed years ago in Santa Fe, New Mexico to accommodate handicapped parking for festivals and weekend activities in downtown Santa Fe. Parking meters around city square were individually covered with blue canvas bags (designating the handicap logo) which were padlocked to the parking meters. This provided temporary increased parking for handicapped without the need to remove meters or paint those areas.

When I mention handicapped parking, a lot of times the actual parking spots do not accommodate handicap vans with a lift which require 8 feet to enter and exit the vans. Please take all of these issues under consideration as you refine plans for developing our city.

Sincerely,

G. Washington, Eames, Jr.

Former president of the Baton Rouge Branch, NAACP

cc: Police Chief Jeff LeDuff, Davis Rhorer

George's health declined while he and I were working with the federal attorneys. More than once, having driven with me to some location, including the Federal courthouse, he wouldn't have the strength to drive home.

"Let me rest a little while," George told me. He'd put a pillow on the steering wheel, and lean on it for twenty minutes, a half hour, or even an hour before he felt he could drive. He insisted on driving his own van. I could not yet persuade him to let me drive. That would come later.

Chapter 19

Southern University

Some had the impression that George hated Southern University. Nothing could have been further from the truth.

George spent much of his energy tackling the more obvious discriminatory practices of LSU, the much larger of the two universities. He loved Southern and wanted only the best for this school. I was privy to his ideas and the deepest intentions of his heart.

On his Web site, he explained:

> Over the years I have attended many events on the Southern University campus. Loving all sporting events, I went to track and field—both high school and college, basketball, and football, especially. I remember when I was younger, with my friends, usually Janis and Jamie Simms or Beverly McNair to help with the chair, parking, etc., we would leave LSU football games at halftime to rush across town to catch the halftime band performance at Southern!
>
> During Marino Casem's tenure as athletic director at Southern University, I really tried to get to the games. "The Godfather"as he was known in the Southwest Athletic Conference, became a close friend. He also got a life membership [in the NAACP].
>
> Basketball coach Ben Jobe and I became good friends during his tenure at Southern University. He visited Kathy and me at our home many times. He attended LSU basketball games with Kathy and me. His beautiful daughter attended Scotlandville Magnet High School, and she was a dancer at Scotlandville and a dancing doll at Southern University. She also participated with her dance groups in many of the Dr. Martin Luther King Birthday celebrations at the Centroplex. Kathy taught English to Coach Jobe's son at Glen Oaks High School. Mrs. Jobe and I discussed on the phone how to make the Dr. Martin Luther King celebrations outstanding.
>
> Jobe and I discussed Avery Johnson, "the Little General," the Southern University basketball player. He eventually became an NBA

player and the head coach of the Dallas Mavericks. The last time I met Avery , I was on my way to Hawaii for an LSU basketball tournament. In Los Angeles, we were able to visit in the airport. He was on his way to a game with his professional team, Seattle Supersonics.

Through the years, Kathy and I and several friends had the good fortune to attend the Bayou Classic, the famous annual competition between Southern University's and Grambling's football teams.[1]

✳✳✳✳✳

Over the years, George was satisfied with many positive dealings with the administration at Southern University, and always tried to be supportive in any way that he could. When former NFL tight-end Greg LaFleur became interested in returning to Louisiana, he wanted to apply for athletic director for Southern University. George worked closely with Greg, having known him well when he worked at LSU, and caring about him personally. George advised him, keeping him abreast of the general atmosphere and working environment at Southern. Eventually Greg was hired.

George also worked with Dr. Dolores Spikes on a case of sexual harassment brought to him by a Southern University student in 1989.

Then in 1990 George complimented Dr. Spikes after the Southern Homecoming:

Compliments to President Spikes on Southern Homecoming

November 10, 1990
Dr. Dolores R. Spikes, President of Southern University
Baton Rouge, La. 70813

Dear Dr. Spikes,
Being in attendance at Southern University's Homecoming, I must say it was the most spectacular event I've ever witnessed of a college game halftime other than the Orange Bowl festivities. Mrs. Helen Williams should be commended for an outstanding exhibit of imagination, creativity, and organization. If you don't mind, the Baton Rouge Branch of the NAACP would like to borrow this lady for our upcoming event in August 1991.

I would also like to compliment Chief Harrison Baptiste of the university's Police Department for an outstanding job of maintaining the type of security second to none that I have seen at a college football game in the history of East Baton Rouge Parish.

G. Washington Eames, Jr.

President, East Baton Rouge Parish Branch, NAACP

I really didn't like attending Southern University football games because the traffic problems were extraordinary there.

George explains:

"Over the years as I attended the football games at Southern University, it became obvious that the traffic snarls entering and leaving the games worked extreme hardships on the fans. My problem was that I had no access to the restrooms, so extra time spent entering and exiting the campus became most uncomfortable. I thought about the problem extensively, and finally proposed a solution to Chancellor Edward Jackson in the summer of 2000. However, Southern never acted on my proposal. See the proposal and Chancellor Jackson's letter acknowledging my proposal."

George's Plan to Ease Southern Football Traffic

July 26, 2000

Office of the Chancellor / Dr. Edward R. Jackson

Southern University

P. O. Box 9274

Baton Rouge, La. 70813

Dear Chancellor Jackson:

After studying parking and traffic problems at Southern University for the last few years, particularly during the last football season, I decided to investigate the three entrances to the campus. Consequently, I came up with this proposal that is attached to this letter. If you have any questions, you can reach me at home. I request your immediate response.

Sincerely yours, a loyal Jaguar fan,

G. Washington Eames

I would like to present a proposal to correct the traffic problems at Southern University before and after football games.

The first thing that should be done is to print three different color parking permits: one blue, one gold, one white. A parking permit should be purchased with each ticket sold at the time the ticket is sold. The color of the parking permit will determine which route the fans would take to go to the game and exit the game. Blue passes would use Scenic Hwy. and Harding Blvd. Gold passes would use Scenic Hwy. and Swan Street. White passes would use Scenic Hwy. and Ave A/Farm Rd.

This scheme will eliminate the cash check points at every entrance to the campus, which have been causing massive delays and jams everywhere on campus.

Two city police officers should be at a check point at Scenic Hwy. and Harding Blvd. Two city police officers should man Scenic and Swan. Two city police officers should man the checkpoint at Farm Road and Scenic for the purpose of directing the white passes to Farm Road, the gold passes to Swan Street, or the blue passes to Harding Blvd. All passes for parking permits should be visible through the windshield [hanging from the mirror].

To eliminate traffic jams, starting at 4:00 p.m., three lanes of traffic should be open on Harding Blvd. going west, starting with the left turn off the interstate, manned by two city police officers.

Starting at 4:00, there should be three lanes of traffic going north on Scenic Hwy. from Hollywood to Southern University manned by two city police officers.

Two lanes on Farm Road should be open for traffic going to the game from 4:00 p.m. till game time. All exits from the campus should be directed to the far right lane going east over the overpass after 4:00 p.m.

Fans must exit the campus the way they entered.

In order for this proposal to be effective, there should be an outline of all the above laid out in a map ASAP to let the fans know that we are about to resolve the traffic problem at Southern University for the first time in its history for this new millennium. The map should also be issued with tickets and published in the local paper with radio announcements.

Sincerely,

G. Washington Eames, Jr.

George turned his attention to Southern. He had achieved phenomenal success in desegregating LSU's athletic department and finding LSU also in complete ADA compliance after years of working with them, His patience was running short. He loved Southern athletic events, yet he was so discomforted while attending them, George knew the students and other handicapped fans were equally inconvenienced—sometimes dangerously.

We began a massive campaign to bring Southern to ADA standards. Armed with my camera, we visited and revisited the problem areas. He explains on his ADA page on his Web site which we began in 2009:

George Identifies Barriers for Disabled at Southern

I have attended numerous activities on the Southern campus, trying to find accommodation the best way I could. For years I have loved track events, following both high school and college events. I went to Mumford Stadium at SU and sat on what I call "the hump" on the student side which is where the events started and where the finish line can be found. Students assisted me to get there because the ramp angle is quite steep. However, several years ago, officials no longer permitted me to sit there, and I had to stop going to SU track events. I literally had nowhere to sit to see the events.

I had a lengthy conversation with the chancellor in 1998, explaining some of the difficulties I had experienced, for track and for football. I said I would be happy to take someone to LSU to see how they had resolved the problem, which I felt SU could also handle. Someone did accompany me to LSU, but nothing came of it. Finally, SU constructed a small wooden platform—not on the student side—but on the east side. Yet the ramps remained long and tiresome to negotiate. The restrooms were not accessible to me, and concession stands were not accessible either.

In the Clark mini-dome, I negotiated a very steep and dangerous ramp to the floor level for years to attend events like basketball and graduation. When I began using my electronic chair, which is very heavy, I began to be more concerned about my safety. When Kathy broke her arm in 2007 and was retiring, Glen Oaks had its graduation there. Kathy was to be honored and was sitting on the stage. I went to be there with her. She could not help me down the steep ramp, and tried to get the security people there to assist us. They just did not respond.

When President Barack Obama spoke in Clark mini-dome, we were denied any access to the floor where I had sat for years for Clark events. The chief of police told us to go to the elevator, but it was not operable. We went home and have never returned.

For these and other reasons, I felt imperative to seek legal redress to get Southern University to comply with the ADA—not just for myself—but for those young handicapped people who will follow.

In 2001, a generous budget passed the legislature for renovations at both LSU and Southern University. I was hopeful that these monies would create renovations on Southern campus which would improve ADA accessibility—especially since I had had more than one visit and lengthy conversations with Chancellor Edward Jackson. I was disappointed.

I brought my letter of complaint first to Federal Court, Middle District, here in Baton Rouge. After investigating, they forwarded it to Washington, DC. My letter came back from Washington with the information that I needed to file my complaint with the Education Department, Civil Rights Division in Dallas, Texas. My case was given a number, and investigation began. It would go on from 2006 through the fall of 2008. Finally, findings came back to me that Southern University was in noncompliance with the ADA in several areas.

Letter to the Civil Rights Division about ADA at Southern
Sept. 12, 2006
To whom it may concern:

I, G. Washington Eames, Jr., have met on numerous occasions about the ADA on Southern University campus with Chancellor Edward Jackson.

As early as 1998, I told him that Southern needed to be in compliance with the ADA, a law that was passed in 1977 by the Congress of the United States mandated by the US Supreme Court. But Chancellor Jackson told me, "George, you don't have to worry about where you can sit. All you have to do is come up in the press box with me and all the dignitaries."

I said, "I want a ramp for the handicapped, so they can enjoy the game with their wives or escorts." I even took it upon myself to call LSU and ask their permission to come and view the handicapped facilities on their campus. In 1999, I took with me a young man named Mr. Simon from Southern University who had been designated by the chancellor, and another young man who worked with parking and grounds at Southern University.

In visiting LSU in 1999, they were shocked to see the outstanding facilities that LSU had for the handicapped. I told them before LSU had these outstanding additions to the east side of the stadium, the handicapped sat in the north end zone.

In 1992, I had met with Joe Dean and the facilities director to inform them that the handicapped seating was inadequate because it was split level, and with these big motorized wheelchairs, the little

Boy Scouts and Girl Scouts who had been assisting the handicapped for years, could not help them on the second level. They understood what I was talking about, and they cut everything down to one level, and staggered the seating arrangement like theater.

The next day I had another appointment with Chancellor Jackson to update him on our visit at LSU. The first thing he said to me, "George, you know we can't compete with LSU."

I said, "I understand that, but you have to do something to make this campus accessible to the handicapped. Do you realize how many young black males have been shot and paralyzed by drive-by shootings? And you have an ROTC on this campus. You should be more sensitive about their well-being when they come back from serving their country with some disparities. Plus, you have a law center here. How can the chancellor of the law center allow this campus to be in noncompliance with the ADA?"

So we decided to go over to Southern's stadium to see where some improvements could be made for the handicapped. We went on the student side, and he told me, "You know, we're getting ready to do some renovations. But you know, in order to do what you want me to do, we'd have to come in here with some big construction air hammers and tear the stadium up."

I said, "Well, you have to build some ramps. And they have to be conducive to wheelchair accessibilities. A lot of people in wheelchairs want to be totally independent with no assistance." On the student side, as we speak, they have nothing. That's the west side.

Then we went to the east side. I had my ruler, of course, so I could do some measuring. What they decided to do was to make a little makeshift ramp [platform] by taking out a half row of seats with the capacity of accommodating about five to seven wheelchairs. Here's the problem I found with that: The ramps coming into the stadium were built in the fifties or early sixties. They are so steep that they are dangerous for motorized chairs, and worse for manual chairs, and you're coming down with hundreds of patrons all around you with no assistance from the security.

The next worse problem for Southern University is that there are no handicap restroom facilities for the handicapped in the sports arenas, stadium or mini-dome.

After riding around Southern University, I also found that the parking facilities for the handicapped, especially for a handicapped van, that needs ten feet to access it, are nonexistent. If a student is handicapped, he cannot attend Southern University at all because Southern University as an institution, has never seen fit to abide by any civil rights law that has been passed in this country, to my knowledge.

With that in mind, I want to file a federal lawsuit against Governor Kathleen Blanco; the State of Louisiana; President Ralph Slaughter, SU; Chancellor Edward Jackson, SU; and chairman of the board, Johnny Anderson.

I would like to have this case filed in the Federal Court, Middle District, in the state of Louisiana, for grossly violating the constitutional rights of the handicapped pursuant to the act of 1977, Americans with Disabilities Act.

Sincerely,

G. Washington Eames, Jr.

Of course, this became headline news when this formerly formidable president of the local branch of the NAACP filed a lawsuit against the primarily black institution. Paul Gates reported "2006 complaint leads to discrimination lawsuit" on Sept. 22, 2009. He explained George's view that Southern University had ignored a federal civil right act for nearly twenty years.[2]

Handicapped himself since 1956, what George found most culpable was that Southern University had a law center, was teaching

2007—I retired early—because of George's health problems—from Glen Oaks High School where I had taught for eighteen years.

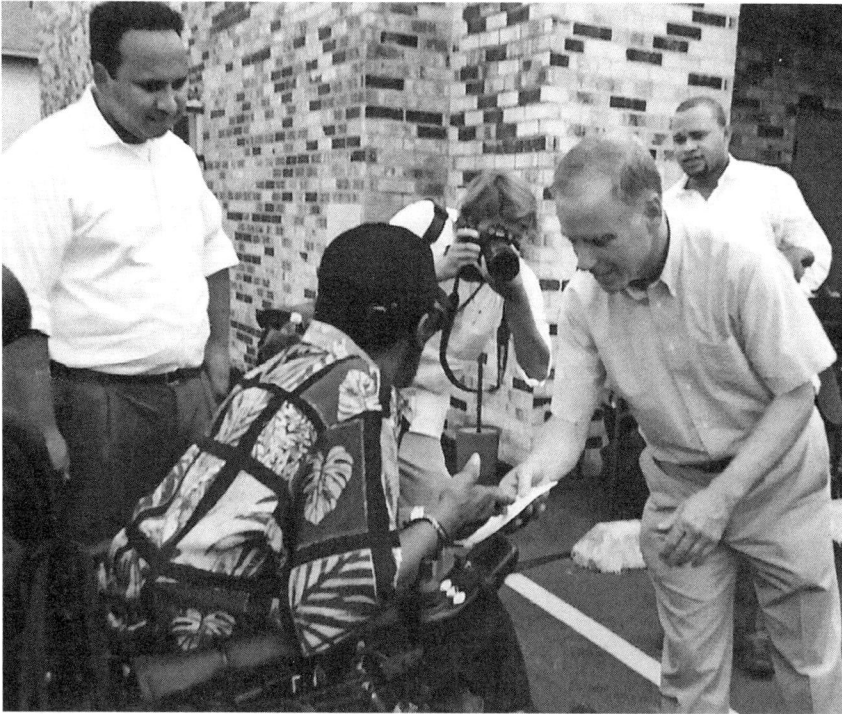

2010—George hands a campaign donation for presidential candidate Barack Obama to Howard Dean, chairman of the Democratic National Committee.

law, but didn't know that they were in violation of the law since 1977.

Attorney Susan Meyers with the New Orleans Advocacy Center represented George. We were criticized by many in the black community for "attacking" this largely all-black institution. Neither George, nor I, nor Susan would back down. Our work with Southern's ADA violations required numerous meetings with Susan, and we met in our home, or drove to New Orleans on many occasions, as well as to the campus.[2]

The handicapped students and fans deserved to be treated fairly, to be able to participate in Southern campus activities along with everyone else. This basic right failed to rouse the leadership at Southern University. George could not understand why.

For example, Southern Chancellor Kofi Lomotey said that the university has been advised by legal counsel not to comment. Then he released a statement insisting that Southern University "continually improves accessibility and comfort for persons with special needs at all of our athletic and educational venues." The federal government thought not.[3]

A week later "Suit: SU campus lacks handicap accessibility," appeared in the *Advocate*, Saturday, Sept. 27, 2009. Southern explained that it had court-side seating for the handicapped at F. G. Clark Activity Center with additional upper-level seating at mid-court. Nevertheless, George Eames was suing the school for alleged lack of accessibility in Clark Activity Center, restrooms and concession areas—a litigation now of three year duration. Seventy-six years old, George Eames, paralyzed for over fifty years, was seeking in a civil suit an unspecified amount of money in US District Court.[4]

Susan Meyers of the Advocacy Center, explained to the press that although some issues had already been addressed, after George initiated his complaint to the US Department of Education's Office for Civil Rights in 2006, many major issues remained. These included needed renovations to Mumford Football Stadium. Southern officials would not comment, saying only that Southern continually tried to improve accessibility and comfort to all its students and visitors in its educational and athletic venues.

In his letter to Southern University on Oct. 31, 2008, Taylor D. August, director of the Dallas civil rights office, noted that George and I had complained about the lack of a working elevator and wheelchair-accessible restrooms in the F. G. Clark Activity Center. Although most of the restroom issues had been addressed, August added that the doors were difficult for the handicapped to open by themselves, since they required more pressure than that recommended by ADA guidelines. Other complaints included lack of accessible parking and restrooms at Smith-Brown Union, and ramps that were too long and too steep at A. W. Mumford Stadium.

At least four hundred and eleven Southern students registered with the school's Office of Disability Services—along with handicapped Southern fans of basketball and football—had endured these inadequacies in the year preceding the letter.

Meyers admitted that the elevator at F. G. Clark Activity Center was finally operational. Still, ramps to the upper levels of the football stadium, built in 1940, remained long and steep. She added that other problems not yet identified by the Office for Civil Rights remained to be investigated. Although Southern provided student assistants at both the basketball center and football stadium, Meyers noted that, while appreciated by the handicapped, that service was not the primary intent of the ADA laws, which mandated that people with disabilities be able to function independently at public events and in public facilities.[5]

Weak and ill, George advised his attorneys that he could no longer assist with the lawsuit. He asked them to drop it in 2010 or 2011.

Both of us were vastly disappointed to let it go after years of intense work and effort, but we truly had no choice.

Chapter 20

A Public Revelation

Commentator Jim Engster was once an adversary, believing that George was trying to destroy LSU's athletic department. Engster had begun to change his attitude toward George. The three of us were becoming good friends.

When the Public Relations Association of Louisiana named him Communicator of the Year, Jim invited us to the awards banquet held in 2012, a banquet which honored other recipients as well.

We were joined by Dale Brown, Eric Guirard, and Steve Myers, who grudgingly conceded to George, "You were definitely right about some things."

We shared a grand meal together, laughing and talking of many common interests. After Jim received his award, he stood to speak. He led with remarks about the questionable progress of the last few decades reflected by the unjustifiable shooting of young Trayvon Martin.

Jim said sharply: "We here in Baton Rouge have our own Trayvon Martin, an unjustifiable shooting, and the victim is right here in this room. In 1956..."

George and I looked at one another, stupefied. We knew where he was going with this—George's shooting in 1956 which had paralyzed him and sullied his good name for the last fifty years. Jim continued recounting the entire episode, citing the newspaper articles which justified the shooter and cast doubt on the victim, reading the letter from the DA's office to the Veterans Administration stating that George would never be arrested because the DA's office doubted that he had done anything wrong. George had been found in a paralyzed condition on a piece of land used for public foot traffic.

Finally, Jim revealed the victim's name.

Guests at our party had been glancing back and forth from Jim to

George and me during this talk. It seemed to last forever. We were certainly shocked to hear Jim declare the truth before hundreds of journalists and their families from throughout Louisiana. Pure joy filled us to see the truth finally revealed to an influential group after so many years.

What a moment for George!

Struggling in a wheelchair, he had lived under this stigma for fifty long years. And despite all his efforts, he felt he would probably carry it to his grave. From a smothering curtain he had cried his message of freedom and justice for all. Under a dark cloud himself, he had proclaimed that all had a right to live in the light.

But today was different. All George could feel was elation. The whole world might not hear that he was innocent of wrongdoing—or even believe it. But the truth was out there, thanks to this courageous and faithful friend.

Jim Engster Gives George a Reason to Smile

Earlier in 2010, Jim gave George another reason to smile, when LSU celebrated its one hundred and fifty year history. The *Tiger Rag*, the bible of LSU athletics, published its selection of the one hundred and fifty individuals who had most influenced the LSU athletic program in its long and illustrious history.

Number one hundred and fifty was "George Washington Eames: A controversial former NAACP leader, he was a surrogate recruiter for LSU for almost fifty years and helped spur integration of LSU sports."[1]

Delighted with this recognition, George carried the little booklet everywhere he went. He showed it to the doctors and medical professionals who became increasingly important in his life lately, as well as to friends and relatives. I had to copy parts of it and insert it on the LSU page of his Web site.

For years, people had been telling us, "You all have to write a book." George agreed. But a book was too labor-intensive and time-consuming—with all the teaching, then the nursing and civil rights work George put to me during these last years of his life.

In August 2009, I sorted tons of material which George referred to as his "archives" and selected some of our most memorable photos—we had thousands—and created his Web site, Mr. Civil Rights–G. Washington Eames, Jr. Satisfied with this achievement, I never dreamed a book might yet one day emerge. I had a new set of business cards made for him, which contained his Web site address, and George happily set about giving them out to everyone he met, proud that at least some of his history was now available.

He loved the Web page we called Timeline which summarized clearly his many achievements going back to 1956. He had me make copies and gave them out everywhere he went. His bio page he dictated to me, and although I had heard much of it earlier, some of it in the seventies right after we met, this section was as meaningful to me as it was to him.

Chapter 21

Gloria

Gloria's feelings about me and about George had been conflicted over the years. She could range from anger, resentment, and shame to pride and deep affection for him. Part of the dynamic between them was the normal interchange between siblings, hateful one minute, devoted the next.

George was shot in 1956, and returned home in 1959. Although she loved her baby brother who was three years younger than she, Gloria felt trapped. She felt obligated to care for him since both of their parents were deceased. She felt she had to put her own life on hold, foregoing marriage and a family of her own. To add to the burden, people gossiped about the reason for the shooting—the news articles alleged he was a prowler or worse.

Gloria was not a witness. I don't think she knew what to believe.

George explained to me that she feared white people and believed whatever they told her. When the relationship between the two of them grew strained, her normally controlled or repressed feelings emerged; and she blamed him for ruining her life. George had no control over the sacrifices she voluntarily made on his account. One day when she was spouting off about how she had sacrificed her whole life for him, he retorted, "Gloria, you know damn well that you didn't have to do a thing for me after 1970 when I met Kathy. She took care of me, and you didn't have to do a thing—so quit lying about what a great sacrifice you had to make for me!"

These two certainly argued.

Gloria created a successful business for herself. A graduate of McKinley High School, she attended Southern University, but excelled in cosmetology which she studied at Carrie's Beauty School. Later, she became an instructor there and before she retired, an instructor at James M. Frazier Vo-Tech and Camelot Career College. I met some of her students who thought the world of her.

One of her most famous clients—believe it or not—was Little Richard, the musician. He was scheduled to perform on the roof of the Temple Theater, and he needed to have his waves done. When he asked around, he heard repeatedly, "Gloria Eames is the best." She did his waves. Little Richard was so happy with her services that he wanted to take her on the road with him; but she was quite young at the time and did not want to leave home.

My relationship with Gloria was minimal at first. When I showed up in the family home in 1970, Gloria was terrified that the Klan or other white people would retaliate against him, burning their home or worse. Her beauty salon was in the front room, and she saw all my coming and going. So did her customers. I can only imagine the conversations which she must have had in that salon, how embarrassed she must have been and furious that George could do that to her.

At the time, I paid little attention to her. She never spoke to me, and I said nothing to her either.

Gloria attended our wedding in 1977, but more than likely, it was with greatest reluctance. However, she did sign the marriage certificate as one of our witnesses. When we moved a year later, she must have felt great relief.

Gloria Helps Us and Son Andre

Things changed in a couple years. When our home was burned in the fall of 1980 and we had to move back temporarily to Van Buren St., Gloria was kind. She let us use her washer and dryer.

She gave much attention to our son, Andre, who was only about seven years old at the time. He stayed upstairs with his Aunt Gloria for hours at a time, where she pampered him. They would have a special relationship for years. As a young adult, he moved in with her.

Eventually, she grew more distrustful of Andre. Gloria grew weary of the arguments. After he tried to steal her automobile one night, she wanted him out of her home—and her life. She told us, "You know what that little bastard did?" Even with this deep disenchantment, she would take Andre back in when he became desperate. She really wanted to help him.

A skilled cosmetologist, Gloria gave me a permanent while we were living on Van Buren St. As her profession had taught her, she knew that an emotional shock such as the burning of our home would have stressed my hair as well; yet she gave me the perm anyway. My hair began to break off at the roots. When I asked her about it, she said she had been reluctant to tell me no since I really wanted the perm. I was unhappy. I let her know in my quiet way that what I really wanted was for my hair not to break off at the roots!

Eventually, in the nineties, George and I convinced her that she would not be able to climb the stairs to her apartment much longer. When her knees began to trouble her, she bought her home on down the street from us. She brought her salon chair with her, and continued to style hair. Gloria would occasionally send mustard greens or some favorite treat to George when she lived down the street from us.

Our family celebrated feasts together. Debra and her family, Joy Mae, and Gloria came over to the house. Gloria usually cooked the dressing and sometimes the turkey; we provided everything else. Complaining of fatigue, Gloria usually didn't stay to eat, but would take a plate home. Debra and her family usually showed up late, as did Joy Mae. Eventually, we just gave up. My own family's traditions differed; we had spent hours together, the whole day, the guests arriving in time for splendid meals. George's family just didn't have traditions—at least not the same kind of traditions mine had—and they seemed unwilling to start anything new.

When George was in prison from 1995-1998, whenever he called her, Gloria always talked kindly to him. She rode with me to visit him every two weeks, and cooked his favorite dishes for our picnic visits.

Things improved between Gloria and me. One day I visited in her new home, helping her to hang pictures and mirrors. She told me, "Kathy, you are not just a sister-in-law to me. You are truly a sister."

We Help Gloria

Before George entered those last two terrible years, a family crisis emerged with Gloria. Sister Joy Mae had died in 1992 with cancer. George told me one day, "I don't know what's going on with Gloria. She must call me fifteen times a day for Greg's phone number." Greg Minor was a friend in our neighborhood who did our yard work, washed George's van, and came to help with many kinds of handy work. George had introduced him to Gloria—and he helped her as well—often when no one else would. She was demanding of the service people who assisted her, and consequently lost their services after one or two calls.

"I gave her the number. Ten minutes later she called me back. I told her I had just given it to her, but she said she couldn't find it. Man, she's been doing that all day!"

It sounded like Alzheimer's disease to me. I suggested this to George, and he agreed.

Gloria had surgery a few weeks later and was hospitalized for a few days.

I went over to Gloria's home to clean and prepare for her return. I was appalled. Garments, dishes, paperwork were in disarray everywhere. George and I spent three days working through the turmoil, finally hiring professional cleaners for two days to help us.

We found also other, more serious maintenance problems, with plumbing, etc. We corrected as much as we could.

When Gloria was released, we had a long conversation with her. I explained that while she was still clear-headed, I needed to take over her checking and business accounts while she could still remember and explain where her significant business papers were.

I spent more precious time trying to organize everything, having her bank authorize my services for her, having extra keys made for the house, installing a light in the carport, and the like.

I continued to see signs of her deterioration.

Her driver's license had expired, and because of her dementia, she could not drive. She insisted on driving, so George took her keys away. She was furious with him. She grew increasingly frustrated at losing control of her daily life. She told George, "I don't like that white woman taking care of my business!"

George was angry. "All that Kathy has done for you over the years and you think of her as some white woman?"

I was unable to handle her business under the circumstances. I immediately returned everything to her and left her alone. George was so angry that he stopped talking to her for awhile.

When Gloria called, he tried to talk to her, but they never agreed on anything. When he began to hang up on her, she cursed him out. At one point, she even called him a peping Ttom and a child molester.

George wanted nothing else to do with her.

I presumed that Gloria's anger was speaking through the dementia.

George corrected me, "That's not her dementia. Gloria's just mean. She's been mean all her life."

Gloria's niece, Debra, assumed responsibility for her.

Tragically, in the fall of 2010 George began a series of hospitalizations totaling 193 days at nine different times, after which he remained homebound in a hospital bed throughout 2012.

During this period Debra found care for Gloria in a facility. We heard that she wanted to see her brother, but George was in no condition to visit her by the time she asked for him.

They never saw one another again.

Chapter 22

Coming Home

When I was 22 years old, I had an intense dream—one that felt more like a vision. This was two years before I left the convent, while I was still at the Motherhouse completing my music degree.

The image is still sharp in my mind. I found myself ascending into heaven, bright with light and clarity. Then, looking down, I saw roiling, dark waters, confusion, melee—and I felt myself slowly stop in mid-air, then begin descending. Frightened, I knew that I would be entering those dark waters feet first, fully able to see, experience, and know where I was. I knew also that it would mean total immersion into the whole mess of humanity, the morass of confusion, dark and ignorant minds, sinfulness, brokenness.

I thought, "This is going to be my life." I didn't know how because at that time I had no intention of leaving the convent. But I reassured myself, no matter what happens, I know Christ is the answer. I will cling to Him and everything will be all right.

All my life, I have been a perfectionist. Mess of any kind disturbs me. I keep a neat house, and I don't like to be around messy people. I discard anything broken or spoiled, so this vision was my worst nightmare. What I did not understand at that time, and have just begun to realize today, is that I also subconsciously rejected the brokenness of people.

What Christ was telling me was that, like Him, I would have to assume a full relationship with my broken brothers and sisters. To reject them was to reject Him. One section of a poem by Gerard Manley Hopkins, *God's Grandeur*, expresses well man's condition. Soon I would be wearing man's smudge and sharing man's smell— what it is to be a human being.

I had already rejected racism, as had George, as we struggled together to improve the flawed society around us.

When I perceived racism in the Catholic Church, I abandoned the church. I could not tolerate it. Resisting those dark waters with all my strength, I refused to step into the flood. I could not—would not—tolerate my flawed and broken brothers and sisters.

After George and I were snubbed at my mother's funeral in the Catholic Church in Brusly in 1995, I left the church and would not return for fifteen years.

During those fifteen years I stumbled around, trying to find a church or spirituality which would support me without offending me.

I investigated Native American spirituality. "The Great Spirit" I could deal with, and I loved the connection to nature which Native Americans shared.

I found Taoism and Buddhism attractive. Here I came to understand and appreciate "be where you are" and going with the flow of life, concepts which helped me through many trials which George and I faced.

I eventually discovered the Unitarian-Universalist Church which respects and pays tribute not only to these but to all other spiritual heritages as well. I felt comfortable there until a couple of negative things happened which showed some members to be narrow-minded and prejudiced. Minister Steve Crump was a warm and loving man who was above reproach, and I had good friends there, but I just could not stomach prejudice in the church itself and stopped attending.

Now, I had nowhere to go. I depended on spiritual reading, relishing especially the wonderful mystical poems of a Muslim mystic, Hafiz, and the poetry of Rumi.

On occasions I attended the Baptist Church with my husband, and I appreciated the services, especially the gospel music at New Hope Church with Rev. Leo Cyrus. He seemed to me to be a faith-filled man, sincere and respectful of others. I attended their communion services, yet this was not the Eucharist I knew and had believed in.

I had gone through many doubts, struggled sincerely to know what was true, doubted in Jesus as the Son of God, yet here I was mentally challenging the Baptist Church because it did not have the real presence in the Eucharist! This is what was missing everywhere, the Body and Blood—the Eucharist. Everywhere I found pulpits, but no altar. I wanted the Eucharist, but my faith was weak, at times, nonexistent. I still had many doubts about God, Jesus as His Son, and the like.

I struggled with faith throughout those years, but I desperately wanted a vibrant faith. In the 1990s, as I explored Native American spirituality, I had written this reflection on Faith:

Faith is such an abstract. How strange we are, or at least how strange I am. I often question *what* it is I believe, yet I never question *that* I believe. Is it because Faith is a posture of the spirit, an attitude, an openness? Let me share with you my reflection on a short poem *"To a Child Running with Outstretched Arms in Canyon de Chelly."*

This poem is written by the noted Native American writer, N. Scott Momoday, a Kiowa Indian born in 1934. Here is my reflection:

This Vision Is Faith

You can see it, can't you?

A little child running into the endless expanse of the great Southwest—black hair streaming, arms wide, running wide open, holding nothing back? This vision is Faith. It's the color and grain of Faith the way a child wears it–close to the skin and in between the toes.

This kind of Faith I can go for: believing with all my heart though I too am small against the immense background of all the people who confuse me with controversy or politics, policy or violence, or the contortions of love that never work out quite the way I have come to expect.

This is my kind of Faith: belief with its hair down, an intense, running, outstretched human being flung open in innocence, vulnerable in delight.

I want this kind of Faith to be the stuff of my life, to believe with all my heart although the world will not stay still, and the spirit (even my own) won't stay put either, but blows like the canyon winds through the wild places. I want to believe although sand shifts, rocks crack, hearts break, heroes fail, friends fall.

I want to believe through all of this and more, through sifting shadows and doubt, through light flickering in ragged ribbons across the garment of my life. I want to wear Faith the way a child wears it—close to the skin and in between my toes.

✳✳✳✳✳

I wrote the reflection on faith in the decade which brought me George's trial, his prison sentence, his aneurysm surgery—some of the most trying years of our lives. Most of the next decade found me unchurched, focused on my teaching, although George gently prodded me about joining a church, any church. But I had lost what little faith I had by that time. I broke my arm in 2007, retired, but could not do more than visit New Hope with George on a few occasions.

Then in November 2009, I discovered Web sites and television shows that explored prophecies about the Last Days. Theories fascinated me about 12/21/12—which, of course, did not materialize.

Then I discovered Quiet Buck's Web site and read Red Elk's great visions from the seventies. All this speculation about the Last Days disturbed me and intrigued me.

I started digging out my old Bibles. In one of them I found a holy card of St. Bernadette. When I was in the convent, my religious name was Sister Mary Bernadette, S.S.N.D. (School Sisters of Notre Dame). This picture showed the incorruptible body of the saint in her crystal casket. I remembered that St. Bernadette, the little girl who had visions of Mary at Lourdes, had died in the 1800s. Her body has never decayed, but remains supple, as beautiful as the day she died. That she died of painful and corrosive bone cancer makes her incorruptibility even more miraculous.

Now I started looking for videos or Web sites on "The Incorruptibles" and located about two hundred and fifty saints who, like St. Bernadette, died as much as 1600 years ago and whose bodies are still supple, intact.

These findings were like a shot of super-adrenaline to my faith— how could this be—except for God's power in Christ Jesus? I wept as my faith came back.

Despite my struggles to maintain a spiritual link to God, I had not reckoned that I could not do so without a faith community, and every faith community is deeply flawed. The human condition may be redeemed, but not perfected. At least, not in time. What I felt, to be gifted again with faith, was total gratitude and humility. I could have stumbled all my life, but God was gracious and full of mercy; and He poured it out on me, restoring to me every spiritual blessing He had ever given me. Rather than the undeveloped faith which I had had as a child and young adult, even in the convent, I now enjoyed the tested faith of a warrior. I had been immersed in the dark waters and emerged again into the light, thanks to God's mercy.

"Mom, I'm Home"

In November 2009, I still could not accept racism—but I could accept the racist, and forgive his brokenness. I was simply ready.

I had a long talk of reconciliation with a young priest at Our Lady of Mercy Church. For my penance, he told me to visit the statue of Mother Mary near the front, to take her hand and say simply, "Mom, I'm home." I was. I wept.

Eventually, I found St. Paul the Apostle Church on Gus Young Ave. again. That's where in the eighties George and I had attended briefly together, where Joe and Precious Delpit had become Andre's godparents during his baptism, where I had sung in the choir for several years, the church with which Andre and I had determined to walk fifty-two miles to protest the death penalty.

I was home.

I immediately began reading everything I could put hands on, reviewing many teachings about my Catholic faith that had been lost in the muddle of fifteen years. I purchased spiritual books I had read years before and read them again. One intense little book above all others taught what I most needed to know to finish this sojourn, a classic of the spiritual life, *Abandonment to Divine Providence*, written by a then-obscure French Jesuit of the 1600s, Rev. Jean-Pierre de Caussade, translated by John Beevers. I had read it back in the early seventies, and I would return to it again and again, reading it every few months. It fed me and taught me, and I, in turn, would minister his teachings to others.

Recently, I had presented a talk at St. Paul in a little ministry, Soul Food, which I started there. Because Father de Caussade's teachings meant so much to me, I simply wanted to share them with others. My little Jesuit explains that most of us live common, ordinary lives filled with daily trifles. Even those who enjoy relative fame endure the constant flow of small, petty actions, insignificant words, every day. All are alternately boring, somewhat pleasant, irritating, or downright tragic.

How did we get here, into our ordinary lives? God put us here, and wants us here, so we should welcome all these events, trifling or not, as the will of God. Father de Caussade coaches us to endure our lives with love and to resign ourselves to anything which causes us "weariness and disgust."[1]

In short, we are to "embrace the present moment," however ordinary it might be, "as an ever-flowing source of holiness."[2]

It's astonishing to think that what happens to us moment by moment is God's way of speaking to us.[3]

Father de Caussade speaks of the "duty of the present moment."[4] Thus, to become holy, all I need to do is to embrace the present moment, my only duty in life, which flows continually, as His will for me. All is bearable, because though we may endure terrible events, all that we need to face is one moment at a time, and we are constantly in communion with our God. That precious moment to which we give our all is a virtual sacrament, as it brings us into union with our God.

I read also, that just as his will is manifested in my life in each moment, so his word also speaks in each event in the history of the world, as incomprehensible or terrible as we may perceive it to be. I became totally convinced, as extraordinarily difficult as many of us may find this to accept, that nothing that happens is outside of his will or at least his permissive will since "every drop of water and every little stream carry traces of their source."[5]

God is speaking to the world in what we do and suffer from moment to moment. We do bring much of our grief upon ourselves, and in many events, we are the victims of the evils that other people willfully perpetrate; but never are we alone.

How manageable our lives become if we face them one moment at a time! God feeds us in each "sacrament of the moment" with His will and his love. Jesus told his disciples, "My food is to do the will of my Father." It is also our food.

In conclusion, Father de Caussade's teaching of the "sacrament of the moment" or abandonment to the Divine Will each moment, is the perfect offering to the Father and can accomplish everything that Jesus asks of us. Every atom, every microsecond containing a fragment of His hidden life and His secret activity in me as I accept and adore God's will, is a tiny stone building the heavenly Jerusalem. I have only to trust perfectly in this tiny moment. Only one moment at a time. As events crowd in upon us, as God feeds us with His divine will moment by swift, intense moment, we eat our destiny one bite at a time. To accept this, our daily bread, with love, can bring us sweetness and joy even in the midst of suffering and misery. Rejection and denial result only in unresolved bitterness.

One of the consequences of my return to the church was to create two Web sites in addition to the one I had created for George, my personal Web site, (livingchrist.webs.com), and a Web site for my church, St. Paul the Apostle. The sites are rich with the spirituality which it has taken me my whole life to discover.

As George and I came to the end of 2010, I was blessed to be gifted again with strong faith.

I would need every support I could find to survive those next two years. Father de Caussade's teachings created for me an unshakeable backbone of spiritual strength and sustenance.

Chapter 23

Final Crises

At Christmastime in 2010, George spiraled into a health crisis. By then I had begun creating the Web site for St. Paul. My prayer, spirituality, and faith deepened. The severe trials which we both would endure would eventually give both of us tremendous strength and endurance.

George did not want professional advice about his weakening health.

I had been caring for his wounds for sixteen years, but now his many problems caused me to beg his doctor to hospitalize George.

His doctors were deeply concerned; he at first refused to be hospitalized, until one of his wound doctors warned him that he was in grave danger—possibly death.

Thus began a series of nine hospitalizations–193 days total–in 2011. Things got worse when George was hurt in the hospital. In May 2011, a nurse in Baton Rouge General Mid-City handled him carelessly, breaking his leg. Surgery did not go well, and we learned that George would have to remain on antibiotics for the rest of his life.

During the hectic schedules of hospitalization, I brought my Bible and spiritual books to the hospital, prayed and read at his bedside, walking outside when I had a few minutes. I stayed close to God. I prayed with George. Father Vincent Alexius, the young Indonesian priest at St. Paul, visited him in the hospital several times, anointing him. They had hit it off from the beginning. They had met when we attended Mass in 2010. Always tenderhearted, George cried, explaining that in his entire life, no other preacher had ever ministered to him the way Father Vincent did. George loved him.

We traveled back and forth to four different hospitals, sometimes in the van, sometimes by ambulance. In 2009 he had realized he could no longer drive, and I had the van altered to drive it safely myself. By the end of 2011, we were both mentally, emotionally and physically exhausted.

The confinement took a deep toll on George who had always been active, sociable, and people loving. He was frustrated and angry. He began taking it out on the people around him—not me so much as his doctors, nurses, and therapists—even friends who came to see him. He demanded that friends bring him "something good to eat" since he hated hospital food.

I could see where this was heading—no one would want to assist him; he drove away physical therapists, refusing to cooperate with them, and nurses actually refused to enter his room. The charge nurse had to tend him herself. I pleaded with him. Some of his remarks seemed to have negative racial overtones—at least the nurses heard them that way.

I Would Never Leave George's Side

The situation deteriorated to the point that in November I began praying and crying for three days to God—what to do?

I was actually considering leaving George, and I told him so. I determined not to be left with him at home, unassisted, to care for him by myself. I seemed unable to reach him.

Finally, at the end of the third day, I heard in my heart in a voice as clearly as someone speaking aloud, *"If you have to err, err on the side of charity."* I would not have chosen that word "charity" myself. My natural instinct would have been to use the more common word "love."

I knew that God had spoken to me. I had an answer. I would never leave George's side. I was all he had, come what may.

Unbelievably, George seemed to mellow from that point. He apologized to his caregivers, and grew more pliant and cooperative.

Yet as Christmas approached, he insisted on going home. He asked the staff if they couldn't just hold his room for a couple of days. No way. He then decided to leave against medical advice, which would create problems with our insurance company as well as Medicare.

Jim Nelson and Herman Brister, Sr. talked to him intensely for hours to convince him to stay. George finally agreed reluctantly. Herman promised a great Christmas dinner if George would only stay. They had been friends more than twenty years. True to his word, on Christmas Day Herman came over before he even sat down to eat his own dinner across the river in Pointe Coupee Parish. He brought bags of food, enough holiday eats to last for two days, at least.

I had bought a tiny dorm refrigerator that the General Medical Center staff permitted me to keep in the small, noisy hospital room. It had a poinsettia on the top. We stashed as much as we could in that little fridge and heated paper plates in the microwave oven.

After his last hospitalization in the New Year 2012, we returned home with a new hospital bed designed for healing wounds.

We hoped that the wounds would continue to heal. George had been going to the wound clinic before all these hospitalizations began in 2011. He was treated by his same wound specialists, beginning with Doctors Mark Silady and Michael Puyau, followed by Dr. Shaun Carpenter and Dr. Jeanne Barnes. George persisted in calling her "Dr. Barnes and Noble," making her laugh. George loved all the wound care nurses there and many of his home care nurses.

✳✳✳✳✳

George began his last year generally homebound except for doctors' appointments. I did all the driving.

George never gave up hope that he would be healed, that he could again become active. I must say here that George hated to talk about illness or pain. He loved life so intensely that he would say nothing at all rather than discuss his personal problems. Though many details of his health in the last two years were horrendous, I will honor his wishes here and not even mention them!

His excellent, regular doctors and specialists included: Dr. Henry Dixon, internist; Dr. "Gertie" Chimeka Anyanwoke, infectious disease specialist; Dr. Siva Yadlapati, a blood specialist for his anemia; and Dr. Clif Richardson, a foot specialist. Home care nurses came two-three times a week. Kurt Soileau, who was so kind to us, supervised or delivered intravenous drugs to us once or twice a week. Medical supplies filled up our pool table in the den.

From wife, mother, teacher, and civil rights activist, I was now nurse 24/7.

Our wonderful friends brought us food—Jim Engster, Dale Brown,

Jim Nelson, Herman Brister, Effie Carter, Gail Coleman, Bessie Landry, and others—some of them numerous times. Jim Nelson tried to come every week or every other week for lunch, bringing George that great Chicken Shack food that he loved, until he could no longer eat. I will never forget their generosity and kindness.

Another visitor who came now to see him and who had come faithfully through the years was George's nephew, Cleveland Bailey, Sr., his sister Olivia's son. Inevitably he and George would evolve into a shouting match, calling each other names; although Cleveland admired much that George did, as a devoted Southern alumnus, he and George disagreed about issues involving the school. They would argue strongly till someone's patience ran thin. Yet he kept coming back. Cleveland's sister, Mary Esther Bailey, also visited George regularly though not as often.

✶✶✶✶✶

When George called me, it was Jesus calling to me.

Wherever I was, I dropped whatever I was doing and ran to assist him. The "duty of the moment," or "the sacrament of the moment" brought me not only to minister to my husband, but to minister to Christ Himself. This I believed, and it brought me joy and comfort in the middle of much distress.

I heard friends, even Father Vincent, marvel at my fidelity as a wife, at the extraordinary witness I gave to the sacrament of marriage. I knew what I was doing. As difficult as it was at times, it didn't seem extraordinary at all. What I did, I felt every spouse should do for their partner. If what I did was extraordinary, then the world is a sad place, indeed.

Believe it or not, George insisted on going to an LSU football game in October. It was virtually impossible for him to dress himself, so I had to dress him. I also had to prop him up with little pillows in his wheelchair and operate it for him. He wanted his beloved games badly, but we had to leave before the half because he began feeling extremely weak.

George wanted to read his Bible daily, but had such a hard time holding it, saying that it was too heavy. I bought a light paperback New Testament including the Psalms for him, but he still could not hold it. I began reading to him myself, and we prayed together every night. When my cousin, Gigi, moved in with us, I invited her to pray with us as well, and she did. She helped during those last few months, sitting with George when I went to Mass on Sunday or ran to the grocery store. I would not leave him for long.

George said an extraordinary thing one night while we were praying. "Kathy, I want to tell you something. All my life you have been my conscience. Every time I was ready to do something, I would ask myself, 'Would Kathy approve of this?' When I answered, 'No,' and I did it anyway, I always got in trouble!" This touched me more than almost anything else he could have said to me.

For months George's voice had been weak—so weak he could barely be understood on the phone. Visitors had to bend low over the bed to hear him. I bought him a little tour guide audio system with speakers. Now we could amplify his voice. I also bought a brass bell that he sometimes used to call for me.

He complained to Dale one morning that he had called and called me, and that I just ignored him; I began sleeping in his room in my leather chair, and when this became too uncomfortable, I set up a canvas cot next to his bed at night.

George and I Prepare for His Funeral

After an abdominal MRI during the late summer, we were told to see an oncologist because of lesions the technician had noticed in the spine and in the liver. I knew that meant cancer, but we had many other issues; we delayed the appointment.

In September Dr. Yadlapati discussed the cancer with us, explaining that George had anywhere from three months to a year.

I told George I wanted him to help me prepare his funeral.

We would call it a "Celebration of Life," because we would be celebrating his life and accomplishments.

He responded with gusto, at least as much as he could muster, as weak as he was.

First, I gathered information and wrote an obit, reading it to him so he could correct any minor errors.

We discussed the church. Father Vincent had been transferred to

Texas. "I don't want to go to St. Paul's. Father Vincent is not there anymore," George said sadly. We finally decided on True Light Baptist Church because his former neighbor was pastor there. He loved Rev. Dennis Hebert, and told me more than once, as he did about many of the young people who had hung around with him at his home on Van Buren St., "I raised that boy."

Then we planned important details, his pallbearers, his mottoes and favorite sayings.

Finally, the music. I knew exactly what he would want: "Jesus is the Center of My Joy," "The Lord is My Light and My Salvation" and "Stand." This last one was the epitome of George; I had bought a CD by Donnie McClurkin which contained that song, and he played it at every opportunity, especially on his way to church every Sunday morning, as long as he was able to attend. How well this song expressed his whole way of being, to do all he could, and when he could do no more, supported or unsupported, just to stand. To refuse to fall down, to bend, or to give in. To endure, with God's help. To endure. This one word, "Stand," meant everything to him. Through the pain, through the hurt, through the shame, through the injustice of it all—stand. Every time I hear the lyrics, I feel his pain in the 1956 shooting, the shameful aftermath, the years in prison, all the months of confinement and suffering with his terrible physical problems.

✶✶✶✶✶

One day he told me, "Get Clarence Jones on the phone for me."

"George, I know what you want to do, but it may be months yet."

"Get Clarence on the phone," he repeated.

Then later, "Clarence, I want to ask you to do something for me." Clarence had done something for George on several occasions; his Heritage singers performed most notably in the great Celebrations for Dr. King's Birthday.

"Anything, George."

"I want you to do the music for my Celebration of Life."

"George, I would be happy to do it, and I won't charge you a dime! Just have Kathy send me the names of any songs you want, and we'll be ready." Clarence would be ready; he sang "Stand" himself, and the song was so moving I cried throughout the piece.

In addition to his favorite poem by Clarissa Pinkola Estes, "A Prayer," which he had read every day during his incarceration, I included a short poem which I wrote:

Contraries
By Kathy Andre-Eames
If water goes
into every hollow place,
what rules the light
to fling so up and far?
Light never yet has run
to fen or bog,
nor water grown
to cosmic life, a star.
Yet something like brightness
brims in every stream;
and dreams of water
soothe the driest eyes.
Even the dark,
skyward, finds its way
as from obedient fire
the smoke must rise.
So, human-wise, as life
in me slows down,
the less I feel,
or understand, or see,
the more I play,
compassion dancing on;
like smoke I rise,
like a dark serenity.

George's Favorite Sayings

Throughout his life, George had a series of favorite sayings and mottoes which explain well his character and philosophy. I entered these also into his order of service to enable family and friends to have them:

"You can't stop progress; you can only detain it."

"Freedom is non-negotiable." [His motto used on his business cards.]

"Be accountable for your space."

"Evil flourishes where good men do nothing" (Burke).[1]

"The Revolution never sleeps." [In those two last years of his life, he answered the phone in this way, even when he had been asleep.]

"You can't do nothing scared: You can't eat scared; you can't sleep scared; you can't make love scared."

"There's no such word as can't."

When confronted with any problem (even his wheelchair and lung cancer) he said: "That's a mild inconvenience."

"That's broke. Fix it."

"I'll take on anybody, any place, any time." [This was the message he used on the NAACP phone.]

At the End, George Wants Gumbo and Music

George suffered a crisis on November 3, 2012, while waiting in Dr. "Gertie" Chimeka Anyanwoke's office.

"Kathy, I can't breathe!"

Overhearing him, Dr. Gertie rushed out with her stethoscope. "Mr. Eames, you may have pneumonia. I want you to go the emergency room immediately."

"I'm all right now. I'm OK." George was afraid of yet another hospitalization.

Knowing George, I wasn't quick to accept that, so I told him, "George, let's keep our appointment with Dr. Gertie. When she's finished, we'll see. One thing I do not want to happen is for us to go home and have another emergency on our hands."

George agreed. When the appointment was over, I took him to the emergency room at the Baton Rouge Medical Center, Mid-City, near Dr. Gertie's office. We soon moved to a regular hospital room. After X-rays and an MRI, three doctors came in to tell us, "We found the primary cancer. George has fourth stage lung cancer. It has metastasized to the spine and liver. This cancer is terminal; we cannot treat it with chemo or surgery."

"How long do I have?"

We were told anywhere from two weeks to a year.

George nodded.

I knew then that he would not last till Christmas.

"All I want is a few weeks to see my friends one more time."

After some discussion, George agreed that he wanted no form of resuscitation if he went into heart failure or any other kind of system failure.

We came home with an oxygen machine.

I began the e-mail and phone calls explaining how things stood with George. Friends began to come and to spend whatever time he had left. The most important call I made was to our son, Andre.

The entire time George had been in the hospital, Andre had not come to see him. He called, as he had been doing for the past few years, but rarely came by. Neither had he come in 2012, when George was home in that last year.

When I finally reached him on the phone and explained that his father was dying, he broke down, weeping so hard that he had to hand the phone to his wife. He couldn't even talk. Although George was not especially anxious to see him, I told him, "Let me tell you something, George; you may not need to see him, but he needs to see you. The two of you need some kind of closure. This will haunt him for the rest of his life, and you can't do that to him." George agreed and we had two or three meaningful visits.

When George was dying, Janice and Jamie Simms came to see him and to assure him that because he had promised to take care of them, they would in turn take care of me. He was not to worry about me.

One visit which I appreciated was that of former NAACP presidents Alvin Washington, Kwame Asante, and Lamont Cole. Together they expressed their thanks and admiration for all that George had done for the people of Louisiana in civil rights. They took pictures with him. The moment was touching and memorable.

During the last few weeks, I often put my laptop on his chest, put earphones in his ears and played some of his favorite gospel music for him. Then sometimes, he woke me at 2:00 in the morning. "Kathy..."

"Yes, George, what do you need?"

"Play music." I knew exactly what he wanted and needed. "Stand." "The Lord is My Light and My Salvation...." His favorites.

In the last week, George seemed to rally a little, as the dying are wont to do; my cousin Lenny and his wife Barbara came to see him, loaded down with food from the country. George heard us mention "gumbo" and said loud enough for everyone in the room to hear him, "I want some gumbo."

He had not eaten anything but liquids for two weeks, and little enough of that, mostly small sips of water.

"George, I'm afraid the gumbo will make you sick."

"I want some gumbo!"

I defrosted enough liquid, and he ate several spoons full.

Then Lenny and Barbara flanked his bed.

"Do you know who I am, George?" Lenny asked.

"The cracklin' man." Yes, Lenny owned a cracklin' factory, and George had always loved his cracklin's. George recognized everyone till the next day when he went into a coma.

Only now did he seem to be in discomfort. He had taken nothing for pain during the last two terrible years. Never did George want to take pain medication; he always refused unless it was a minor headache, claiming that he wanted a clear head with no addictions. He had seen patients in the Veterans Hospital in New Orleans become addicted over fifty years ago, and still adamantly refused any relief. I began giving him morphine to be sure that he could rest without pain. His breathing did not seem troubled.

When I woke at 2:00 in the morning on December 8, 2012 to give him his morphine, his breathing had slowed to only one or two breaths a minute; I knew that the end was near. I stood by his bed, telling him I loved him, would miss him, but encouraging him to "Just let go into the wild blue yonder as soon as you are ready."

I realized that this was one of the greatest holy days in the church, a feast day of Mary. Being devoted to her, I told her, "Mother, I want you to come and get him. If you take him with you, I know he won't be afraid."

Then I prayed the Chaplet of Divine Mercy for the dying, and by the end of the twenty minutes, as I completed the prayer, George had stopped breathing. "Like smoke I rise, like a dark serenity."

Standing by George's bed, I held his hand, loving it, loving his peaceful face. I prayed my rosary, the Glorious Mysteries, including the Resurrection and Ascension.

Chapter 24

Celebrating Life

Many of our arrangements had already been made, but I delayed the funeral a week because I knew many would want to be there and had to work during the week. Jim Engster had already asked to pay for his obit to be published. It was long, so he was most gracious to contribute several hundred dollars just for this.

George Washington Eames, Jr. 1933-2012

G. WASHINGTON EAMES, JR. passed away on Saturday, December 8, 2012 after lengthy illness including lung cancer. He was a lifelong resident of Baton Rouge, LA. George was born General W. Eames, Jr. on March 12, 1933. He attended McKinley High School, and after tenth grade entered the US Army which promptly changed his name to George W. Eames because "the Army can't have a Private General." For this reason he adopted G. Washington Eames, Jr. as his official nomenclature, though family and friends always called him "Junior" or "George."

In the Army in 1954, he became an excellent radar tracker at Ft. Meade, was honorably discharged in 1955, and entered Spalding Business College where he was in attendance when he was shot in 1956. He was in the Veterans Hospital for three years. The experience of being shot and paralyzed while in egress on public property stirred his sense of injustice. His favorite nurse told him as he left the hospital, "Junior, you go home and see to it that this injustice never happens to another young man." Thus began his lifetime work in civil rights.

1956—One of the original plaintiffs in the desegregation lawsuit between the NAACP and the East Baton Rouge Parish School System.

1965—Desegregated Baton Rouge Police Department.

1968—Became office manager of the NAACP Baton Rouge branch.

1969—Became program director of the branch.

1976—Became first vice president of the branch.

1979—Became interim president of the branch.

1980—Elected president of the branch.

In the intervening years he desegregated the fire department; interceded for people's jobs; desegregated LSU athletic department and interceded for athletes; investigated and resolved issues of violence against unarmed blacks; investigated and resolved issues of discrimination in hiring in various businesses, in transportation, in education, in BREC, in the penal system, etc.

He was instrumental in getting recognition for Dr. King's birthday in the parish and school system, establishing annual birthday celebrations, Freedom Fund banquets, and finally activating a Youth Council of over three hundred youth and establishing Capital City Baseball which, in the last year of its operation served forty-five teams of youth with Leap counseling and sport competitions.

Even as his health began to fail in late 2006, he began a last campaign on behalf of the handicapped, targeting Southern University for poor accessibility, the city of Baton Rouge, (especially downtown public facilities), restaurants, and even a cemetery.

He is survived by his wife, Theresa (Kathy) Andre-Eames; his son, Wardell Andre Buckner Eames and his wife Anne; his grandsons Andre DeVonte Kinchen and Michael; several nieces and nephews, etc. He was preceded in death by his parents General W. Eames, Sr. and Alsie Buckner Eames, and by several beloved brothers and sisters, including Joy Mae Eames and Gloria E. Moore.

Visitation will be held at Resthaven Funeral Home at 11817 Jefferson Hwy. on Friday, December 14, 2012 from 5-9 p.m. Visitation from 12:00-1:00 p.m. at True Light Baptist Church, 3762 North St, followed by the funeral at 1:00 at True Light Baptist Church. Interment at Resthaven following the service and repast after interment at True Light Baptist Church.[1]

I determined to have George's Celebration of Life, as he always called it, on the next Saturday. We had already planned our speakers, the church, pallbearers, the songs, all the essential elements. I called Rev. Dennis Hebert at True Light Baptist Church to inform him that George had died. Dennis had grown up in the house next to George's home on Van Buren St.

We held the wake on the Friday evening before, displaying many of the pictures which had graced George's office for many years.

At the funeral the next day, since I wanted our son Andre, with his family, to sit with me, we chose others for George's pallbearers. These were close friends who had been such a comfort to both of us during many of the previous years: Herman Brister, Sr.; Jim Engster; student minister Rashid Muhammad; Jim Nelson; Tracy Porter and Lyman White.

Honorary pallbearers: Herman Brister, Jr.; Dr. D'Orsay Bryant; Jamaican Dartez (Tracy Porter's son-in-law); Mabra Holeyfield (Janis' husband); Tic Price (Jamie's husband); and attorney Domoine Rutledge.

I invited Tracy Porter to give his remembrances. He was a successful businessman in California, a lifelong friend and former LSU football player who had been drafted by the Detroit Lions in 1981. Tracy had a prior business commitment and could not be with us for the funeral, so his mother, Ivory Porter, represented him and his long and loving relationship with George:

Tribute

By Tracy Porter

To Kathy, Andre and the entire Eames family, please accept heartfelt sympathies regarding the loss of our community leader, George Washington Eames, Jr. Thank you for coming today to celebrate and share the life of this amazing person. George was a change agent who was on the forefront of the desegregation movement here in Baton Rouge.

I first met George while in high school attending Southern University Laboratory School. I really began getting to know him the spring of 1984 when he asked me to attend an NAACP meeting in south Baton Rouge. As you know, George was a direct person. During the meeting, he told me that I needed to get involved "in the Revolution" and that it could be done by running for first vice president of the local chapter of the NAACP. He said, "If you submit your name as a candidate, I will support you and you should win the office."

George gave a speech in support of my candidacy, and I was voted by the membership for this position. Of course, everything happened just as George said, and at that point I became a lieutenant of George. I was immediately put to work selling ads and Freedom Fund tickets.

However, working closely with George, I learned several key traits, such as leadership, strategic thinking, and the value of relationships. These valuable traits have proven to be vitally important in the development of my character and in other areas of life as they have transferred into my careers both in sports and business.

As our relationship developed over the years, George took over the role as a mentor-father to me—informing me that throughout my business travels I needed to stop in Baton Rouge to see him and Kathy. However, he would always tease me about leaving Baton Rouge by telling me that once I left, I needed permission to return back to my own hometown. I can recall on one occasion when he told me to come and visit him at his house; he referred to it as the "Potter's House." I guess I am the clay.

When spending time with him, one of the things that made him unique is that he never minced his words. You knew exactly what George's opinion was on any topic or person. Whether you asked him or not, he told you where he stood in a convincing style. He was direct and to the point.

George Washington Eames, Jr. took on many controversial issues in Baton Rouge that many of us wouldn't dream of tackling. He not only took them on, but was successful in winning most of them. The input he had in desegregating LSU and specifically LSU Athletics has helped make LSU the powerhouse it is today. All of us who are former or current student-athletes of this institution owe him recognition for his work in helping to open doors for us.

George and Kathy loved attending LSU athletic events, especially the football and basketball games. I've had the pleasure of attending some of these events with him and I can tell you that he thoroughly enjoyed being in the midst of these events. It was as if he could see the fruit of his labor right before his eyes.

One of George's greatest fetishes was fashion. He prided himself on being one of the best dressers in Baton Rouge. You could count on him being one of the sharpest dressers at any event he and Kathy attended....George will be sorely missed by his family, my family, and the Baton Rouge community.

Lyman White spoke, followed by Jamie Simms Price and Janis Simms Holeyfield.

Former LSU head basketball coach Dale Brown, a close friend and compatriot for many years also shared words:

Expressions about George Eames

By Dale Brown

The summation of anyone's life is a most difficult task and George Washington Eames' life was complex and controversial, yet in many ways simple, because he recognized that there is only one power greater than fear—and that is faith. A weak faith is weakened by predicaments and problems, whereas strong faith is strengthened by them.

On March 26, 1956 on his way home from school, his faith was challenged because he was shot in the back and for fifty-six years lived with the stigma that he was an intruder but was actually a victim. No one publicly ever stated the facts until Jim Engster was honorable and courageous enough to expose the truth this year. George spent two years [actually three] in the hospital and the rest of his life in a wheelchair but never ceased being a tenacious warrior for civil liberties and in the process alienated some folks in the white and black communities with his blunt and curt approach. His motto was "Freedom is non-negotiable and I'll take on anybody, any place, at any time."

Let me give you a paramount example.

MLK gave a sermon titled "The Drum Major." I feel this describes George's life on earth. "If any of you are around when I meet my end, I don't want a long funeral and if you get someone to deliver the eulogy, tell them not to talk too long. Just say I was a drum major. Say that I was a drum major for justice; that I was a drum major for peace; that I was a drum major for righteousness. And—all the other things won't matter. I won't have any money to leave behind. I just want to leave a committed life behind."

Thanks, George, for doing your best to be a drum major for Baton Rouge.

Before Dale spoke, Kwame Asante, representing the NAACP, summarized what the many years of service in civil rights had meant to the state of Louisiana, and especially to East Baton Rouge Parish. Looking at me, he said words that will stay with me forever: "Kathy, if George was Mr. Civil Rights, then you are Mrs. Civil Rights."

Other beloved friends and relatives participated in the service, Effie Carter with scripture readings; Rev. James R. Barrett, Sr., cousin, giving words of comfort; Jim Engster reading the obituary;

Rev. Dennis R. Hebert, Sr. with the eulogy; and Gloria High-Steward with the "Prayer" and my poem.

Because he was an Army veteran, the military honored George with a salute, presenting the American flag to our son at the burial.

"George Eames Belongs to No One but God"

Beth Bryant sent me several e-mails. This one was especially revealing about George:

> My sister and I were with him in that big blue van hundreds of times. He would pick us up at our dad's office in Baker. Nothing ever happened except a whole lot of laughter; George was hilarious.
>
> The short of it is that years later I was working for WBRZ, and I would come in on the weekend to make extra money. I was about twenty when I was graduated, so it must have been around 1989. WBRZ used to have this program on Sunday called *Sunday Journal*. When Mr. Eames rolled in he yelled across the newsroom "Hey, Beth, come give me a hug." Of course I did, and it was innocent.
>
> John Spain, the news director at the time, hated Mr. Eames, and made no bones about it. After the program was produced, I said goodbye; and Spain calls me into his office and chews me out. I said that he was my friend, and, if you don't like him, that is fine; but I am going to continue being his friend. I've known him for years.
>
> A few years later, my dad, who loved George, called me to tell me he was arrested on sex offense charges and he believed he was set-up. He said that constantly until the day he died. I was late visiting him when he was in the BRG-Bluebonnet and had to tell him that George had died.... George always invited Dad to go with him to the Final Four. Dad would always say that he couldn't because he didn't have a ticket. George would rely that he didn't need a ticket if he went with him. I visited regularly knowing that he was dying.
>
> There is so much more to tell about George. The fact that he is remembered as a sex offender just breaks my heart. Even Coach Brown called me when it happened, and said, and I quote, "George Eames belongs to no one but God." Coach is a pretty good judge of character and doesn't tolerate immorality. He and George were longtime friends. George helped him integrate the LSU basketball program...I just wanted to offer that to you. I have never been to an

open casket funeral and looked at the body. I went up to George, and kissed him on the forehead. He was a kind man and didn't mind a couple of little white girls hanging around on his floor seats with all his buddies. He would get mad if we didn't come by and at least say hello. He never expressed one ounce of anger about what happened to him, and he worked hard for equality and peace. The white establishment at the time had it out for him, and I know that for a fact.[2]

Another Funny Story about Dale and George

On Oct. 4, 2013, Beth e-mailed to me another funny story of Dale and George which she witnessed:

One day when I was shooting baskets at the LSU Field House, Mr. Eames and I already had met, and he rolled over to visit. Coach Brown was in the Field House, as, I believe, they were having camp or practice. Coach doesn't remember me as a child, as I was just one of many, but he and I have become closer since I returned to Baton Rouge. However, I followed Coach with diligence through my adulthood. He reminds me a lot of my Dad.

Mr. Eames was talking to me while I shot hoops, and all of the sudden Coach Brown comes up from behind, no warning, grabs the handholds of the chair and starts sprinting around the track at the field house as fast he can with Mr. Eames holding on for dear life. It was so funny! I think Mr. Eames' hat blew off in the race. It is one of these pictures in my mind that I will never forget.

For some reason, I know when special, meaningful things happen, and, I make a note to myself. I say to my brain, "Don't ever forget this." Then I let it register. Coach had on khaki pants and a yellow LSU shirt, and Mr. Eames had on a pair of black pants and a white shirt. I still remember the expression on his face and it was a mixture of surprise and hilarity. Coach had this "man on mission" look on his face running as fast as he could."[3]

Beth recently told me one more story about George:

There is something that you must know, and I never have told you. Mr. Eames never told my sister and me what really happened to him— he did not mention it at all.

Children are so honest and direct and we asked him why he was in a wheelchair. I still remember the look on his face, and, even in my young mind it registered that there was more to this story, when he repeatedly told us he was hit by a drunk driver. With us being white, I suppose he wanted to spare us from the horror that he endured.

It wasn't until I was in college that I found out what really happened to him. I never saw him angry or bitter, and I learned from him to never be angry or bitter, but to live my life waking up each day looking for a new adventure.

I am so happy your story together will be told. It is one that so many could benefit from, and I had the good fortune to have that dear soul in my life, and, now you.

My mom and dad loved him so, as well as my sister. I just told my mother the other day that he had passed away while they were in the hospital. She asked me if I had seen him recently, and she shed a few tears. He meant a lot to all of us.

With love,
Beth Bryant[4]

Chapter 25

Memories of a Warrior

Lyman White, a football linebacker who played for LSU, was drafted by the Atlanta Falcons in 1981. He later left the professional football league after a severe injury. Lyman has been another brother to me. He and I finally talked in mid-October 2013, as Lyman shared his history with George:

Lyman White Shares Stories about George

My first encounter with George was in 1977 or 1978 as a student athlete when an incident happened around homecoming week. It was a cartoon in the *Reveille* [the LSU student newspaper] that showed, in a derogatory way, a black woman, then state NAACP President Rupert Richardson, wearing the Aunt Jemima kerchief on her head. This cartoon profoundly upset the black student population. Even non-students and other black adults were irate at the insensitivity.

Specifically, women students went to the chancellor—who did nothing. They went to the NAACP. That was my first time seeing George W. Eames, at a meeting at the outdoor Greek theater. Our head coach, Charlie McClendon, encouraged all black athletes to stay away. Most black athletes went anyway. A large group of black students showed up that evening for the meeting.

As we stood around waiting in the Greek Theatre, a man in a wheelchair was escorted there. He couldn't get down the steps, so he sat at the top with Susan Matthews, I believe it was.

We wanted justice, we wanted apologies from the *Reveille*_and from LSU for their insensitivity for this cartoon. From there we couldn't participate anymore because the coaches prohibited us. It was homecoming week. That was my first encounter with George. Not only did George ask for and receive a public, published apology for this editorial, but he was instrumental in changing the chain of command in the *Reveille* office.

My next encounter was after graduating, after playing pro football, and after my injury. I went to a football game around 1983 or '84. At the beginning or in the middle of the game, when I walked out of the chute onto the field at Tiger Stadium, George beckoned to someone to call me to him. When I came to him, sitting at the gate in his wheelchair, he asked, "Boy, do you know I am?" He knew me right off the bat, but I didn't know him.

All I had heard were some negative remarks about George Eames, some people even saying that he had ruined the relationship between whites and blacks. All I had heard was negative—that he was not good for race relations, for the black community, or the white community, and that the best thing to do was to stay away from him. Being from a different part of the state, I didn't know anything; so I stayed away from him.

My third encounter, around 1989, came when I opened a restaurant, Buffalo Wings Express off Lee Dr. George stopped in late one evening to dine, first time in the restaurant; and it happened that day, that a friend of mine, Judge Darryl White, dropped in also. He was a white judge in Baton Rouge from the 19th Judicial District. Part of the restaurant's ambiance was for guests to sit and talk about events in the community, as our staff conversed with our customers. It brought us close to our customers, so they would tell us the truth about the food, and the like.

Judge sat down with me and George. It was one of the first times I had ever conversed with George on a level where I gained much respect for him. I learned quickly that he was not an ignorant black man, nor was he afraid to speak his mind to anybody. Judge White, George, and I began to dialogue about the court system. I soon realized that George had a deep knowledge about the legal system. It became kind of heated because Judge White began to realize that George had his own perspective of the legal system and was able to articulate his points quite well.

In the restaurant, we had Christian religious tracts and played religious music. My brother is a minister and would often pray with people there. But at the same time, it became a heated debate between George and Judge White. I sat there listening.

Judge White, who was a Christian himself, had strong religious convictions on life and justice. George's view was that justice in the legal system was one thing, and that the Bible was something else; but Judge White felt they were on equal footing. George asked the judge, "You're telling me if Lyman got into trouble right now and showed up in your court, and he pulled out the Bible and started quoting scripture, you would free him or not based on the scripture passages?"

"That's not what I'm saying. You still have to follow the law," White said.

George responded, "That's the point I'm making. You still have to follow the law."

What happened with me in that experience is that George, speaking as a peer would speak, with a judge no less, became a man whom I held in high regard and respect. At that time, hearing a black man speak to a white man, and not just a white man, but a judge, without any hesitation or reservation, gave me a revelation about this black man, George, whom I had been taught to avoid at all cost, because he had been labeled a troublemaker and agitator to white people.

This is the day I learned that here was a man who had great understanding, wisdom, insight, purpose, and drive. I had no clue where he was or where he was going, but I knew I wanted to know more about him.

✼✼✼✼✼

About three days later I showed up at George's house. That was the first time I met Kathy. When I reached his house and we began to talk, he was in his wheelchair. Welcoming me warmly, he eased my entry. He began discussing his history, and we began to debate.

He told me he had integrated LSU.

I told him no.

"How do you think Ron Abernathy got there? How do you think Charles Alexander and Greg LeFleur got their jobs?" George said.

I commenced to explain to him that one of the reasons was that our organization which we had formed, the Fifth Quarter Club which we had formed in 1989, was quickly becoming a threat to LSU's football department once they realized that former black athletes had formed an organization with Ron Abernathy, LSU assistant basketball coach, being the president, and Mel Renfro, another officer. At that time the LSU football department had no black employees in administration. My contention was that the Fifth Quarter Club, made up of all former athletes of LSU, mostly football players, was the cause of LSU's hiring Charles Alexander and Greg LaFleur in 1991 or so.

George said, "No, that ain't right. Boy, I had already been dealing with those people over there."

George had sitting in his office about four or five fifty-gallon trash bags that I assumed were full of trash. He told me to look in one of them, "That bag over there." I grabbed one. "Not that one. That one over there... not that one," till I finally grabbed the right bag. "Open the bag." He told me to look through the bag. "You're going to see a letter that I wrote to the LSU administration around 1988 or so." He told me to read the document, which I did. He told me to bring it to him; then, looking at it, he said, "Boy, see when this letter was written?"

That's when I realized that he had written notes for a press release followed by a news article in Feb. 1988 challenging LSU's athletic department for not having blacks in athletic administrative positions.

I remember him telling me through the years, "Some are guilty, but all are responsible. Now which way did that white man go, because I know he done something wrong."

✹✹✹✹✹

The first time I met Kathy was a shocker, "Man, I thought to myself, he *is* married to a white woman!" We in the younger generation knew George was married, but weren't sure if the rumors that she was white were true or not. But when Kathy walked in, all my doubts were dispelled.

Now all I wanted was the right opportunity to ask him, "How can you call yourself a black activist, leader of black people, fighting for all our causes when you're married to a white woman?" Many months later, while sitting in my restaurant, I had the opportunity to ask him that question.

"That's my secret weapon. She can go out there and get secret information from the white folks and bring it back to me," George answered.

From this day forward, George became a regular at the restaurant—almost daily.

He had a way of calling people at all hours, even early in the morning, to share his new ideas, plans. Our relationship grew to the point that people started asking me, "What are you doing? You're friends with George Eames?"

I could also see his power with young people whom he wanted to involve in the struggle. Any and all projects he had going on, he wanted to get everyone involved. One project was Capital City Baseball. I became a sponsor, and so did my brother—but that wasn't enough for him. He wanted us to go to the "field of dreams" to coach and help out. Not only did he want our money; he wanted our presence.

By the time George was released from prison, I had already moved into his neighborhood. When I saw that he had been released, I came by to visit with him and bring him some money; then too, I had not seen Kathy in several years. George was all excited. He told me, "That little woman of mine doesn't stop. She renovated the bathroom, she's got a botanical garden. We have a place where we can come relax and enjoy our lives together." At that time, I don't think George realized he would get right back into the struggle. He really couldn't stay away.

I stopped by a few years later. George felt he was not a good provider for his family. I was shocked that he had little income, so I began to give him money. He would come by my office in Melrose East, where I had a youth substance abuse program. George would come by my window, and I would walk out to the van to talk to him. I wanted him to come in to talk to my children, but at that time I didn't realize that because of his conviction, he could not come anywhere near a child.

*****

A few years later I would end up in prison for Medicare fraud, charges related to my youth program. The government said I ran a storefront program bilking Medicare funds—doing nothing for children. Nothing could have been further from the truth.

As I'd done for George, he did the same for me. He called me within a month or two after I was released. He and Kathy invited me to lunch, kind and concerned about how I was doing. There, George gave *me* some money.

Near the end of his life, when he was in the hospital, he told me, "I'm glad that white man shot me. This wheelchair has not been a handicap for me, only an inconvenience. I'm in a wheelchair, and everybody who came to me for help, came walking. I've helped many people in this town. God gave me a strong constitution such that I never let any problems conquer me. When God calls me, I will be ready because I have done all I can do. There is nothing else I can do to help you or anybody else."

Although George was in a wheelchair, to me, he stood tall among men.

Cousin Rashid Muhammad Remembers George

More memories of George came from his second cousin Rashid Muhammad in October 2013, months after George's death on

December 8, 2012. Rashid was a Black Muslim student minister. He had become a brother to me, over the years—especially in the absence of my own brothers. Rashid spent a few hours with me filling in the years between the shooting in 1956 and the time that I met George in 1970—and the years of their activism beyond.

I was fascinated to learn how this keen observer and family member had viewed George's progressive relationship with me and with civil rights.

Rashid began:

I was raised around the corner from George, who was my second cousin, on Sonora St. In 1965 when I was around sixteen years old, as I would walk back and forth from McKinley High School, George would be on his front porch near his front door. He would call out, "Hey, boy, do you know who I am?" Actually, my sister Janice, a year younger than me, would be with me; and George would holler at both of us, "Come here!"

Janice would keep walking because she was afraid of him, but I would go over to him. As he began to talk to me on a daily basis, I could see that he had a unique connection with young people. He always would offer words of advice and encouragement.

In some of my first remembrances of him, he would ride us around in his 1957 Chevrolet which he drove with a cut-off broom or mop; and he taught us how to drive. He had no hand controls then, but he was a master with that stick! [Hand controls were invented in 1954, but George would not have them till the seventies.] Once he taught me how to drive, and he was convinced I could drive, he would allow me and some of my friends to drive him all over the state of Louisiana, mostly to athletic events for McKinley High School. [Loved by many black people in East Baton Rouge Parish, McKinley High School is listed on the National Register of Historic Places. It was, at one time the only high school for blacks in East Baton Rouge Parish. McKinley students who did not ride in the back of the city bus to get there had to walk—regardless of how far they might live from the school.]

I recall going to Bogalusa, where we were stopped by the state police on the highway and ordered out of the car. Asked where we were going, we replied that we were going to see McKinley High School play football against Bogalusa High School. When we got there, we met the Deacons of Defense which is like the Black Panther party. Someone yelled out from that group: "That man [George] is H. Rap Brown!"

They surrounded us and provided us with security. We laughed about that all the way home—George laughing louder than anyone else.

We also attended football games in Monroe, LA when McKinley played Monroe's Carroll High School, another large black school in the northeastern corner of the state. Each place we went, he was teaching us how to drive on the highway. Another city was the westernmost city, Lake Charles—McKinley vs. Washington High School, another large black high school. We also attended games with McKinley High School vs. black St. Augustine in New Orleans.

When I and my friends and cousins wheeled George into the gyms and such arenas for sporting events, we would try to roll him to the area where other handicapped persons were sitting. George would tell us, "I don't want to sit here; I'm not handicapped like them. I'm just in a wheelchair!"

During each trip that we would take, we would have to stop about every fifty miles to put more oil and water in the car, because it leaked; George was not afraid to drive that car.

I can remember that in 1968, H. Rap Brown was supposed to be coming to Baton Rouge to participate in a civil-rights rally at Capital High School. Once the officials found out, they put out a curfew—8:00 p.m. Born in Baton Rouge, Brown was somehow related to George. His activism during the early sixties included work with the Student Nonviolent Coordinating Committee of which he was named chairman in 1967. In those early years, he was a role model to us young compatriots in Baton Rouge.

A bunch of us were with George: me; my brother, Melvin; Patricia, my sister; G. Baby [Edward G. Robinson, our cousin]; and Leslie Brown, my future brother-in-law. George told us when he found that Rap was coming to town, "We're going to the rally."

My brother-in-law told us, "You know we have an 8:00 p.m. curfew."

George said, "I don't give a damn about the curfew. I'm a free black man. I go where I want to go."

We crowded into the '57 Chevy, and attempted to drive to Capital High. We were stopped by the police on North St., on the way. We were ordered to get out of the car with our hands up. All of us proceeded to get out but George.

Once they saw that all of us were out but the driver, George, they hollered at him, "Nigger, didn't we tell you to get out of the car?"

George answered, "Man, I can't walk. I'm paralyzed."

The police then told him, "Put your hands up!"

George raised his hands, gesturing, "Where do you want me to put my hands, over here? [In front.] Over there? [Left side.] Or over here?" [Right side.]

"Put your hands over your head or we'll blow your brains out. You better not move," the police told him. They lined the rest of us up against the wall of a building, kicked us around, telling us that if we moved, they would kill us.

From the car, George was hollering out, "Leave them alone; they're good kids, never been in any trouble."

They asked us our names. We began telling them. When they got to G. Baby, he told them his name was Edward G. Robinson. One cop told him, "And my name is Santy Claus." E.G. Robinson was a movie star at that time. "How would you like to have a blood stain on the side of your head, your smart-ass nigger?"

When they got to Leslie Brown, "What's your name? You look like a smart ass nigger too."

He told them, "My name is Leslie Brown. I go to Dillard University in New Orleans. My daddy's name is Newt Brown, and he works at Exxon. My mama's name is Bernice Brown..."

The police interrupted him, "Nigger, we didn't ask for all that. You a smart ass nigger! We just might blow your brains out."

About then the first two black police officers who had ever been hired in the city drove up. Both of them knew George. They told the white cops, "We know him. They good people; why don't you let them go?"

To our amazement—we thought we would be dead that night—they warned us to go straight home and let us go.

On the way home, George told us, "You know, I wasn't born to obey no law, but I'm gonna' take you home."

After that, we were all afraid to ride with George.

✶✶✶✶✶

This seemed to me to be a turning point in George's life; he decided to dedicate his life to civil-rights activism. A few days later, we were talking on his front porch where he always sat. Gloria, his sister, had her beauty shop in the front room there—and she would participate in hair-styling contests downtown, winning contests year after year, hosted by Emmitt Douglas, state president of the NAACP. Douglas also had a statewide black beauty product distribution business, and he drove up, wanting to see Gloria.

Seeing George on the front porch, Douglas asked, "Young soldier, do you want to join the NAACP?" I was the only other one on the porch at the time.

Douglas told him, "I have a lot of work for you to do." George was excited to join and to be active in civil rights.

Douglas immediately made him the office manager of the local branch of the NAACP.

George was able to help establish an active youth council. George had a way with young people, having made himself a friend of many young people at sporting events. It was the first time, as far as I know, that the local branch had a youth council.

The local NAACP office was housed in the Douglas building from which he managed Douglas Barber and Beauty Supply Company and Douglas Fine Foods.

Thus began George's organized activism. From this point we could see a transformation of George that would last for the rest of his life. We respected him more, not just as a cousin, but as a role model. He was like a father to me—and not only to me—but to many of us young people throughout the city of Baton Rouge.

What I admired about him most was his fearlessness. He feared no one but God, this despite the fact that he was in a wheelchair. In my opinion, this was why he was successful as the president of the NAACP.

*****

Around 1969, when I went into the service, George was not as conscious of civil rights as he would become later in the seventies.

He had a problem with black militancy. He told me about Muhammad Ali, calling him Cassius Clay. "If I could go in the Army, why can't he? He's no better than me."

Also, George had a problem with people like Marvin Gaye jazzing up the National Anthem, "They messing that up!" He listened only to Ray Charles and Nat King Cole, Miles Davis and the jazz classics. He also had a problem with Angela Davis.

When I returned from Vietnam, I came to visit him. What did I see on the wall? Posters of Angela Davis with her big Afro, and Muhammad Ali!

"What are you doing with these pictures on your wall?" I also heard him playing "black" music, Marvin Gaye whom he had formerly despised. "What's going on with you? This is not the George Eames that I know!"

That's when he mentioned Kathy to me.

He explained "My woman hooked me up with all that, Kathy."

"Who is Kathy?"

"A pretty, young white woman who teaches at LSU. She used to be a nun. She'll never be a nun again!" Because he knew I was courting

Stephanie, a Creole girl, he told me that I "needed to get the real thing instead of a half-breed." At this point we quit talking for a few years. I was angry at his comment.

Years later, I had to revise my thinking after meeting Kathy and seeing his total physical and mental progression; for one thing, he had been physically healed.

In the sixties George had been seeing Dr. Noto nearly weekly, with constant stomach problems. I wasn't surprised; George lived on canned Spam sandwiches made on white bread with Mayo, eating that with canned peaches. Sometimes, when she wasn't mad at him, Gloria would bring him a hot plate in the evening. He could cook some things well. I never ate better mustard greens cooked with okra than that cooked by George. He taught Kathy how to cook greens; but overall, he was eating much better food now with Kathy.

My family said that Kathy was good for him. Their assessment was that "No black woman would put up with him anyway!"

People, including family, felt that George was a radical. Some believed that he would cause trouble for black people, and they were actually afraid of him. As he continued to work in the NAACP, he gained more and more respect from family and from people in the community.

I saw also that Kathy was increasing his exposure to black culture. An English teacher, as she read more and studied for herself, she shared black literature with him, exposing him to a deeper understanding of Malcolm X, Ralph Ellison's *Invisible Man*, which she began teaching on LSU campus, and other great writers like Langston Hughes. She gave him more access to the black music popular during the seventies. George told us that Kathy herself was *becoming* the NAACP. When black relatives and friends asked him, "How can you call yourself a black leader when you're with this white woman?" he set them straight. "I believe in integration—this is integration!" George practiced what he preached.

Around this time I began my own brand of activism, a way different from George. I became a Black Muslim, practicing separatism whereas Brother George believed in integration. But our level of respect for one another increased because I saw George practice what he believed, and I practiced what I believed.

✴✴✴✴✴

Around 1989, when I returned to Baton Rouge from Chicago, Minister Farrakhan made me the student coordinator for the city of Baton Rouge. Knowing George both as my cousin and as fearless leader of the NAACP, I asked all the young Muslims to join the NAACP under George's leadership—and to register to vote. We all began attending NAACP meetings, and he asked me to join his executive board, for which I ran and won.

Later on around 1992, our young Muslim brothers were confronted, attacked and locked up for selling newspapers close to LSU campus by almost 300 police officers, who were on the scene in a matter of minutes. George immediately came to our aid. He organized a meeting between the Nation of Islam [the black Muslims]; and the mayor; the police chief; all the black political leaders such as council members, state representatives, and ministers in the Fourth Southern Baptist District led by Rev. Leo Cyrus. We all attended that meeting at the mayor's office.

That year was the most progressive year for civil rights in the city of Baton Rouge because that year the NAACP, the Southern Christian Leadership Conference, and the Nation of Islam all united, forming a coalition of over 300 people. This had never happened, certainly not in Louisiana, and probably nowhere else in the nation. It was headed by us three cousins, myself, George, and Rev. Reginald Pitcher, the local president of SCLC. We began working together for race relations in BR. Our coalition that year called for a selective buying campaign in Baton Rouge because the police had killed several unarmed black men. That selective buying campaign was the most talked about event in the state; it was no wonder that the police began harassing George and that he was arrested in December 1992. All the black political people active today, judges and other black political officials in 2013, were part of that coalition. Also in 1992, encouraged and advised by George, I became the first Black Muslim to run for office in the Deep South.

When I left Baton Rouge to go to Chicago, I had to resign from the NAACP board; and Kwame Asante took my place on the board. Asante said at George's funeral in 2012 that what inspired him the most was this coalition in 1992, inspiring him to join the NAACP and later become the state president of the NAACP 2005 to 2007.

How Son Andre Remembers George

Later, in October 2013, I asked our son, Andre, to put together some memories of his father. As we read over these, I was profoundly moved to hear first-hand some of his earliest memories which included some of our most troubled times as a family:

I remember the day I was adopted by George and Kathy. I had just turned six. I really didn't understand what was going on, but I was pretty smart for my age and knew I wasn't going back to my biological mother.

I have a brother and a stepsister and will always wonder where they are and if they think about me. I think about them—not my mother so much. I was told that she (my biological mother) gave me up because she couldn't take care of us, but I think the adoption agency knows more. The adoption is a closed adoption which means the biological mother doesn't want to be found, contacted, or heard from. Do I hold any resentment towards her? Maybe. Do I forgive her? Somewhat. As I got older I understood better what was going on.

Don't get me wrong. I don't hate my mother. Just want answers, but as the saying goes, some things are best left alone.

Growing up, I found out quick that George Eames was the dictator of our house—not saying that in a negative way. But what George Eames says, goes! At the same time, even though he didn't always show it, he had a big and caring heart.

I guess the discipline came from his time in the Army. He wanted me to be what he wanted me to be, but I wanted to be my own man. That's why we bumped heads almost every day, and I don't think he understood that, or he didn't want to. The majority of my rebelling was that I needed somebody to blame. I held a lot of emotions in and didn't talk to nobody. I could have talked to my parents, but being a young kid, I didn't think they would understand.

As I go through life, now I understand what my father, George Eames, was trying to do. He was trying to make me a better man. Even though I wasn't what he wanted me to be, I know he was still proud of me and knew he loved me. Even though I was in and out of prison for the majority of my life, he was still there for me. And after catching butt whippings every day, one thing I learned, that life hurts!

I learned something early about my Pops, that he was an important figure in the community. I had a chance at an early age to sit in on NAACP meetings and phone conversations. I guess I learned from him how to cuss worse than a sailor. One thing about my Pops was that he told you what was on his mind, and even though I was adopted, I feel that I picked up traits from him and my Mom. If you ask me—or if I feel something is not right—I'm gonna tell ya what's on my mind.

I was a quiet person growing up. As I went through years of therapy and growing pains, I realized that my Pops was not the enemy. He was just trying to mold me into the young man of the future. As I mentioned before, my Pops and I bumped heads a lot of times.

We did have some good times. I remember going to Colorado Springs, Colorado. My parents checked me out of school. I was in Villa Del Ray Elementary. They called my name over the PA system, and I thought I was on top of the world. [I'm not sure what he's remembering here. We actually left for Colorado in early August 1983. We would never have taken him out of school for two or three weeks!] In my opinion, that was the best family vacation ever. My Pops was happy—never seen him smile so much.

✳✳✳✳✳

As time went on, getting older, I felt like he couldn't tell me anything—started smelling my behind, as it were; so I stole a gun from him. My mother was in fear that he was going to kill me—or I was going to kill him.

Truth be told, I wasn't going to kill him, but people who were close to him knew George Eames. He demanded respect and struck fear in the hearts of the fainthearted. This was my first taste of life, my first taste of tough love, and it hurt. This was the first time I realized that my Dad wasn't going to be there, but at the same time, he was there. I went to juvie.

I missed my home, I missed my Mom, but most of all, I missed my Pops. I think I was about fifteen or sixteen; that's when everything went downhill for me. Like I said, even though I was the black sheep of the family, George Eames was still there for me. While I was in prison he still sent me money, still gave me advice. You can't tell me that's not a father's love. He never turned his back on me. Any time I needed something, he was there. Even though I was a mama's boy—and I don't have no shame to say that—he still understood. He didn't like it, but he understood that I was going to be my own man.

✳✳✳✳✳

We kind of lost touch with each other. I would call on holidays. It took me thirty something years to realize where he was coming from, that he was not to blame for my outcome in life, and that he was only trying to help me.

I got married in July 2012. My Pops used to tell me to marry a beautiful woman, marry a smart woman, a woman with an education.

They say you can't change a person, but I feel if you believe in

God, you can. My wife was an addict; she's been four years removed from drugs. I'm proud of her, but this is not about me or her. This is about Dad. At our wedding, I remember coming out of the office [of the church building] to stand at the podium waiting for my wife, Elizabeth. My Pops gave the biggest smile and the warmest hug. Even though he didn't say it, I knew he was proud of me.

What a lot of people don't know and don't realize is what my Pops did for LSU and SU. He also played a big part in creating handicapped parking, services, and accessibility for the handicapped for the games.

A lot of things my Pops did that I don't know about—and a lot of things I still don't know about him. But I can say this: I miss his advice. I miss him. I miss his discipline. Whenever I needed something, he was there. He taught me to be strong, a man, and how to be independent despite everything.

How Andre Is Like George

As we went over what Andre had taken the time to write for me and chatted briefly afterwards, his face filled with something like longing and grief; he teared up briefly.

Every word had come from his heart.

Andre's father truly would be proud of him. He and Elizabeth, whom I know as Ann, have suffered a great deal themselves. Both of them have had a hard life; Ann's mother had many problems, and Ann had no mother to speak of, except a beloved grandmother. Yet the two of them have carved out a loving life for themselves and their two sons, one each, both from previous relationships. Andre's great ambition and drive is to be a good father to them, and I have to laugh when I hear Ann telling him that he's too hard on them!

George used to make Andre come into the kitchen with him so he would learn to cook. How well he succeeded! Andre is an excellent cook, and generally cooks for the family—as George did for me many years ago.

George would feel at home in their apartment, especially on Saturdays when Andre and his friends sit glued to the television, watching the collegiate football games!

Chapter 26

Inspired

I had been here before; after all, I have been a poet and a writer all my life.

You really cannot imagine what it is like unless you have been in the spirited embrace of a piece you are writing that penetrates your whole will, mind, and body. It drives you with passion and fire.

The project started innocently enough. I had gone to a special meeting at the East Baton Rouge school board office on Monday, August 26, 2013. I wanted to learn more about the new medical insurance plan which the school board planned to implement in the next year.

I was surprised to see George's nephew, Cleve Bailey, Sr. and his tiny wife, Susie! We embraced; and since the meeting was over, I offered them a ride home. Before we could leave the building, their son, George's great nephew, Cleve Bailey, Jr. strolled in. We chatted briefly.

"Kathy, we have to talk before I go back to the West Coast," Cleve Jr. said.

"Fine," I said. "When do you want to come by?"

"How about Thursday next week?"

"It's a date," I said.

On September 5, 2013, Cleve rang my doorbell. After we had taken our seats in my little office, in front of my computer, he eased into his topic. "After my divorce, I stayed with my parents a while. My aunt and uncle were also there trying to begin putting their lives together after Katrina. When they returned to New Orleans, I went with them to help them out. There, in the *New Orleans Times-Picayune* I read an intriguing article claiming that Louisiana would be the Hollywood of the South. 'Wow,' I thought. Then it occurred to me that this was what I should do, go to San Francisco to film school [Academy of Art University]. Making up my mind that I would be the best film school graduate they had ever had, I studied long and deep into the night. Most mornings I saw the sun rise. I was driven. When my teachers asked me what themes I was most interested in exploring, I told them social justice and sports. For my final project I produced a fine little documentary about a woman martial arts fighter, Katrine Alendal, *Bad-Kitty-Kat!* A finalist in the Epidemic Film Festival, it won Best Documentary; I then pursued other documentary material. I also produced another film, *Inclusion Illusion,* which will be aired on LSU campus in February," he said.

"But what I came to talk to you about is this: the whole time I was in film school, you kept coming to my mind. I said to myself, 'I must tell this story above all!'"

Then Cleve dropped his bombshell: "Kathy, I want to do a full length feature movie on you and George."

Flabbergasted, I was speechless for a few moments.

"Terrific, Cleve. But tell me how you are going to do this. As you know, George died in December. I guess we can use pictures. Maybe we can request some clips from the news media here. He was in the news all the time...."

"Kathy, you don't understand. I want to make a movie about you! You will be the protagonist. George's life will be seen through your eyes. Actors and actresses will portray you and George and the other characters. I want to know and show how this Southern white woman born in the forties in one of the most racist areas of the South could become who you are today. A fighter for civil rights, married to George."

I was floored!

"Do you and George have a book? We usually work from a book," Cleve said.

"No. For years people have been telling us we should write a book, but with the teaching, civil rights work, and then having to care for George 24/7 in the last two years—no way. However, he has a Web site which I put together in 2009. Can you use that?"

"Certainly, but I also need to know more about your childhood."

"Tell you what. Have a good look at the Web site—and I'll begin writing what I think you will need."

I found early photo albums of my childhood and of George's and my early life together. Cleve said he would scan the material and mail them back to me. Finally, we set up an appointment one week hence when he would do a camera interview with me.

I was still in a state of shock. I began thinking about the project. That night, on September 5, during my regular prayer time, I prayed about it. The beginning of my writing sprang from that moment with Psalm 40.

The next day, I believe, I called Dale, telling him about the project.

"Kathy, if you are going to do this, do it with full transparency. Tell all, the whole truth about George. If you are doing it for fame, it will not be successful. If for money, even worse. If you are going to do it at all, do it to help people." Dale was clearly intrigued.

I had already determined not to restrain my tongue—it would be all truth, to the best of my ability, or nothing. As for fame or money, neither had entered my mind.

Cleve had come to me—I had not gone to him. I was convinced God wanted this project to move forward. I knew that if His hand was on it, the project would succeed. The writing that I planned to do was to give Cleve more material to use for the film. A book had not entered my mind.

My writing went slowly for a couple of days, then gathered momentum as I began to remember, taking notes so I would not forget what I meant to put into the narrative. As memories began to flow, I did research. Above all, I wanted complete truth, context. Yet the more I wrote, the more I remembered; and the pages poured out of me.

After a few days, I now knew it would be a book. It would not let me sleep. I would lie down at night, but the thoughts kept coming, insistent that I spit them out. I would have to turn the light on once again, type the thought on my computer which stayed on day and night. As soon as I would lie down again and try to sleep, the book would prod me again, inflaming my mind, pleading for air.

On the weekend of October 5-7, I typed furiously till the wee hours of the morning, pushing out sixty single-spaced pages. During the next few days, whether I took a moment to eat, tried to rest for a short while in my recliner, the book kept writing itself in my head. It gushed out in perfectly formed sentences. If I did not reach my computer, they would be lost. I no longer belonged to myself, but to the book.

Throughout this period, Cleve and I e-mailed one another almost daily. We talked on the phone several times, a half hour at a time.

Engaged with the film, he was similarly driven, and kept egging me on, "Keep it coming!"

He was working on the story line using first the Web site, then the story which I continued to send him in updates. He kept wanting to print it. The story grew so quickly through the middle and end, with multiple additions, that he finally stopped trying. He told me he would wait till I finished the manuscript before trying to print it.

Help from the Holy Spirit with this Story

Again on the weekend of October 12-14, I don't know how, the book intensified yet again, keeping me up at night, till I reached what I thought would be my ending. In and out of bed, I would type, then lie down. The book shamelessly yanked me out of bed at 4:00 in the morning of October 11. I finally reached the last paragraph—I myself learned even as I revealed.

I was physically and emotionally overpowered by what I was writing. I wept as I typed. My mind, my heart, and soul were ringing with the truth of what I was feeling and writing.

The vast power was not coming from me but from the Holy Spirit.

As I had begun, so I finished.

After the conclusion, the tempo eased. I read and reread the entire book, polishing, making small corrections, moving a few paragraphs to improve the flow, even adding a few small sections, but it was generally finished.

On that Sunday I called a few close friends. I tried Marie Weiss, but could not reach her. I called Fannie Godwin who was excited. As I shared the whole project, I eventually read several passages including the ending to her. She wisely told me, "Kathy, while this whole process is fresh in your mind, you need to write some of this down, how you were driven. People are going to invite you to speak, and they will ask you about how you came to write the book."

Hours later, as I try to relax in my recliner, here it comes again, the book, begging for one more chapter, about the writing itself.

Of course, I had to give in. The date was October 14, 2013, just about one month from the date I had started.

I was amazed.

Chapter 27

The Beloved

To remember is to celebrate.

I find joy talking to Lyman, Rashid, and Andre, in learning more about their relationship with George, and George himself, even now.

To know more is to have more cause to celebrate, to see the pattern of George's extraordinary life as from a single strand it began to intertwine with mine, and to have been present to experience most of it with him.

How remarkable is the pattern of all our lives! How intricate the weaving of ignorance and knowledge, error and correction, lightheartedness and sobriety, suffering and glory. "What a piece of work is a man!" Shakespeare nailed it.[1]

Years ago I had entered the convent determined to serve God as a religious sister. I left in 1969, not too sure where God was leading me. A close friend, Sister Martha Mendizabel from Guatemala, asked me then: "What I want to know is how will you serve?"

I knew precisely what she was asking me. From our earliest teen years we had been led to serve God. We knew that what that entailed—more than anything else—was to serve the people of God. Not just Catholics, but all people in their most essential needs. I presumed that I would teach; and of course, I did. But what I could not know then and know now, is that God is perfect Justice; and it was Justice calling me to serve His cause. To fight for the right and to do right as well.

In George I saw a man "more sinned against than sinning."[2]

I loved him fully as my equal. He won my compassion—though he never pitied himself.

Because George's passion was also justice, we could not fail to bind together in a marriage stronger than any vows could affect. We agreed in the most essential values; and together, we could take only the high ground if we did not fail ourselves and our God.

"The best secret weapon that black people in this parish have is me. They just don't know it yet." I told George this often.

I did not think of myself then as a warrior for justice.

I thought of George as a warrior for justice. It was George who, for justice, lay his body on the line, having to struggle every day for over fifty years from a wheelchair; who, for justice, lay his honor and his good name on the line, suffering the desecration of character that haunted his every move.

All I could do was to lay myself on the line for him and with him.

When he rejoiced, I rejoiced. When he suffered, I suffered. He was my companion in arms and the love of my life. As Winnie Mandela would say of Nelson, wherever he went, "My soul went with him."

I stand in the Resthaven Chapel of Faith, beneath the impressive rising window in the mausoleum where his body rests today, looking at the bronze plaque, "George W. Eames, Jr. – 1933-2012." His life is complete at nearly eighty years old.

The inscription on the other side of the marble slab says, "Kathy Andre-Eames–1946 -."

I wonder at my life and at George's. We were married 35 years, our anniversary on Nov. 21, mere days before he died. We had lived together precisely seven years before that.

Only God Could Have Pulled This Off

On the day of our anniversary, George was still conscious. I told him, "We made it, George, thirty-five years married, forty-two years together."

I have to think that only God could have pulled this off. We always marveled at the day we met, the way we met. How could God have brought together two such diverse people? But he did. How did he give us such an intense sense of vocation—mine utterly different from everything I had dreamed? Yet he did.

Our sense of doing God's work remained with us to the end. Through the struggle, through the pain, through the victories and successes as well.

George lived with deep faith: "The Lord is My Light and My Salvation; Whom should I fear?"[3] George feared no one. And when I stood by his side, I, too, feared no one. When he could do no more, he stood. He was as tall—taller—than any man I knew, my warrior. What was not to love?

✶✶✶✶✶

How can we begin to thank the God of our hearts, the Heart of our God?

Deepest thanks to the many people who have touched us on this mighty sojourn. I can't begin to name or thank them all, but a Catholic missionary, Marino Restrepo, gave me a little phrase which I use every day. All those whose lives cross our path in any way throughout our lives are in our "territory of souls." For these souls we are responsible. If kind, they have supported, comforted, and consoled us; and we owe them for the greater beings which we have become. If mean, vengeful, or hurtful, they have tested and toughened us, strengthened our resolve, our courage and perseverance, and deepened our souls. For every one of these we should also thank God—and pray for all.

This one thing I do, indeed, I must do—pray for everyone in my territory of souls daily. With forgiveness, every one of these can be precious to our hearts. God forgive and bless them, everyone: the racists, the rapists, the shooters, the arsonists, the jailers, the calumniators, those who bear false witness. We don't have to associate with everyone, but we can love and remember.

How can I begin to thank you, George, for the miraculous journey we shared? With all our faults, falls, strivings, it was always God we strained after—whether we recognized it at the time or not. If we saw anything good, anything just, anything admirable or lovable in the other, and for me, it was you—it is not the beloved that we loved, but the Beloved.

We saw, but did not always recognize Him. In eternity, everyone's vision will be 20/20.

God is not only Perfect Justice, but also Mercy; yet before all else, He is Love.

Notes

Chapter 1

1. "Psalm 40," *The New American Bible* (New York: Catholic Book Publishing Corp., 1992) vs. 8-11. Scripture texts in this work are taken from the *New American Bible*, with revised New Testament and Psalms copyright 1991, 1986, 1970 Confraternity of Christian Doctrine, Washington, DC and used by permission of the copyright owner. All rights reserved. No part of the *New American Bible* may be reproduced in any form without permission in writing from the copyright owner.

2. "Southern Gentlemen Fight Desegregation in Louisiana," Corpus Christi: *Corpus Christi Times,* (Saturday, April 9, 1955), p. 7.

3. "Pro-segregation unit in La. still in mystery class, *the Times News,* Hendersonville, N.C. *(Oct. 25, 1955), p. 4.* Retrieved Sept. 20, 2013 from http://news.google.com/newspapers?nid=1665&dat=19551025&id=I0IaAAAAIBAJ&sjid=hyMEAAAAIBAJ&pg=4413,6201880.

4. Adelson, Bruce, *Brushing Back Jim Crow* (Charlottesville: University Press of Virginia, 1999), p. 189.

5. Andre, Theresa K., "Bio," *Mr. Civil Rights.* Retrieved on Oct. 1, 2013 from http://mrcivilrights.webs.com/bio.htm.

6. Rapaport, David, "Jim Crow Laws: Louisiana." Louisiana Jim Crow. Retrieved on September 20, 2013 from http://www.findingsources.com/sitebuildercontent/sitebuilderfiles/jimcrowlawslouisiana.pdf, p. 2.

Chapter 5

1. Cook, Kevin, "Dale Brown prays for Bob Knight," *Playboy* magazine (April 1990), p. 136.

2. Cook 136.

3. Didier, Karen. "Eames says LSU discriminating in hiring," the *Advocate,* (Baton Rouge, La., Thurs. Feb. 25, 1988), p. C5

4. Didier C5.

5. Guilbeau, Glen, "LSU officials answer racism charges," *Alexandria Daily Town Talk,* (Dec., 8, 1989), D1.

6. Ellerbee, Tim. "NAACP pushing for changes," *New Orleans Times-Picayune* (Sunday, Dec. 3, 1989), Special Report: LSU at the Crossroads, p. C10.

7. Ellerbee C10.

8. Andre, Theresa K., "LSU," "*Mr. Civil Rights,*" Retrieved on Oct. 10, 2013 from http://mrcivilrights.webs.com/lsu.htm.

Chapter 7

1. Cullen, Ed, "Eames naturally part of desegregation suit," the *Advocate* (Sat., Oct. 4, 1980), p. B1.

2. "Brown v. Board of Education." *Wikipedia the Free Encyclopedia,* Retrieved on Aug.15, 2014 from http://en.wikipedia.org/wiki/Brown_v._Board_of_Education.

3. Cullen B1.

4. Cullen B1.

5. Eysink, Curt, "President calls for federal probe of East Baton Rouge school system, Baton Rouge, Louisiana." the *Advocate*, (Friday, June 2, 1989), p. A1.

6. Eysink A1.

Chapter 8

1. "75 pilgrims walk 52 miles to reject state death penalty," *Catholic Commentator*, (April 24, 1985) Baton Rouge: Catholic Diocese, 1985, p.15.

Chapter 9

1. "First they came…," *Wikipedia the Free Encyclopedia*. Retrieved on Aug.14, 2014 from http://en.wikipedia.org/wiki/First_they_came_….

Chapter 10

1. Bielawa, Michael and Janice, *Baseball in Baton Rouge* (Charleston SC: Arcadia Publishing, 2006), p. 79.

2. Andre, Theresa K., "Baseball," *Mr. Civil Rights*. Retrieved on Oct. 1, 2013 from http://mrcivilrights.webs.com/baseball.htm.

3. Schiefelbein, Joseph, "Inner city youths revived by league." the *Advocate*, (Thursday, Aug. 18, 1994), p. 8C.

4. Schiefelbein 8C.

5. Andre, Theresa K., "Baseball," *Mr. Civil Rights*. Retrieved on Oct. 1, 2014 from http://mrcivilrights.webs.com/baseball.htm.

6. Andre, same page.

7. Eames, George. "Bring back Baton Rouge youth baseball." the *Advocate* (Editorial, Mar. 11, 2008), *p. B2.*

Chapter 11

1. Douglass, Frederick, "Our destiny is largely in our hands: An address delivered in Washington, D.C. on 16 April 1883." John Blassingame & John R. McKivigan, ed., The Frederick Douglass Papers, 5 vols. (New Haven: Yale University Press, 1992), pp. 68-69.

2. Andre, Theresa K., *"Speeches," Mr. Civil Rights*. Retrieved on Oct. 1, 2013 from http://mrcivilrights.webs.com/speeches.htm.

3. Andre, same page.

4. Ehrmann, Max, "Desiderata," *Wikipedia the Free Encyclopedia*. Retrieved on Aug. 14, 2014 from http://en.wikipedia.org/wiki/Desiderata.

Chapter 14

1. Hale, Edward Everett, "Edward Everett Hale." *Wikipedia the Free Encyclopedia*. Retrieved on Oct. 2, 2013 from http://en.wikipedia.org/wiki/Edward_Everett_Hale.

2. Andre, Theresa K. "Winding Fingers," edited by Elnora A. Old Coyote and Jon Reyner,
Teepees are Folded (Billings, Montana: Indian Council of Education, 1991), p. 5.

3. Andre, Theresa K., *Louisiana Visions*, "Poetry—Humanity." Retrieved on Oct. 2, 2013 from http://mimosalouisiana.webs.com/poetryhumanity.htm.

4. Wilde, Stuart, *Weight Loss for the Mind* (Sydney, Australia: Nacson & Sons, Pty., Ltd., 1994) p. 22.

Chapter 16

1. "Legal Notices," the *Advocate*, (Wed., Dec. 13, 2000), p. 5C.

2. Talley, Tim, "Eames resigns NAACP Position." *the Advocate (March 25, 1995), p. A*

Chapter 17
Estes, Clarissa Pinkola, "A Prayer." *Faithful Gardener.* (San Francisco: Harper, 1995), p. 76.

Chapter 18
1. Elliott, Dwayne, editor and publisher, "A Conversation with George Eames." the *Urban Leader* (August 14, 1998, Vol. 1, Number 1), p. 3.
2. Quotation taken from my photograph of the sign itself, located on Beale Street, Memphis Tennessee.
3. "Bo Bahnsen." LSU Sports Net, Athletic Department. Retrieved on Oct. 1, 2013 from http://www.lsusports.net/ViewArticle.dbml?&ATCLID=174045&DB_OEM_ID=5200.

Chapter 19
1. Andre, Theresa K., "Southern University," *Mr. Civil Rights.* Retrieved on Oct. 1, 2013 from http://mrcivilrights.webs.com/southernuniversity.htm.
2. Gates, Paul, WAFB, "2006 complaint leads to discrimination lawsuit" (Posted: Sept. 22, 2009, 2:41 p.m. PDT Updated: Sept. 22, 2009 2:41 p.m. PDT).
3. Gates.
4. "SU campus lacks handicap accessibility." the *Advocate* (Sat., Sept. 27, 2009), p. B1.
5. "SU campus," B1.

Chapter 20
1. Engster, Jim, "The top 150 Most Influential People in LSU athletics history," *Tiger Rag* (Baton Rouge: Tiger Publications, Inc., 2000), p. 3.
2. Andre, Theresa K., "Bio," *Mr. Civil Rights.* Retrieved on Oct. 2, 2013 from http://mrcivilrights.webs.com/bio.htm.

Chapter 22
1. De Caussade, Jean-Pierre, Translated and introduced by John Beevers. *Abandonment to Divine Providence* (New York: Doubleday, 1975), p. 20.
2. DeCaussade 36.
3. DeCaussade 20.
4. DeCaussade 29.
5. DeCaussade 42.

Chapter 23
1. Burke, Edmund. "All that is necessary for the triumph of evil is that good men do nothing," *Quotations page.* Retrieved on Oct. 2, 1013 from quotationspage.com.

Chapter 24
1. "G. Washington Eames, Jr.," Obituaries. the *Advocate, (Dec., 12, 2012).*
2. Bryant, Beth, Personal communication, Sept. 12, 2013.
3. Bryant, Oct. 4, 2013.
4. Bryant, Oct. 4, 2013.

Chapter 27
1. Shakespeare, William, "What a piece of work is man!" *Hamlet, (Prince of Denmark, Act. II, Sc. 2), Wikipedia.* Retrieved on Aug. 14, 2014 from http://en.wikipedia.org/wiki/What_a_piece_of_work_is_a_man.
2. Shakespeare, William, "A man more sinned against than sinning," *King Lear (Act III, Sc. 2), Shakespeare Quotes.* Retrieved on Aug. 14, 2014 *from* http://www.shmoop.com/shakespeare-quotes/more-sinned-against-than-sinning/.
3. Psalm 27:1. *New American Bible.*

Bibliography

Adelson, Bruce. *Brushing Back Jim Crow*. Charlottesville: University Press of Virginia, 1999: 89.

Andre, Theresa K. "Winding Fingers," edited by Elnora A. Old Coyote and Jon Reyner, *Teepees Are Folded*. Billings, Montana: Indian Council of Education, 1991: 5.

Andre, Theresa K. Living Christ: http://livingchrist.webs.com/ ; Mr. Civil Rights: http://mrcivilrights.webs.com/ ; Louisiana Visions, http://www.mimosalouisiana.webs.com; St. Paul the Apostle Catholic Church: http://stpaulbr.webs.com/.

Bielawa, Michael and Janice. *Baseball in Baton Rouge*. Charleston SC: Arcadia Publishing. 2006.

"Bo Bahnsen." *LSU Sports Net*. Athletic Department. Retrieved on Oct. 1, 2013 from http://www.lsusports.net/ViewArticle.dbml?&ATCLID=174045&DB_OEM_ID=5200.

"Brown v. Board of Education." *Wikipedia the Free Encyclopedia*. Retrieved on Aug.15, 2014 from http://en.wikipedia.org/wiki/Brown v. Board of Education.

Bryant, Beth. Personal communication: July 14, 2013, Sept. 12, 2013, Oct. 4, 2013.

Burke, Edmund. "All that is necessary for the triumph of evil is that good men do nothing." *Quotations page*. quotationspage.com. Retrieved on Oct. 2, 1013 from quotationspage.com.

Cook, Kevin. "Dale Brown prays for Bob Knight.: *Playboy* magazine, April 1990, p. 136.

Cullen, Ed. "Eames naturally part of desegregation suit." the *Advocate*, Baton Rouge, LA. Sat., Oct. 4, 1980: B1.

De Caussade, Jean-Pierre. Translated and introduced by John Beevers *Abandonment to Divine Providence*. New York: Doubleday, 1975: 257-258.

Didier, Karen. "Eames says LSU discriminating in hiring," the *Advocate*, Thurs. Feb. 25, 1988: C5.

Douglass, Frederick. "Our destiny is largely in our hands: An Address Delivered in Washington, DC on 16 April 1883." John Blassingame & John R. McKivigan, ed., *The Frederick Douglass Papers*, 5 vols. New Haven: Yale University Press, 1992: 5:68-69.

Eames, George. "Bring back Baton Rouge youth baseball." the *Advocate*. Editorial, March 11, 2008.

"G. Washington Eames, Jr." Obituaries. the *Advocate* , Dec., 12, 2012.

Ehrmann, Max. "Desiderata." *Wikipedia the Free Encyclopedia*. Retrieved on Aug. 14, 2014 from http://en.wikipedia.org/wiki/Desiderata .

Ellerbee, Tim. "NAACP pushing for changes," the *New Orleans Times-Picayune*, Sunday, Dec. 3, 1989, Special Report: LSU at the Crossroads: C-10.

Elliott, Dwayne, editor and publisher. "A conversation with George Eames." the *Urban Leader*. August 14, 1998, Vol. 1, Number 1: 3.

Engster, Jim, President. "The top 150 most influential people in LSU athletics history." *Tiger Rag*. Baton Rouge: Tiger Publications, Inc., 2000: 3.

Estes, Clarissa Pinkola. "A Prayer." *Faithful Gardener*. San Francisco: Harper, 1995: 76.

Eysink, Curt. "President calls for federal probe of East Baton Rouge school system, Baton Rouge, Louisiana." the *Advocate*, Friday, June 2, 1989: A1.

"First they came...." *Wikipedia the Free Encyclopedia*. Retrieved on Aug. 14, 2014 from http://en.wikipedia.org/wiki/First_they_came_....

Gates, Paul, WAFB. "2006 complaint leads to discrimination lawsuit" posted: Sept. 22, 2009 2:41 p.m. PDT Updated: Sept. 22, 2009 2:41 p.m. PDT.

Guilbeau, Glen. "LSU officials answer racism charges," *Alexandria Daily Town Talk*, Dec., 8, 1989, Sec. D.

Hale, Edward Everett. "Edward Everett Hale." *Wikipedia the Free Encyclopedia*. Retrieved on Oct. 2, 2013 from http://en.wikipedia.org/wiki/Edward_Everett_ Hale.

"Legal Notices." the *Advocate*, Wed., Dec. 13, 2000: 5C.

"Pro-segregation unit in La. still in mystery class." the *Times News*. Hendersonville, N.C.: Oct. 25, 1955, 4. Retrieved Sept. 20, 2013 from http://news.google.com/ newspapers?nid=1665&dat=19551025&id=I0IaAAAAIBAJ&sjid=hyMEAAAAIBAJ &pg=4413,6201880.

Rapaport, David. "Jim Crow laws: Louisiana." *Louisiana Jim Crow*. Retrieved on September 20, 2013 from http://www.findingsources.com/sitebuildercontent/ sitebuilderfiles/jimcrowlawslouisiana.pdf: 2.

Schiefelbein, Joseph. "Inner City youths revived by league." the *Advocate*, Thursday, Aug. 18, 1994: 8C.

"75 Pilgrims walk 52 miles to reject state death penalty," *Catholic Commentator*, April 24, 1985. Baton Rouge: Catholic Diocese, 1985: 15.

"SU campus lacks handicap accessibility." the *Advocate*, Sat., Sept. 27, 2009: B1.

"Southern gentlemen fight desegregation in Louisiana." Corpus Christi: *Corpus Christi Times*, Saturday, April 9, 1955: 7.

Talley, Tim. "Eames resigns NAACP position." the *Advocate*, March 25, 1995: A1.

The New American Bible. New York: Catholic Book Publishing Corp., 1992. Psalm 40: 8-11, Psalm 27:1.

Wilde, Stuart. *Weight Loss for the Mind*. Sydney, Australia: Nacson & Sons, Pty, Ltd, 1994, 22-24.

Author's Publishing Credits

Fiction

"The Snake-Caller," *The Snowy Egret*, Vol., 54, Spring and Autumn 1991, Bowling Green, IN: Snowy Egret Press, 1991: 43-37.

Poetry

"Bird parts," "What is Most Tender," *Louisiana Literature*. Fall 1990: 38-39.

"Bodies stir," "Mosquito-hawks," "Mosquitoes bite," edited by Robert Spiess, *Modern Haiku*, Vol., XXI, Winter-Spring 1990: 30.

"Close your eyes for this boy," *Fantasies*. Pittsburgh, Texas: Poetry Press, May 1989.

"Falling to Sleep," *Windows on the World*, National Library of Poetry, May, 1989.

"First Six Weeks," *The Lyric*, Summer 1991, Vol., 71, Number 3: 73.

"Groundswells," "Pines in July," *The Word and Image*, Spring 1991, Vol. VI, Issue No. 11: 34.

"Losing Sight," *New Beginnings*. Mt. Pleasant, Texas: *Poetry Unlimited*, May 1989.

"Louisiana Man: Midwinter Reflections," Freeman's Point, *Riveries*, edited by Walt Franklin, Great Elm Press, 1991: 14-15, 17-18.

"Louisiana, the Image," "On Coffee," and "Achille, the Barrel-Maker," *Louisiana Literature*, Fall 1989, Vol., 6, Number 2: 53-56.

"Notes after dark," *New York Poetry Anthology*, April, 1989.

"On City Park Pool," "Street Poems," "disquiet," *Southern Review*, Autumn 1972, Vol, VIII, No. 4: 909-911.

"Snow," edited by Michael Scearce and Mark Van Tillburg. *Gulfstream*, 1972: 5.

"Song of the Decadent," *Journeyman*, edited by Richard Powers, Unitarian Fellowship of Baton Rouge, 1971.

"The Aftermath," *American Poetry Annual*, The Amherst Society, June 1989.

"To Jonathan," the *Mediterranean Review*, Spring 1971: 86- 88.

"Under Mimosa," *Mainichi Daily News*, Tokyo, Japan, July 23, 1989.

"Under the Sun," *The Wilderness*. Washington, DC: The Wilderness Society, summer 1991: 30. *Wildsong*. Athens, Georgia: The University of Georgia Press, 1998: 34.

"Undersides," and "Birdsong at Night," *Journal for College Writing*, Vol., 1, No. 1.

Louisiana Tech University, Ruston, LA., May 1994: 28.

"Winding Fingers," edited by Elnora A. Old Coyote and Jon Reyner, *Teepees Are Folded*. Billings, Montana: Indian Council of Education, 1991: 5.

"Wooden Stairs," "Once I taped painted fake tulips," "After four days," *Certain Days are Islands* 1971: 3, 5, 31.

"Yet Sappho Still," "Snow Leopard," "Arrested," "The Crepe Myrtle," *Thirteen Poetry Magazine*, April 1991, Vol. IX, Number 3: 24-25.

Index